UNDERSTANDING SECTARIAN GROUPS IN AMERICA

REVISED

UNDERSTANDING SECTARIAN GROUPS IN AMERICA

REVISED

THE NEW AGE MOVEMENT • THE OCCULT
MORMONISM • HARE KRISHNA • ZEN BUDDHISM
BAHA'I • ISLAM IN AMERICA

GEORGE W. BRASWELL, JR.

BROADMAN
& HOLMAN
PUBLISHERS

Nashville, Tennessee

4210-47
ISBN: 0-8054-1047-3
Dewey Decimal Classification: 280
Subject Heading: CULTS // SECTS // UNITED STATES — RELIGION
Library of Congress Catalog Number: 93-24941
Printed in the United States of America

Unless otherwise stated, all Scripture quotations are from the *King James Version* of the Bible.

Scripture quotations marked RSV are from the *Revised Standard Version* of the Bible, copyrighted 1946, 1952, © 1971, 1973.

Library of Congress Cataloging-in-Publication Data
Braswell, George W.
    Understanding sectarian groups in America / George W. Braswell. —
[New rev. ed.]
      p.   cm.
    Includes bibliographical references.
    ISBN 0-8054-1047-3
    1. Sects—United States. 2. Christians sects—United States.
3. United States—Religion. I. Title.
BL2525.B72 1994
291.9'0973—dc20

                                93-24941
                                CIP

99 00 01   4 3

Dedicated to my students
who have sought to understand peoples of other religions
by studying their beliefs and practices
and by visiting their worship places and study centers.

TABLE OF CONTENTS

∎   ∎

INTRODUCTION

■   ■

For several years I have taught courses in the areas of world religions and nontraditional Christian communities in America. Often, classes have been held off-campus in the worship and educational facilities of those communities, in which we engaged their leaders and followers in conversations about their beliefs and practices and our own. I have found the people of these communities to be friendly and hospitable. Although differences in doctrines and practices have emerged, there has been open discussion based on honesty and integrity.

In recent times various books have been written on the nontraditional Christian communities, as well as those of the world religions. Various descriptive titles have been given to these communities, including cults, new consciousness groups, sects, new religions, and Christian deviation groups. This volume presents religious communities that have (a) sprung out of traditional Christian belief and practice and (b) altered certain of those beliefs and practices. They have deviated from orthodox Christianity. This volume also presents religious communities that represent orthodox world religion thought and practice. These communities have not had origins in Christianity, but they have settled down in American society.

Thus, two major representative religious communities are the focus in this volume. The nontraditional Christian communities, sometimes referred to in the literature as cults or sects, usually center on an individual who has received special revelations that result in new interpretations of the Bible, new sacred writings, a different world view, different principles and laws of behavior, and a new community. Often, the leader and the community take one or several

1

orthodox Christian teachings and change them to fit their own new revelation and interpretation. They often castigate Christianity, separate themselves from it, and claim their religion as the absolute truth.

The other religious communities in this volume have had their origins in world religion communities outside the United States. They have arisen in America due to immigrants' needs and the responsiveness of Americans to their teachings and practices. Some of these communities have accommodated to American Judaic-Christian backgrounds to attract followers from the traditional religious communities.

Religious freedom in America allows for religious pluralism. Religion appears to be healthy in America, given its visibility and extensiveness across the nation. Worship attendance, buildings, budgets, publications, mass media, and missionary outreach all point to religion's strength. Before World War II, America was usually pictured as a nation whose main religious communities were Protestants, Roman Catholics, and Jews. Although the traditional religious communities have remained strong, numerous others have come to prominence or have even been born since the 1950s.

The first two chapters of the book concern the Church of Jesus Christ of Latter-day Saints, known as the Mormons, and the Jehovah's Witnesses. Both groups have grown rapidly and visibly during the last several decades. These two religions, both native to America and born of the nineteenth century, have offered alternatives to traditional Christianity. The Mormon ideas of eternal marriage and man becoming a god and the Jehovah's Witnesses' anticipation of the end of the world have appealed to many millions. The Mormons now number over eight million, and the Witnesses have over four million followers. Mormons have over forty thousand missionaries, while the Witnesses circulate tens of millions of their religious periodicals monthly.

The third chapter deals with the Unification Church, which is a post-World War II phenomenon. The Unification Church, founded by Sun Myung Moon, was brought from Korea, preaching the unification of world Christianity and the need for a new messiah. The church's followers, known as Moonies, are encouraged to be married by Moon and to be missionaries for the church.

The fourth chapter includes three religious communities in America. The Christian Scientists and the Unity School of Christianity have their roots in the nineteenth century. Mary Baker Eddy began the First Church of Christ, Scientist (Christian Science) with emphasis on the Bible and her book *Science and Health With Key to the Scriptures*. The Unity School emphasizes the importance of mind over matter. The Church of Scientology, founded by Ron Hubbard, is a post-World War II growth movement. Hubbard's Scientology offers a blend of religion and science with therapeutic courses. Altogether they are not as numerous as the Mormons and Jehovah's Witnesses.

The fifth chapter deals with astrology, witchcraft, and Satanism. These expressions of the occult include leaders, followers, and community life. Jeanne Dixon in her use of astrology and Anton LaVey in his Church of Satan use and often manipulate Christian symbols and practices.

Chapters six, seven, and eight deal with Hindu, Buddhist, Muslim, and Baha'i communities in America. These communities basically began in America in the early twentieth century with the immigrant population's religious needs. Particularly after World War II, various sectarian groups emerged, led by Hindu gurus, Buddhist monks, and Muslim imams. Many Americans were attracted to religious communities and teachings such as Transcendental Meditation, Hare Krishna, Zen Buddhism, Soka Gakkai, and the Nation of Islam (Black Muslims).

The last chapter is on the New Age. New Age thinking and practice has its foundations both in some of the nativistic American religions and in religions beyond America. Its themes include pursuit of the higher consciousness of self or God; realization of one's own potential; holistic health; and paradigm shifts in education, economics, politics, psychology, and religion.

Tens of millions of Americans are influenced by these religious communities as they build their churches, kingdom halls, temples, centers, societies, and mosques in inner cities, in suburbs alongside traditional Christian churches, and on prime real estate in developing population centers. Americans are influenced by these groups through their (a) mass media worship; (b) educational and promotional programs on television and radio; and (c) books, journals, magazines, and videos. Other millions of Americans are attracted to these communities in partial participation or in full membership. Thus, historic and orthodox Christianity is challenged by alternate religious communities claiming new revelations, new scriptures, and new doctrines and practices.

This book contains sample religious communities from both the Christian deviation groups and the world religion communities. Brief histories and major teachings and practices are included. Primary sources are often used to allow the groups to speak for themselves. Issues and challenges within the groups are stated as they face transitions in American society, as well as their interactions with traditional Christian teachings and practices. A Christian view of each group, which attempts to state briefly Christian distinctives and their differences with those major beliefs and practices of the groups, is projected.

Thousands of religious communities are classified as nontraditional Christian groups across America. Some have a leader and few followers, and some have millions of members. I have chosen selective groups to give a substantial sample within a brief volume. Also, these particular groups have been included on the basis of their rapid growth and influence in America and/or on their missionary thrust and appeal to traditional church members, their families, friends, and neighbors. A later volume may well present a fuller theological critique from a Christian perspective on the major teachings of the religious groups.

Hopefully this book will be read by people in churches, by students in the classroom, and by those interested in knowing about groups from Mormons to Moonies to Muslims. A goal of the writing is to sensitize the traditional church communities to the teachings and practices of many of their neighbors who belong to these alternate religions.

Once I was teaching a senior citizen group in my church about religious pluralism in America. One woman spoke up and said, "I know there are differences between Christians and Muslims, but Methodists, Mormons, and Baptists believe about the same thing." The book intends to offer facts and insights into the differences between Mormons and Baptists, but more particularly between traditional Christianity and alternative religions across America.

Many people have aided in stimulating thought for this book. Students in the classrooms, church folk in workshops, and persons in the nontraditional religious communities have raised questions and offered insights. Of course, I take full responsibility for the format and content of the book. I thank my family for allowing my empty place at times in the home while writing occurred. I hope the reading will bring understanding of the religious communities presented and a commitment by the reader to seek the truth and to follow it in the Christian context of obedience and reconciliation.

1

THE CHURCH OF JESUS CHRIST OF LATTER-DAY SAINTS

■   ■

The People Called Mormons

The coffee and banana plantations of Western Guatemala reached as far as an eye could see. My daughter and I, together with a missionary colleague, had set out on foot to visit an Indian church. After an hour's walk through the luscious fields, we rounded a bend in the path. Coming toward us on bicycles were two young men dressed in dark trousers, white shirts, and blue ties. They were Mormon missionaries. They had preceded us to visit the Indians and were hastening on to other visits. Mormons have over forty thousand missionaries scattered around the globe. Their church numbers over eight million individuals. They seem to be omnipresent.

The sun was setting on a lazy summer evening in North Carolina. We had friends around our dinner table. A knock sounded loudly on the door. I greeted two Mormon missionaries dressed in neat suits. After telling them of my interest in them and their church, I got their telephone number for contact for a later visit. As they left, one said to me, "How do you feel about the Savior?" At another time we would talk about their understanding of the Savior whom they call Jehovah.

A group of senior citizens was meeting over a hot lunch at my church. They had invited me to speak to them on the challenges of religious pluralism in America. We were talking about Roman Catholics, Protestants, Jews, Muslims, Hindus, and Buddhists. One lady said, "I know there are differences between Christians and Muslims, but Methodists, Mormons, and Baptists believe about the same thing." Little did she realize that Mormons do not classify themselves as Protestants and that they view all other churches as apostate.

These three examples about the followers of the Church of Jesus Christ of Latter-day Saints indicate at least two things. Mormons are a very mobile and missionary people, spreading their teachings over the globe and establishing their churches and temples in villages, cities, and the far reaches of the earth. They project their growth to ninety million by 2030. Secondly, non-Mormons have little knowledge of the substance of Mormon doctrine and practice. The Mormon church sends missionaries to all peoples, including Baptists and Methodists, to encourage them to join the true church on earth. They do not include themselves in the Protestant wing of Christianity, and they see themselves as the true restored church for this age.

This study of the Church of Jesus Christ of Latter-day Saints will revolve around several interests. First, it is an indigenous American church movement, having been born in America in 1830. It is celebrating over 150 years of continuous history. What were the social and religious conditions in the early nineteenth century that influenced the birth of the Mormon church? Did they include revivalism, the question of the origin of the American Indians, the restoration of the true church, the perfectionism of human nature, Masonism, millennialism, and theocratic thought and practice? Scholars continue to debate the issues, such as Masonic influences on Joseph Smith, who was a Mason.

Second, the Mormon church is not only a religious movement native to American soil, but it is founded on an American, Joseph Smith (1805-1844), who claimed to be a prophet and receiver of new revelations. The study of the Mormon church is inseparable from the study of its prophet.

Who and what influenced his early life in Vermont and New York? What were the sources of his visions of God and angels that led him to unearth golden plates and transcribe them into the *Book of Mormon?* Why did he leave New York for points west? What were the circumstances for his new revelations of vicarious baptism for the dead, of exclusive temple rites, of marriage for eternity, of God being flesh and bone, of humans being able to become gods, and of polygamous marriages? What were the events surrounding his death in the jail at Carthage, Illinois? Perhaps these revelations are the points of most concern in non-Mormon discussions with Mormons.

A third interest is the religious writings of the movement. Visions and revelations to Joseph Smith are collected in the *Book of Mormon,* the *Doctrine and Covenants,* and *The Pearl of Great Price.* As one examines the doctrines of the Mormon church, one will compare the words of the Bible (*King James Version* is preferred by the Mormon church) with the church's three other sacred written traditions. Many changes have been made in the *Book of Mormon* over 150 years. Two in particular are the denial of polygamous marriages in a revelation in 1893 and the admission of black males into the priesthood in 1978 after they had been denied priesthood by the *Book of Mormon* since 1830.

What is the basis for revelation and authority in the Mormon church? Is it the Bible or other sacred scriptures? Is it all of them? Are there contradictions among the four sacred writings? Mormon leaders often state that the veracity of their religion stands or falls on the revelations and the words of Joseph Smith.

A fourth major interest concerning the Mormon church is temple work. It is within the temple that ceremonies such as marriage for eternity, baptism for the dead, and the endowments occur. Only Mormons who have a temple recommendation from a church leader may participate. About half of all Mormons qualify for temple work, according to estimates. One must participate in temple work if one is to become a god and if one is to have marriage and the procreation of children throughout eternity. What is the source for the idea of temple work? How does temple work affect the Mormon church at large? Joseph Smith began the first temple in Kirtland, Ohio, the second in Nauvoo, Illinois, and over forty-five have been built around the world.

Joseph Smith led the early Mormons from New York through Ohio, Illinois, and Missouri, and founded a strong community of Mormons. After his death, Mormons were lead by Brigham Young, prophet and president successor to Smith, across the west to the Utah basin. They founded a new community and built their temple in Salt Lake City.

The story of the Mormons is filled with heroic and pioneer efforts of courage, bravery, and fortitude in settling in the West. The story also includes their hardships and persecution. Why were they besieged with hostility by other Americans? Was it because of their clannish ways, their plural marriages, their strange doctrines, or the threats of their economic and political power in the emerging West? What factors enabled them to grow? It appears that Mormons, at critical junctures of their religious history, have been able to be flexible and to accommodate to cultural and political contingencies surrounding them.

Thus, the Church of Jesus Christ of Latter-day Saints has become a visible, vocal, and viable religious institution with global impact. Prophets have succeeded Joseph Smith and have had new revelations. Magnificent temples have been built around the world. Strategies for continuing worldwide outreach to Africa, Latin America, the Middle East, and

Asian countries have been mapped by the leadership. Mormons appear to be a future-oriented people.

Their history is brief in comparison to the long lineage of the Christian churches since New Testament times. However, their history is deep and rich in doctrine and practice, and they have become one of the fastest-growing religious groups in the world.

Many of the questions that have been raised above will now be pursued. Since Mormons view Roman Catholic churches and Protestant churches as apostate, they will not be considered in the mainstream of historical Christianity. They themselves state this position. Churches in the mainstream view Mormons as a deviation group from the mainline orthodox teachings and practices of historical Christianity. These deviations shall be noted and discussed as the study progresses.

Joseph Smith: Prophet and President

The Mormon church is rooted in the authority it places in Joseph Smith and his successors, the prophets. Mormons have had thirteen prophet/presidents, including the present Ezra Taft Benson, but Joseph Smith is the primary theologian and founder of the church.[1]

Joseph Smith was born in Vermont in 1805 and moved with his family to Palmyra, New York, at an early age. His parents were sometime schoolteachers who held other jobs and struggled for economic survival. Both in Vermont and New York revivalism was in the air. Smith later reported that the subject of religion was flourishing around Palmyra:

> Religious discussion soon became general among all the sects in that region of the country. Indeed, the whole district of country seemed affected by it, and great multitudes united themselves to the different religious parties, which created no small stir and division amongst the people, some crying "Lo, here!" and others "Lo, there!" Some were contending for the Methodist faith, some for the Presbyterian, and some for the Baptist.[2]

At about age fourteen, being troubled by religious questions, Joseph had a vision while he prayed in the forest near his home. (This vision, which occurred in 1820, is now referred to as the "first vision.")

> I saw a pillar of light exactly over my head. . . . When the light rested upon me I saw two personages (whose brightness and glory defy all description) standing above me in the air. One of them spoke to me, calling me by name, and said, (pointing to the other), "This is my beloved son, hear him." . . . I asked the personages who stood above me in the light, which of all the sects was right, . . . I was answered that I must join none of them for they were all wrong, and the personage who addressed me said that all their creeds were an abomination in his sight; that those professors were all corrupt, . . . He again forbade me to join with any of them; and many things did he say unto me which I cannot write at this time.[3]

Out of this experience Smith declared all churches (sects) to be apostate and their ministers corrupt. He was on the way to establishing the true church. Recently, several letters have emerged from Mormon files that describe the first vision differently. The two letters are in Smith's handwriting. One letter reports he saw angels when he was sixteen. The other letter states he saw angels when he was fourteen. Scholars argue that there are three versions of the same first vision with differences in ages and in personage/angel appearances.

Smith continued to have visions in which the angel Moroni appeared to him and told him of buried golden plates in a nearby hill. By 1827 he had dug up these plates from the hill Cumorah and translated them into the *Book of Mormon*. By 1830 he had a sacred scripture revealed to him and had begun the true restored church.

Life was not easy for Joseph Smith, the self-proclaimed modern prophet. Citizens of Palmyra ridiculed him as a fortune-teller, a "peep-stone gazer" or "glass-looker." His wife

Emma's family distrusted him in his new finding. Lawsuits on indebtedness and some convictions hounded him. However, he persevered to found his church. Three of his early and faithful friends, Oliver Cowdery, David Whitner, and Martin Harris, gave official affidavits that they had seen the golden plates from which Smith had translated the *Book of Mormon*. Their names, together with eight other names, are included in the preface of the *Book of Mormon* to indicate their testimonies of seeing and handling the golden plates from which Smith made his translation.

If the birthplace of the Mormons could not tolerate this growing church, then perhaps the West would. Smith began his westward movement through New York and on through Ohio, Illinois, and Missouri. He was a prophet, and he had his twelve apostles. Included among them was Brigham Young. The Mormons were missionaries from the beginning. Between 1837 and 1846, Mormon missionaries who were sent to England baptized English citizens into the church. Some 4,733 of these eighteen thousand English Mormons emigrated to Nauvoo, Illinois, in the early 1840s. Between 1846 and 1887 European Mormons numbering over 85,000 emigrated to Utah.[4] Believers were aggressive in their outreach, and Mormon faith and practice were attractive to the thousands.

By the time Joseph Smith arrived in Nauvoo in the early 1840s, several definite characteristics gave flavor to his church. He had left intolerance and persecution in New York. In ten years he had gathered thousands into his church, and the frontier in Illinois offered opportunities for settlement and growing organization. Most importantly, the Mormons were rapidly becoming a temple-oriented people. Revelations had continued to come to Smith through the 1830s and into the 1840s. These revelations and visions were incorporated into two other sacred written traditions, the *Doctrine and Covenants* and *The Pearl of Great Price*.

Temple work became prominent. Revelations to Smith indicated that God had flesh and bones like humans and that humans could become gods.[5] The idea of a plurality of gods emerged in his teachings. The teaching that a man and woman whose marriage was sealed in the temple (marriage for eternity) emerged. Husband and wife could then become gods, ruling over a celestial heaven and having spirit children throughout eternity.[6] Mormons who gained entrance to the temple could also vicariously baptize for the dead, aiding the deceased to gain merits they neglected in this life.[7] And temple work included the endowments that brought purification to Mormons to prepare them for the celestial heaven.

Only those Mormons having permission to enter the temple could participate in these ceremonies. One had to receive a temple recommendation from a church leader saying that financial and moral obligations had been met. Mormons took vows of secrecy and wore special undergarments as they merited these special sacred temple works. Also, Smith began to tell his closest apostles and his wife Emma of the new revelation of plural marriages where a man might take more than one wife.[8] This revelation brought much dissension within the Mormon church as well as outside it. Plural marriages were sanctioned by the church until 1893, when another revelation from God to the prophet/president Wilford Woodruff abrogated the revelation of Joseph Smith.[9]

The Mormon church was growing in Nauvoo, but all was not well. There was turbulence within, but more so without. Mormons formed business co-ops, and this solidarity agitated non-Mormon businesses. Mormons favored candidates who favored them. Joseph Smith even ran for president of the United States. He called for the rights of American Indians and the freedom of slaves. He was accused of attempts to establish a theocracy. Smith was said to use Masonic rituals in his temple rites, and there was much anti-Masonic bias against the Mormons. Smith's practice of polygamy and Mormon clannish behavior brought suspicion, distrust, and hostility from outsiders.

In 1844, Smith and his brother Hyram were jailed in Carthage, Illinois. They were both killed when a mob rushed the jail. Reports said Joseph had been smuggled a gun, which he fired at the mob in his own self-defense. The Mormons, however, were not to be without a prophet. Brigham Young, the chief of the twelve apostles, stepped forward to lead them from confusion and persecution further westward to the Salt Lake basin. Some Mormons were not to follow, including Joseph Smith's wife Emma. She was to remain behind, together with other family members and Mormons, to help form the splinter church, the Reorganized Church of Jesus Christ of Latter-day Saints.

Mormon beliefs and practices, as formulated and organized by Joseph Smith, challenged more orthodox religious patterns in the United States. There appeared to be three ways to deal with them. They could have been protected by the government, but order broke down in the death of the Smiths. They could have been exterminated. Or they could move on to less-populated regions either by expulsion or by voluntary means. Mormons chose to move to a less-populated region.

Smith's vision was more fully realized under the leadership of prophet/president Brigham Young. Salt Lake City became the headquarters of the church. The great temple was begun. The church grew. By the time of Brigham Young's death in 1877, there were 140,000 Mormons. By 1893 the temple was completed. Utah gained statehood in 1896 with a majority Mormon population. However, there had been much dissension between the United States government and Mormons. The revelation by prophet/president Wilford Woodruff to discontinue polygamy paved the way for better relations between the emerging state and the nation.

A People of Books

Authority for Mormons rests in four writings—namely, the Bible, the *Book of Mormon,* the *Doctrine and Covenants,* and *The Pearl of Great Price*. However, this authority is qualified by interpretations made on these writings by the prophet/president of the Church of Jesus Christ of Latter-day Saints.

The Bible

Joseph Smith was influenced by the Bible. He stated that he claimed the biblical promise in James 1:5 before he received his first revelation in the forest, "If any of you lack wisdom, let him ask of God, that giveth to all men liberally, and upbraideth not; and it shall be given him." However, the view of Joseph Smith and the Mormons toward the Bible is contained in Smith's Articles of Faith, "We believe the Bible to be the word of God as far as it is translated correctly; we also believe the *Book of Mormon* to be the word of God."[10] On one occasion Smith said, "I told the brethren that the *Book of Mormon* was the most correct of any book on earth, and the keystone of our religion, and a man would get nearer to God by abiding in its precepts, than any other book."[11]

Mormons usually refer to the *King James Version* of the Bible when they quote. However, they turn to their other books more often; and whenever there is a choice between both data and interpretation of belief and practice, they accept Smith's visions and revelations as found in his books. Smith began his spiritual pilgrimage in distrust of the churches and Scriptures of his day, and it was he who formulated a new church and new scriptures.[12] The *Book of Mormon* became the bridge between Christianity and Mormonism.

The Old Testament passage of Ezekiel 37:15-20 is cited by Mormons as a biblical reference to the *Book of Mormon*. From these verses they interpret the stick of Judah as the Bible (Jews) and the stick of Ephraim as the *Book of Mormon* (Nephites). Non-Mormon interpreters point out that the passage in Ezekiel depicts the spiritual restoration of Israel by God. Whereas Joseph Smith claims that the sticks are scrolls, another word in Hebrew is used for scroll. Also, it is pointed out that Ezekiel was commanded to write on two sticks. Does this mean that he wrote part of the *Book of Mormon?* Mormons use the Bible to support the validity of their other sacred books.

The *Book of Mormon*

The *Book of Mormon* was first published in 1830. As previously indicated, Joseph Smith had several visions, as a young boy and into manhood, of the corruption of the Bible and of golden plates buried in the hill of Cumorah near his home. In 1827 he was led to the hill by the angel Moroni. He found the golden plates and translated them in three years. Much debate has occurred among non-Mormons about the veracity of the plates and the translations, of borrowings by Smith from writings of his day, and of the history and archaeology of the civilizations referred to in the book.

The *Book of Mormon* claims to be the official history of the early inhabitants of the Americas and includes the historical era of roughly 600 B.C. to A.D. 421. The scriptures are composed of fourteen books with some five hundred pages. Its main story concerns the two sons of Lehi, who are Laman and Nephi. Laman leads the Lamanites, who are sinful and rebellious, while Nephi leads the Nephites, who are the righteous. These peoples have migrated from the places and times of the Tower of Babel and the destruction of Jerusalem to the New World.

Because of their sin the Lamanites are punished by God with dark skin, and they become the American Indians whom Columbus discovers. Jesus Christ appears to these peoples in the New World after His resurrection, preaches the gospel, and His church flourishes among both peoples. After a period of peace, conflict arises between the Lamanites and Nephites. The Lamanites destroy the Nephites, who by this time have become sinful in the eyes of God. The Nephite prophet, Mormon, and his son, Moroni, are responsible for the collection and preservation of the golden plates, which are hidden about A.D. 421 in the hill of Cumorah until they are revealed to Joseph Smith in the 1820s. This main story is found in the *Book of Mormon* in the chapters of Mosiah, Alma, Helaman, and 3 and 4 Nephi.

In the chapter of Ether, the history of the Jaredites is given. Jared and his people traveled to the Americas in saucer-like submarines during the time of the Tower of Babel. They were destroyed, however, because of their sin. In this account the word *Deseret* is used, meaning "honey bee." Later the Mormons were to use this word for the name of the state of Utah and their publishing press.

Thomas F. O'Dea in his book, *The Mormons,* points out that the key theme in the book is the "arrival and settlement of Hebrews on this continent before the Christian era, a theme that serves the obvious purpose of explaining the origin of the American Indian, a subject upon which there had been much speculation."[13] O'Dea also states other key themes in the book, including the problem of good and evil, repentance, America as the Promised Land, millennial thoughts on the building of Zion in America, and practices similar to those of the Masonic order. He concludes that "the *Book of Mormon* was admirably suited to become what it did in fact become, the scriptures of an American church."[14] It is also noted that much attention has been given by Mormons to the civilizations and great cities noted in the book.

Mormons claim there are many translation errors in the Bible, but the *Book of Mormon* contains none. Anthony Hoekema writes out of his research that since 1830, some three thousand changes have been made in the *Book of Mormon,* "the most correct book on earth," as stated by Joseph Smith.[15] A most recent change occurred in 1978. Then prophet/president Spencer Kimball received a new revelation concerning the admission of black males into the Mormon priesthood. Blacks had been prohibited from the priesthood since 1830. Through this new revelation Kimball admitted black males. In doing so, he changed 2 Nephi 30:6 in the *Book of Mormon* from "a white and a delightsome people," which had been the reading since 1830, to "a pure and a delightsome people." Editions of the *Book of Mormon* since 1978 show this new translation.

The *Doctrine and Covenants*

Many revelations attested to by Joseph Smith are contained in the *Doctrine and Covenants*.

> The Doctrine and Covenants is a collection of divine revelations and inspired declarations given for the establishment and regulation of the kingdom of God on earth in the last days. . . . Most of the revelations in this compilation were received through Joseph Smith, Jun., the first prophet and president of The Church of Jesus Christ of Latter-day Saints. Others were issued through some of his successors in the Presidency.[16]

The collection of sacred writings contains some 138 sections and two official documents. Sections 135, 136, 138, and Official Declarations I and II concern matters other than revelations to Joseph Smith. Smith received these revelations as he left New York and took his followers through Ohio, Illinois, and Missouri.

> In the revelations the doctrines of the gospel are set forth with explanations about such fundamental matters as the nature of the Godhead, the origin of man, the reality of Satan, the purpose of mortality, the necessity for obedience, the need for repentance, the workings of the Holy Spirit, the ordinances and performances that pertain to salvation, the destiny of the earth, the future conditions of man after the resurrection and the judgment, the eternity of the marriage relationship, and the eternal nature of the family. Likewise the gradual unfolding of the administrative structure of the Church is shown with the calling of bishops, the establishment of other presiding offices and quorums. Finally, the testimony that is given of Jesus Christ—his divinity, his majesty, his perfection, his love, and his redeeming power—makes this book of great value to the human

family and of more worth than the riches of the whole earth.[17]

More specifically, the *Doctrine and Covenants* includes the theology of Joseph Smith and the organizational structure of his emerging church. Section 130, for example, explains the nature of God, indicating that God has a body of flesh and bone as that of man. Section 128 describes the need for and the rites of baptism for the dead, which is a temple work. The church at present maintains millions of genealogical records for use in this baptismal practice. Section 132 describes celestial marriage, also a temple work, which enables the husband and wife later to become gods and have spirit children. This section also describes the revelation to Smith concerning plural marriage and his initial telling of the revelation to his wife, Emma, and her reaction to it.

Official Document I states the revelation and circumstances surrounding the issue of polygamy and its official resolution by the prophet/president Wilford Woodruff in 1893. Official Document II concerns the new revelation to the prophet/president Spencer W. Kimball in 1978 extending priesthood privileges to all worthy males in the church, which in effect opened up the priesthood for the first time to black males.

The Pearl of Great Price

The fourth major written authority for Mormons is *The Pearl of Great Price,* which in sixty-one pages contains the *Book of Moses,* the *Book of Abraham,* the writings of Joseph Smith, and the Articles of Faith. The *Book of Moses* deals with data from Genesis. The *Book of Abraham* is a translation by Joseph Smith of Egyptian papyri containing writings from Abraham. Much controversy has centered over the validity of Smith's claims in the translation of the *Book of Abraham.*[18] The writings of Smith include portions of the Book of Matthew and some of his personal history and testimonies. The Articles of Faith are the thirteen belief statements first published by Smith in 1835.

The Mormon church stands on four written authoritative sources for its faith and practice. However, no one source appears final and absolute in and of itself. Prophet/presidents who have succeeded Joseph Smith have received revelations that have altered past faith and practice in the church. Even Joseph Smith continued to receive revelations after the *Book of Mormon* was complete, when he had testified it was the most perfect book on earth. The ensuing study will now consider more fully the major doctrines and practices of the Mormon church as found in their sacred scriptures, pointing out the harmony and the deviations in their written traditions.

The Organization of the Mormon Church

The concept and practice of priesthood is central to the organizational framework of the Mormon church. Only males are admitted into this priesthood, and it is composed of two categories. The Aaronic priesthood was given to Joseph Smith and his friend Oliver Cowdery in 1829 by John the Baptist. *Doctrines and Covenants* 13 states,

> Upon you my fellow servants, in the name of Messiah I confer the Priesthood of Aaron, which holds the keys of the ministering of angels, and of the gospel of repentance, and of baptism by immersion for the remission of sins; and this shall never be taken again from the earth, until the sons of Levi do offer again an offering unto the Lord in righteousness.

The higher priesthood of Melchizedek was given to Smith through Peter, James, and John, but the date is uncertain.

The two priesthoods are divided into councils or quorums and serve as a stepladder for males to progress from youth to adulthood in maturity and leadership in the hierarchy of the church. In the Aaronic priesthood one may be a deacon at age twelve, a teacher at fifteen, and a priest at eighteen.

In the Melchizedek priesthood one may become an elder at age twenty, a member of the seventy (quorum) with maturity in the church, and a high priest in middle or later life.

Twelve deacons form a quorum, which has a president and two counselors. At about age eighteen a Mormon youth is ordained a priest, whose "duty is to preach, teach, expound, exhort, and baptize and administer the sacrament."[19] The priests are organized into a quorum of forty-eight with a high priest. The office of bishop is the highest order in the Aaronic priesthood. The bishop must be a high priest, and he is assisted by two counselors or high priests. The bishop is the unpaid leader of the ward, the local congregation.

At age twenty, one may be ordained into the Melchizedek order and may become an elder. This ordination signifies the arrival at maturity of the male and his possession of supernatural powers to handle all important and necessary affairs of the church. The elders compose a quorum, which has a president and two counselors. The next rank in the Melchizedek order is the seventy. This rank includes those Mormon young men who become missionaries for several years, paying their own expenses either in the United States or another country. These quorums of the seventies are headed by seven presidents, and the senior president presides. The top rank of the order is the high priest, and most of the top offices both locally and nationally are held by high priests.

At the top of the Mormon hierarchy is a body of men called the General Authorities. The first presidency consists of the president and two counselors. The president is still considered the divinely inspired prophet, seer, and revelator of the restored church. The first presidency oversees the Quorum of the Twelve, the patriarch of the church, the Seven Presidents of Seventy, and the presiding bishopric. The president/prophet appoints all members of the General Authorities, whose tenure is voted on by Mormons who attend the two general conferences held each year in Salt Lake City.[20]

Two key communities in the Mormon church are the stake and the ward. The ward is the most local expression of the church and is presided over by a bishop. The stake is headed by a stake president and is subdivided into a number of wards. Both in the ward and the stake, members gather to hear addresses, to worship, and to conduct the affairs of the church.

The Women's Relief Society was organized in 1842 in Nauvoo, Illinois. Today it is composed of over 1.5 million adult ladies. Its purpose is:

> to care for the poor, the sick, and the unfortunate; to give assistance in times of death; to give guidance and training to the sisters in homemaking arts and skills; to foster love for religion, education, culture, and refinement; to develop faith and to study and teach the gospel.[21]

This society provides women some of the functional equivalents of the male priesthood from which they are barred. The Women's Relief Society meets each Sunday at the same time as the priesthood meetings.

The Deseret Sunday School Union provides religious education for all ages. The Church Welfare Plan includes the Storehouse, a place of goods and services for needy Mormons. The Mormon temple is one of the foremost organizations in the church, and a forthcoming section will discuss temple work.

From male priesthoods to women's relief societies to temple work, Mormons are called on for commitment to church practices and organizations. President/prophet Spencer W. Kimball stated that the whole program of the church may be included in three categories: missionary work, temple work, and keeping church members active and faithful. A typical week in the life of a Mormon teenager might include the following: a priesthood meeting, one-and-a-half hours; Sunday

School, one-and-a-half hours; Sacrament meeting, one-and-a-half hours; Young Men, Young Women, one-and-a-half-hours; Seminary, five hours; Fireside social, two hours; and Family Home Evening, one-and-a-half hours. These activities would total fourteen hours in church-related functions.[22]

God and Man as Flesh and Bones

What do Mormons believe about the nature of God and man? The *Book of Mormon* in 2 Nephi 31:21 states, "And now, behold, this is the doctrine of Christ, and the only and true doctrine of the Father, and of the Son, and of the Holy Ghost, which is one God, without end." Also, in the *Book of Mormon* in Alma II 26-31 it is written,

> Now Zeezrom said unto him: Thou sayest there is a true and living God? And Amulek said: Yea, there is a true and living God. Now, Zeezrom said: Is there more than one God? And he answered, No. Now Zeezrom said unto him again: How knowest thou these things? And he said, An angel hath made them known unto me.

These statements indicate that the revelation to Joseph Smith in the *Book of Mormon* included a trinitarian view of God and the oneness of God. In the testimony of the three witnesses to the introduction to the *Book of Mormon*, they conclude their testimony to the truthfulness of the contents with the following words: "And the honor be to the Father, and to the Son, and to the Holy Ghost, which is one God. Amen."

Later revelations to Joseph Smith and various statements of succeeding prophet/presidents and Mormon theologians demonstrate different views of God and man than those found in the *Book of Mormon*. In *Doctrine and Covenants* 130:22 concerning the nature of Father, Son, and Holy Ghost, it is stated, "The Father has a body of flesh and bones as tangible as man's; the Son also; but the Holy Ghost has not a body of flesh and bones, but is a personage of Spirit. Were it not so, the Holy Ghost could not dwell in us."

Joseph Smith continued to speak on the nature of God in discourses he delivered in 1844, fourteen years after the publication of the *Book of Mormon*. He said:

> I will preach on the plurality of Gods . . . I have always declared God to be a distinct personage, Jesus Christ a separate and distinct personage from God the Father, and the Holy Ghost was a distinct personage and a Spirit: and these three constitute three distinct personages and three Gods. . . . Many men say there is one God; the Father, the Son, and the Holy Ghost are only one God. I say that is a strange God anyhow—three in one, and one in three! It is a curious organization. . . . All are to be crammed into one God, according to sectarianism. It would make the biggest God in all the world. He would be a wonderfully big God—he would be a giant or a monster.[23]

In his famous King Follet address, delivered at the funeral of an elder in 1844, Smith said of God:

> God himself was once as we are now, and is an exalted man, and sits enthroned in yonder heavens! . . . If you were to see him today, you would see him like a man in form . . . He was once a man like us; yea . . . God himself, the Father of us all, dwelt on earth, the same as Jesus Christ himself did . . .[24]

Brigham Young, who followed Smith as prophet/president, said:

> How many Gods there are, I do not know. But there never was a time when there were no Gods and worlds, and when men were not passing through the same ordeals that we are now passing through. That course has been from all eternity, and it is and will be to all eternity.[25]

Lorenzo Snow, the fifth prophet/president of the church, said of God and man, "As man is, God once was; as God is, man may become."[26] Also, in the King Follett address Smith described the nature of man as that of a god:

> Here, then, is eternal life—to know the only wise and true God; and you have got to learn how to be Gods yourselves, and to be kings and priests to God, the same as all Gods have done before you, namely, by going from one small degree to another, and from a small capacity to a great one; from grace to grace; from exaltation to exaltation, until you attain to the resurrection of the dead, and are able to dwell in everlasting burnings, and to sit in glory, as do those who sit enthroned in everlasting power.[27]

The belief of man becoming god is also found in *Doctrine and Covenants* 132:19,20,37. In verse 37 Abraham and other patriarchs "have entered into their exaltation, according to the promises and sit upon thrones, and are not angels but are gods." In verses 19-20 those whose marriages are sealed for eternity shall become gods in the afterlife.

In 1852 Brigham Young introduced the Adam-God doctrine into the Mormon church. He said, "When our father Adam came into the garden of Eden, he came into it with a celestial body, and brought Eve, one of his wives with him. . . . He is our Father and our God, and the only God with whom we have to do."[28]

Bruce McConkie, a leading Mormon theologian of recent times, wrote:

> Implicit in the Christian verity that all men are spirit children of an Eternal Father is the usually unspoken truth that they are also the offspring of an Eternal Mother. An exalted and glorified Man of Holiness (Moses 6:57) could not be a Father unless a Woman of like glory, perfection, and holiness was associated with him as a Mother. The begetting of children makes a man a father and a woman a mother whether we are dealing in his mortal or immortal state.[29]

The Mormon understanding of God and man is predicated on the ideas of a plurality of gods, the eternal progression of man becoming a god, of God having been a man of flesh and bones, of man and woman becoming gods and creating spirit children, and of spirit children taking earthly bodies to continue the progression to exaltation and godhood. Thomas O'Dea in his study of Mormonism writes:

> It combined Trinitarianism and anti-Trinitarianism confusions, and the result was tritheism. It combined materialism and visions, and the result was the conception of a God of flesh and bones, which later led to the doctrine of polytheism. It combined this-worldly hopes for a reformed society with the doctrine of the Second Coming of the Lord and produced the Mormon idea of building the kingdom on earth in preparation for the millennium. It combined secular progress and evangelical enthusiasm, and the result was eternal progression. It combined anthropomorphism and the universe of nineteenth-century science as common men were beginning to understand it, and the result was a finite God.[30]

Jesus Christ, Exaltation, Salvation

Mormons view Jesus Christ as Jehovah, the firstborn of the preexistent spirits. *Doctrine and Covenants* 93:21-23 has Jesus saying:

> And now, verily I say unto you, I was in the beginning with the Father, and am the Firstborn; And all those who are begotten through me are partakers of the glory of the same, and are the church of the Firstborn. Ye were also in the beginning with the Father.

James Talmage, the noted Mormon theologian, in his *Articles of Faith* writes further:

> Among the spirit-children of Elohim the firstborn was and is Jehovah or Jesus Christ to whom all others are juniors. Jesus Christ is not the Father of the spirits who have taken or yet shall take bodies upon this earth, for He is one of them. He is The Son as they are sons or daughters of the Elohim.[31]

As has been noted, Mormons do not advocate belief in the Trinity. They believe that God has been man and that man may become a god. In this context, Jesus is seen as a god in the preexistent spirit along with other preexistent spirits such as Lucifer and others. Besides being the firstborn spirit, the distinction of Jesus from all other spirits may be questioned. Mormon theology points to the physical birth of Jesus as a significant distinction. Thus, the virgin birth must be discussed.

In the *Book of Mormon* in Alma 7:10 it is written,

> And behold, he shall be born of Mary, at Jerusalem which is the land of our forefathers, she being a virgin, a precious and chosen vessel, who shall be overshadowed and conceive by the power of the Holy Ghost, and bring forth a son, yea, even the Son of God.

Although the first part of the passage about the birthplace is inaccurate, the rest stresses the virgin birth and the power of the Holy Ghost in the conception. However, Brigham Young wrote concerning the virgin birth:

> When the Virgin Mary conceived the child Jesus, the Father had begotten him in his own likeness. . . . And who is the Father? He is the first of the human family; and when he (Christ) took a tabernacle, it was begotten by his Father in heaven, after the same manner as the tabernacles of Cain, Abel, and the rest of the sons and daughters of Adam and Eve. . . . Jesus, our elder brother, was begotten in the flesh by the same character that was in the Garden of Eden, and who is our Father in Heaven.[32]

Brigham Young appears to have implied that the Father of Jesus was Adam. Mormon leaders have attempted to disassociate themselves and the Mormon church from the Adam-God doctrine preached by Young, the immediate successor to the founder, Joseph Smith.

Joseph Fielding Smith, the tenth prophet/president of the church, said, "They tell us the Book of Mormon states that

Jesus was begotten of the Holy Ghost. I challenge that statement. The Book of Mormon teaches no such thing! Neither does the Bible."[33] Smith went on to say:

> Our Father in Heaven is the Father of Jesus Christ, both in the spirit and in the flesh . . . I believe firmly that Jesus Christ is the Only-Begotten Son of God in the flesh . . . Christ was begotten of God. He was not born without the aid of Man, and that Man was God.[34]

James Talmage supports Smith's theology when he writes:

> Elohim is literally the Father of the spirit of Jesus Christ and also of the body in which Jesus Christ performed his mission in the flesh. . . He (Christ) is essentially greater than any and all others, by reason . . . of His unique status in the flesh as the offspring of a mortal mother and of an immortal, or resurrected and glorified Father.[35]

Orson Pratt, an early apostle of the church, attempted to elaborate on the way God could begat Jesus through sexual relations:

> It was the personage of the Father who begat the body of Jesus; and for this reason Jesus is called "the Only Begotten of the Father, ". . . But God having created all men and women had the most perfect right to do with His own creation, according to His holy will and pleasure: He had a lawful right to overshadow the Virgin Mary in the capacity of a husband, and beget a Son, although she was espoused to another; for the law which He gave to govern men and women was not intended to govern Himself, or to prescribe rules for his own conduct.[36]

Mormon theology indicates that God the Father has a body of flesh and bone, literally. It also infers that God the Father had a physical relation with Mary from which Jehovah or Jesus Christ was born. One may raise questions with the Mormons of the use of virginity in reference to the virgin

Mary. One may also raise the issue, "Who is the real father of Jesus?" according to the Bible, the *Book of Mormon*, Brigham Young, or other prophet/presidents and theologians of the church. Mormon writings and theology obviously portray Jesus Christ quite differently in terms of His preexistence, divinity, and virgin birth than historical and traditional Christian sources.

The question of Jesus Christ's possible marriage has surfaced within the Mormon church's discussions. A marriage of Jesus is not mentioned in the stated books and doctrines of the church. However, Mormons teach, believe, and practice that if one is to attain the highest levels of heaven, one must be married and that marriage must be performed and sealed in a Mormon temple. Also, Mormons through their history have believed and practiced polygamous marriages. In this context one of the top leaders of the church, Orson Hyde, who served as a member of the first Council of Twelve Apostles, has been quoted:

> If at the marriage of Cana of Galilee, Jesus was the bridegroom and took unto him Mary, Martha and the other Mary, it shocks not our nerves. If there was not attachment and familiarity between our Saviour and these women, highly proper only in the relations of husband and wife, then we have no sense of propriety.
>
> We say it was Jesus Christ who was married whereby He could see His seed. Before the Saviour died He looked upon His own natural children as we look upon ours. When Mary came to the sepulchre she saw two angels and she said unto them, "they have taken away my Lord or husband."[37]

Mormons do have a doctrine of atonement in Jesus Christ. They believe that the fall of Adam and Eve, and consequently sin, was necessary. In 2 Nephi 2:22-25 in the *Book of Mormon* it is written:

> And now, behold, if Adam had not transgressed he would not have fallen, but would have remained in the

Garden of Eden. . . . And they would have had no children; wherefore, they would have remained in a state of innocence, having no joy, for they knew no misery; doing no good, for they knew no sin. . . . Adam fell that men might be; and men are that they might have joy.

Apparently, the sin of Adam and Eve provides the way for preexistent souls to have physical bodies. This is necessary for man's final pilgrimage to become god.

At the same time the fall demands an atonement to satisfy divine justice. This is the paradox. Mormons believe that the fall brought physical death. The atonement provides deliverance so that man may be resurrected from the dead. Atonement is made possible through the voluntary death of Jesus on the cross. Jesus became the sacrifice for the sin of man. Adam's role in the fall was necessary to help man become exalted to godhead, as was Jesus' role in atonement to overcome death.

The atonement through Jesus Christ provides two kinds of salvation or redemption. General salvation is universal and is provided for everyone through the death and resurrection of Jesus. Individual salvation is through Jesus Christ also, but rests on individual efforts through morality, obedience to law and codes, baptism, and temple works.

Mormon theology holds that there are three heavens: telestial, terrestrial, and celestial. All humankind will enter one of these heavens or kingdoms after death. The dishonest, liars, sorcerers, and adulterers will enter the telestial heaven. This is the low road in eternity. The good and honorable people who, however, have been blinded by the craftiness of men and are not Mormons will enter the terrestrial heaven. This is the broad way throughout eternity.

The third Mormon heaven, the celestial heaven, includes those who place faith in Jesus Christ, who repent, who are baptized, and who hold fast to morality and duty as taught by the Mormon church. This is the straight and narrow way. The celestial heaven is divided into realms for those who have been temple Mormons and those who have not, and for those who have had their marriage for eternity performed in the temple and those who have not. This heaven is also divided into areas for those who have performed rites of baptism for the dead and the rites of endowment. More shall be discussed on temple work, on heaven, and on celestial marriage in succeeding sections.

Jesus Christ provides both universal and individual salvation for man. However, salvation in the general sense does not enable one to enter the celestial heaven. It is individual salvation through Jesus Christ and one's own work ethic and righteousness that enables one to enter the celestial heaven. Thus, one is exalted through stages of obedience and rituals in the Mormon temple to attain the highest levels of the celestial heaven. One is exalted to a god. An attractive Mormon pamphlet describes salvation and exaltation as follows:

> By revelation, our Saviour made known again the plan of salvation and exaltation. Resurrection comes as a gift to every man through Jesus Christ, but the reward of the highest eternal opportunities you must earn. It is not enough just to believe in Jesus Christ. You must work and learn, search and pray, repent and improve, know his laws and live them. This is the way to peace and happiness and the fullness of the everlasting life. It is your Heavenly Father's way.[38]

For the Mormon, faith and works are essential in salvation and exaltation. In fact, faith in Jesus Christ and faith in Joseph Smith are necessary. For it was Joseph Smith who introduced the ideas of the three levels of heaven, temple work, eternal progression, man's exaltation into godhood, and God's nature of flesh and bones, as well as celestial marriage. *Doctrine and Covenants* 135:3 states, "Joseph Smith, the Prophet and Seer of the Lord, has done more, save Jesus only, for the salvation of men in this world, than any other man that ever lived in it."

Temple Works

A Mormon prophet, Spencer W. Kimball, has said that temple work is one of the most important programs of the Mormon church. There are over forty temples around the globe with many more in the planning stages. By the time of the building of the temple in Nauvoo, Illinois, in the early 1840s, Joseph Smith had received two particular revelations according the baptism for the dead as well as other revelations pertaining to temple works.

Baptism for the Dead

In *Doctrine and Covenants* sections 124 and 128, revelations are recorded concerning baptism for the dead. Joseph Smith cited such Scriptures as Matthew 16:18,19; 1 Corinthians 15:29; and Malachi 4:5-6 to support his doctrine on baptism for the dead. Since Smith had been ordained into the priesthood and held the keys of the kingdom, he felt it was his duty to set up baptism for the dead in the temples.

> Now the great and grand secret of the whole matter, and the summum bonum of the whole subject that is lying before us, consists in obtaining the powers of the Holy Priesthood. For him to whom these keys are given there is no difficulty in obtaining a knowledge of facts in relation to the salvation of the children of men, both as well for the dead as for the living. (*D. & C.* 128:11)

> Herein is glory and honor, and immortality and eternal life—The ordinance of baptism by water, to be immersed therein in order to answer to the likeness of the dead, that one principle might accord with the other; to be immersed in the water and come forth out of the water is the likeness of the resurrection of the dead in coming forth out of their graves; hence, this ordinance was instituted to form a relationship with the ordinance of baptism for the dead, being in likeness of the dead. (*D. & C.* 128:12)

> And now, my dearly beloved brethren and sisters, let
> me assure you that these are principles in relation to the
> dead and the living that cannot be lightly passed over,
> as pertaining to our salvation. For their salvation is nec-
> essary and essential to our salvation, as Paul says con-
> cerning the fathers—that they without us cannot be
> made perfect—neither can we without our dead be
> made perfect. (D. & C. 128:15)

Joseph Smith once said that the greatest responsibility in
this world that God has given Mormons is to seek after the
dead. Thus, an elaborate temple work has been instituted to
facilitate the ceremonies surrounding the baptismal for the
dead. A baptismal font, resting on the backs of oxen, is
included in each temple for the ceremonies. The faithful
Mormon enters the temple to be cleansed, dressed, and baptized in proxy for the dead one. John Taylor, the third
prophet/president of the church, said, "We are in fact the
SAVIOURS OF THE WORLD, if they ever are saved."[39] Wilford Woodruff, the fourth prophet/president of the church,
wrote that he had saved John Wesley, Columbus, and all the
presidents of the United States except three.

To support the doctrine and practice of baptism for the
dead, the Mormon church has established a genealogical
society. This society employs over five hundred workers and
supervises the microfilming of birth data over the world. The
birth data are placed in a huge subterranean storage facility
twenty miles southeast of Salt Lake City. According to estimates, over five billion names are in the storage files that are
housed in a vault whose size is one and a half acres. Genealogical research is a multimillion dollar enterprise for the
church. Thus, this research furnishes Mormons the necessary data on deceased family and friends to be used in the
ceremonial font baptism. Without this earthly proxy baptism, the dead would be unable to receive the restored gospel. However, to be fully realized, the dead must accept the
gospel along with the baptism.[40]

Endowment Ceremonies

The endowment ceremonies are also temple work. Men and women are segregated for special bathing and cleansing rituals. They are anointed with oil, beginning at the head and including all important organs. The procreative organs are anointed and blessed to serve their functions. An undergarment is provided each worshiper that is to be worn forever, and a secret name is given to each one. Then robes are provided the participants to continue through the ceremonies. Certain dramas are enacted with the participation of the worshipers, including the creation of the world, the fall of Adam, and passing through the veil of Solomon's temple. The endowment ceremonies usually take the greater part of a day to fulfill.[41]

Thomas O'Dea in *The Mormons* comments on endowments:

> The tendency toward polytheism, the eternity of matter, the new and restored priesthood with its power to bind and loose on earth and in heaven, the new marriage doctrines . . . the eternity of man, and the duty to bring waiting spirits into the world by having children—all these Mormon beliefs are symbolized in the temple ceremony. It has the effect of increasing the loyalty of the church member by initiating him into secrets and thereby making him a privileged sharer in holy mysteries and by his promising in impressive ceremonial circumstances to be loyal to the church and obedient to the priesthood.[42]

O'Dea indicates the close association between Mormon symbols and ceremonies with those of the Masons.

> To find appropriate materials for ritual development, his own non-liturgical religious background made it necessary to look outside strictly religious practices. Joseph went to Masonry to borrow many elements of ceremony. These he reformed, explaining to his followers that the Masonic ritual was a corrected form of an

ancient priesthood ceremonial that was now being restored.[43]

Celestial Marriage

Mormons believe that one must be married in the temple in the sacred ceremony in order to be married throughout eternity and to be exalted as a god. Before marriage in the temple, one must receive one's endowments, and a male must hold the Melchizedek priesthood. This marriage enables one to have spirit children in eternity. Joseph Smith received the revelation on celestial marriage in *Doctrine and Covenants* 128:15-20:

> Therefore, if a man marry him a wife in the world, and he marry her not by me nor by my word, and he covenant with her so long as he is in the world and she with him, their covenant and marriage are not of force when they are dead, and when they are out of the world; therefore, they are not bound by any law when they are out of the word. (15) Therefore, when they are out of the world they neither marry nor are given in marriage; but are appointed angels in heaven, which angels are ministering servants to minister for those who are worthy of a far more, and an exceeding, and an eternal weight of glory. (16) For these angels did not abide my law; therefore, they cannot be enlarged, but remain separately and singly, without exaltation, in their saved condition, to all eternity; and from henceforth are not gods, but are angels of God forever and ever. (17) And again, verily I say unto you, if a man marry a wife by my word, which is my law, and by the new and everlasting covenant, and it is sealed unto them by the Holy Spirit of promise by him who is anointed unto whom I have appointed this power, and the keys of this priesthood . . . and shall inherit thrones, kingdoms, principalities, and powers, dominions, all heights and depths. . . and they shall pass by the angels, and the gods which are set there, to their exaltation and glory in all things as hath been sealed upon their heads . . . (19) Then shall they be gods, because they have no end; therefore shall they be

from everlasting to everlasting, because they continue; then shall they be above all, because all things are subject unto them. Then shall they be gods, because they have all power, and the angels are subject unto them. (20)

Thus, the Mormon church teaches that one's marriage must be sealed properly in the temple in order to have the highest exaltation in celestial heaven.[44] Joseph Fielding Smith, the tenth prophet/president, said, "If you want salvation in the fullest, that is exaltation in the kingdom of God, so that you may become his sons and his daughters, you have got to go into the temple of the Lord and receive these holy ordinances which belong to that house, which cannot be had elsewhere."[45] Bruce R. McConkie wrote:

Those who gain eternal life (exaltation) also gain eternal lives, meaning that in the resurrection they have eternal "increase," "a continuation of the seeds," "a continuation of the lives." Their spirit progeny will "continue as innumerable as the stars; or, if ye were to count the sand upon the seashore ye could not number them." (D. & C. 131:1-4; 132:19-25,30,55)

"Except a man and his wife enter into an everlasting covenant and be married for eternity, while in this probation, by the power and authority of the holy priesthood," the Prophet says, "they will cease to increase when they die; that is, they will not have any children after the resurrection."[46]

The sealing of a marriage in the temple enables a man and woman, as well as the children, to be bound for eternity, to continue to procreate spirit children, to attain the highest exaltation, and to become gods. Thomas O'Dea writes, "As progress to glory in the world beyond the grave will be greatly enhanced by the size of a man's family, for one will become king and eventually a god over his progeny, the importance of sealing is obvious."[47]

Not all Mormons have their marriages sealed in the temple. An estimated 48 percent of Mormons in the United

States have their marriages sealed in the temple.[48] The sealing ceremonies, however, may be performed by proxy for the dead, similar to baptism for the dead. Many Mormon leaders, both past and present, have decried the neglect of temple marriages by Mormons. Therefore, for at least half of Mormons in the United States, exaltation to the highest heaven remains only an ideal. Spencer W. Kimball wrote in the context of marriage for eternity:

> Are you willing to jeopardize your eternities, your great continuing happiness, your privilege to see God and dwell in his presence? . . . Are you willing to make yourself a widow for eternity or a widower for endless ages—a single, separate individual to live alone and serve others? Are you willing to give up your children when they die or when you expire, and make them orphans? . . . I sincerely pray you stop today and weigh and measure and then prayerfully proceed to make your happy marriage an eternal one.[49]

From a brief overview of the three major ceremonies held in the temple, one may see that much Mormon thought and practice is geared to the other world. Many Mormons attend the ward and stake meetings in the life of the church. Mormons are baptized through immersion into the church. But many do not go to the temple.

A Mormon must be "worthy" to attend the temple and to participate in the ceremonies. One must appear before the bishop and be examined as to doctrine and practice before one can receive a temple "recommend" or "pass." Not only the bishop but also the president of the stake must pass on the qualifications of the applicant. A Mormon must be morally clean, must support the General Authorities of the church, and must obey the church's rules. One must be a full tithe payer. One must keep the Word of Wisdom (D. & C. 89). This means one will abstain from alcohol, tea, coffee, caffeine products, and tobacco. One is asked to wear the undergarment once the endowments ceremony is experienced. The temple recommend is issued as a plastic coded card and must be renewed yearly.

The basis for temple works (baptism for the dead, endowments, celestial marriage) comes from specific revelations as recounted by Joseph Smith in the *Doctrine and Covenants* and from further interpretations made on them by leading Mormon prophet/presidents, theologians, and church officials. Some Mormon church officials admit that the Bible is silent on some of these works. Many non-Mormon scholars refute the interpretations given by Joseph Smith on certain Scriptures that he used to buttress his ideas and practices.

Jesus neither taught nor practiced baptism for the dead. The apostle Paul referred to a group in 1 Corinthians 15:29 that practiced baptism for the dead and gave no indication of his approval of, or the practice of, such a ceremony in the early church. As for marriage throughout eternity and the procreation of spirit-children, the Bible is silent. Jesus said that those who attain resurrection from the dead will neither marry nor be given in marriage. Thus, temple works in the Mormon theology and practice are basically founded in extrabiblical sources of the Mormon church.

Temple works, themselves, segregate the exalted and the gods from an average Mormon church member. No visitors may enter a Mormon temple after its initial period of dedication, and only worthy Mormons may enter and participate in the ceremonies it offers and its heavenly rewards. Thus, true and ultimate Mormonism is reserved for those Mormons who have been declared worthy and have been issued a temple pass.

Issues and Challenges in Contemporary Mormonism

The growth and progress of the Church of Jesus Christ of Latter-day Saints have made it one of the largest and wealthiest indigenous religious communities in the United States. Recently, it has sent out over forty thousand missionaries globally to serve eighteen-month terms of service. The church membership numbers over eight million. Recently bishops have baptized a new convert every three minutes. The church flourishes because of voluntarism. Missionaries raise their own support from family and friends. Mormons of retirement age give years voluntarily and freely to serve as hosts and hostesses in temples, visitor's centers, and other organizations. Most local leaders, including bishops, are non-salaried. The church believes in the "pay as you go" plan; and ward, stake, and temple buildings are paid for before they are built.

Estimates place the yearly income of the church at over one billion dollars; and its holdings are vast in insurance investments, properties, and diverse businesses. The great temple at Salt Lake City, the Tabernacle Choir, and singers Donny and Marie Osmond are representative of Mormon public relations. In a meeting between Protestant seminarians and Mormons in the Atlanta area, Dale Murphey, who then was the star of the Atlanta Braves baseball franchise, was included on the program to give his account of attraction to the Mormon church. He spoke of his hope in celestial heaven and marriage for eternity.

Numerical growth and increased status in the economic, social, and political arenas of the nations have brought some peculiar challenges to the church. Its early teachings and practice of polygamy brought growth to its membership as well as stigma. The revelation of the practice of polygamy to Joseph Smith in *Doctrine and Covenants* 132 prepared both his wife, Emma, and the church to accept polygamy under dire threat of judgment. Reacting to the hostilities of the public, as well as the legal and social customs of the land, in 1893 prophet/president Wilford Woodruff declared,

> Inasmuch as laws have been enacted by Congress forbidding plural marriages, which laws have been pronounced constitutional by the court of last resort, I hereby declare my intention to submit to those laws, and to use my influence with the members of the Church over which I preside to have them do likewise.

. . And I now publicly declare that my advice to the Latter-day Saints is to refrain from contracting any marriage forbidden by the law of the land.[50]

The church had faced one of its great challenges and had made an accommodation, although not all of its members followed Woodruff's call.

Mormon missions around the world brought continuing growth patterns both in members and in temples. On June 8, 1978, prophet/president Spencer W. Kimball announced a revelation enabling males of all races to attain the priesthood and consequently enter the temple for all its rights and privileges, including celestial marriage.[51] This action broke a 130-year ban denying the priesthood to blacks. As indicated earlier, the *Book of Mormon* was changed to eliminate the former racist policy (2 Nephi 30:6).

The Mormon church had faced dissension and protests both at home and abroad over its racist policies. Intermarriages between Europeans and Blacks in Brazil caused problems for the church. The church's missionary thrust into Africa faced difficulty. In 1963, Nigeria refused to grant visas to Mormon missionaries. Blacks protested a tour of the Tabernacle Choir to New England in 1974. Several universities refused to play athletic events with Brigham Young University because of the church's racial policy. Again, the church's leadership demonstrated its accommodational spirit to change in the 1978 decision.

Leadership in the church takes a conservative stand on the role of women both in the church and in society. Female Mormons are denied the priesthood, which is open to males beginning at age twelve. The church has opposed the Equal Rights Amendment, arguing that it is a moral and family issue so important that sides must be taken. A basic view that emerges from the writings and teachings of Mormons is that the role of women is in the home to tend family needs and to have children. The ideal family is the one whose marriage has been sealed in the temple, together with the children, and whose marriage and childbearing continues throughout eternity.

The key leadership role in the church rests in the office of "Prophet, Seer, and Revelator." Spencer W. Kimball served in the office from 1973 until 1985. Kimball, who died in his nineties, was formerly in the realty and insurance business. He was an active president although he suffered heart trouble, three brain operations, and cancer. He and his wife, Camilla, lived in the Utah Hotel across the street from the Mormon temple in Salt Lake City. They lived in the church-owned hotel with a modest stipend.

Ezra Taft Benson became the thirteenth president in 1985. Benson had served as the president of the powerful Quorum of the twelve apostles. The head of this Quorum has become the church president in each transition since the founder Joseph Smith.

Benson served as United States Secretary of Agriculture in the Eisenhower administration. From the 1950s into the 1990s he was an outspoken critic of Communism and was associated with the John Birch Society. Now in his nineties, he has been sickly and hospitalized.[52] At other leadership levels from bishops to presidents there is much transition and shuffle due to the nature of the offices, voluntarism, and the nonclerical aspects. For the most part there appear to be smooth changes among the leaders in the church.

Mormons tend to exclusivism in favoring, protecting, and aiding their own church members in good times and bad times. The bishop's storehouses, located in strategic places across the United States, serve as processing plants, canning industries, supermarkets, and distribution points for goods and services to needy Mormons. Meat, milk, cheese, canned goods, and fresh produce bear the Deseret label, and Mormon-owned and operated trucks stand ready to ship goods to other distribution points. The ward bishop has authority to give permission for the needy to obtain necessary foods from the storehouse, and in return the needy may offer hours of work under the auspices of the bishop. Also, each

Mormon family is encouraged to stockpile in the home a year's supply of foodstuffs for emergency use.

In good times Mormons look out after one another. While Secretary of Agriculture, Ezra Taft Benson reportedly hired many Mormons. The voting record of Mormons has traditionally been conservative. For example, they supported President Reagan, and he named Mormons to key positions. James B. Conkling, the president of Bonneville Entertainment International Productions, a corporation affiliated with the Mormon church, was named by President Reagan to lead Voice of America. Richard Richards, a Mormon of Ogden, Utah, was named chairman of the Republican National Party. Rex E. Lee, dean of the Brigham Young University law school, was nominated by President Reagan to be the United States solicitor general. Other Mormons who served in the Reagan administration included Terrel H. Bell, Secretary of Education; Ray Buchanan, treasurer; Richard Beal, director of the Office of Planning and Evolution; and Richard Wirthlin, the president's pollster and strategist. General Brent Scrowcroft, a Mormon, served as National Security Advisor to President George Bush.

Mormonism demonstrated significant growth under the Kimball presidency. The church grew by 5 percent yearly, increasing from 3.3 million to 5.5 million. However, the number of convert baptisms decreased from 224,000 in 1981 to 207,600 in 1982 and 189,419 in 1983. Thus, in the fall of 1984, Kimball raised the term of service for missionaries to two years. This action was intended to increase the baptism and convert rate by the missionaries who served in some 179 missions in 90 countries.

Under President Ezra Taft Benson, the church has continued to grow. Through 1991, membership stood at 8,120,000. There were 43,395 missionaries serving in 138 countries. According to Church News (LSO), April 11, 1992, there were 267 missions and 297,770 converts.

A recent publication by Robert Gottlieb and Peter Wiley, America's Saints: The Rise of Mormon Power, describes

Mormonism as the nation's fastest-growing religion, with great wealth and expanding influence. However, the authors predict a difficult future for the church as they discuss its aging and authoritarian male hierarchy, its thirst for engaging in politics, the unrest among certain of its women, and questions and confusion among its foreign members. Mormon officials have rebutted this critical analysis, yet cracks are apparent in the Mormon fabric. Despite their high moral standards, their emphasis on family, family night each week, and close supervision of members by visits, Mormons still face—across the nation and even in Utah where they command the majority of the population—the plights of divorce, crime, and immoralities.

Like any large and prospering religious body, Mormons face the tests of success—the interaction, or lack of it, of large and often impersonal bureaucratic structures with the personal needs of individuals, and the discrepancies between their visions and ideals and the practical and pragmatic functions of everyday life. Historically Mormons have often met challenges through accommodation and change. Their future suggests that other issues and challenges, perhaps greater than those of the past, will come to bear.

Mormon scholarship and Mormon missionaries through the years have claimed archaeological data to support the authenticity of the *Book of Mormon*. Critics have refuted the claims. In recent years some Mormon scholars have tempered their claims. In copies of the *Book of Mormon* before 1981, a picture of the ruins of Monte Albans, supposedly dating to 800 B.C., was found at the front. That picture is no longer included. In an address at Brigham Young University in 1964, Fletcher B. Hammond stated, "There does not yet appear any artifact that we Latter-day Saints can present to the world—and prove by any scientific rule—that such artifact is conclusive proof of any part of the *Book of Mormon*."[53] Critics point out that no ancient manuscripts of the Mormon scriptures have been found. No artifacts, inscriptions, cities, names, persons, nations, or places mentioned prominently in the *Book of Mormon* have been discovered through new world archaeology. Thus, the debate continues concerning the authenticity of Mormon archaeological claims.

Mormonism and Christian Belief and Practice

The beginnings of Mormonism are predicated upon the assumptions that the theology, practice, and the clergy leaders of the Christian churches since the first century have been erroneous and corrupt. Joseph Smith, in his early visions and subsequent revelations, sought to establish and restore the true gospel, the true church, and the true priesthood. Thus, in the Mormon perspective the Church of Jesus Christ of Latter-day Saints is that church which preserves and demonstrates the very truth of the gospel.

Therefore, through visions, revelations, and the affirmation of them by his followers, Joseph Smith claimed the proper baptism and priesthood under God. He claimed to receive revelations from God that corrected and superseded those recorded in the Bible and which were translated into the *Book of Mormon,* the *Doctrine of Covenants,* and *The Pearl of Great Price.* He became the true priest, prophet, and president of the true church. Smith's followers became witnesses of his teachings and validated his claims. Joseph Fielding Smith, who served as the tenth prophet/president from 1970-72, said, "We reject and damn all who do not accept 'Mormonism' and the ministration of our elders."[54]

Bruce McConkie has written, "There is no salvation outside the Church of Jesus Christ of Latter-day Saints."[55] By salvation McConkie means "exaltation" or "godhood" in the celestial heaven. Basically, non-Mormons have the possibilities of existing in the telestial and terrestrial heavens, as well as through proxy arrangements by temple Mormons to attain these existences beyond death. One may be moral and live a good life both within and without the Mormon church and still be excluded from the highest rewards the church offers in the upper realms of the celestial heaven.

Mainstream Christian theological beliefs and church practices differ widely with those of Mormonism. Mormonism stands or falls on its faith in and acceptance of Joseph Smith as true prophet, on his account of receiving the *Book of Mormon,* on his word of receiving revelations, and on his interpretation and implementation of revelation into church practices and organizations such as the priesthoods of Aaron and Melchizedek, temple works (baptism for the dead, endowments, celestial marriage), polygamous marriages, and the three eternal kingdoms.

The biblical witness in Deuteronomy 18:21-22 and 1 Thessalonians 5:20-21 indicates several things about a prophet. When someone speaks as a prophet in the name of God, hearers should test and prove all things and determine whether there is substance and consistency in what the prophet says.

Critics point out that the *Book of Mormon* predicted the discovery of America by Columbus (1 Nephi 13:12), the Puritans (1 Nephi 13:16), and the Revolutionary War (1 Nephi 13:18-19)—all after they had happened. In *Doctrine and Covenants* 84:1-5, a revelation and prophecy is given to Joseph Smith of the building of the temple in Missouri, but the construction never occurred.[56]

The *King James Version* of the Bible is used by Mormons. Their church publishes it with explanatory notes and cross references to the standard works of their faith. Mormons, taught by Joseph Smith, say they believe the Bible as far as it is translated correctly. Some critics write that if Mormons would believe the biblical data as found in the *Book of Mormon,* they would not be too distant from the main theological tenets of orthodox Christianity. Christians believe that the Bible is inspired by God and is trustworthy (2 Tim. 3:16; Mark 13:31; John 17:17). The *Book of Mormon,* "the most correct book on earth," has gone through over 2,100 deletions, additions, and word and phrase changes since its inception in 1830. Some point out that there are significant theological changes from one edition to another.

In the 1830 edition in 1 Nephi, page 25, line 4, it reads, "the virgin which thou seest, is the mother of God." In the 1963 edition 2 Nephi 11:18 (verses were added in 1879) reads, "the virgin whom thou seest is the mother of the Son of God." In the 1830 edition 1 Nephi, page 26, lines 10-11 read, "Behold the Lamb of God, yea even the Eternal Father." The 1963 edition had edited 1 Nephi 11:21 to read, "Behold the Lamb of God, yea, even the Son of the Eternal Father." Mormons do not believe in the Trinity.

According to *Doctrine and Covenants* 18:1-5, the *Book of Mormon* contains "all things written concerning the foundation of my church, my gospel, and my rocks" (clarification in *D&C* 1:37-39).

Concerning God the *Book of Mormon* teaches

- one God (Alma 11:21-22,28-31; 2 Nephi 11:7; 31:21; 3 Nephi 11:27,36; Mosaih 15:1-5)

- God the Father and Son have been God eternally (Alma 11:38-39,44; 2 Nephi 26:12; Mosaiah 16:15)

- God is unchanging (Mormon 9:9-11; Moroni 7:22; 8:18)

- God is Spirit (Alma 18:24-28; 22:9-11).

Critics who examine Mormon writings such as *Doctrine and Covenants, The Pearl of Great Price,* and the statements and interpretations made by prophet/presidents and General Authorities point out discrepancies between the *Book of Mormon* and those writings. The *Book of Mormon* does not contain the doctrines and practices that are explicit in the Mormon church such as Aaronic and Melchizedek priesthoods, the plurality of gods, God as an exalted man, the human potential to become a god, the three heavens (telestial, terrestrial, celestial), the Word of Wisdom, the pre-existence of the human spirit, eternal progression, baptism for the dead, celestial marriage, and the plurality of wives. Joseph Smith received revelations after the *Book of Mormon* and established these beliefs and practices.

The Church of Jesus Christ of Latter-day Saints views itself as the restored and true church. Consequently, other churches are forms of corruption and apostasy. The Mormon church sees little, if any, necessity for participating with other churches in ecumenical or joint endeavors. It does not include itself as a part of Christianity or denominationalism. The Bible is not sufficient in and of itself as the guide to faith and practice for the Mormon church; therefore, it has extra-biblical sacred texts that provide the basic substance for church life. The church provides non-Mormons, called Gentiles, value as moral beings and acknowledges an eternal condition for them exclusive of the exalted conditions of Mormons. The Mormon church actively proselytizes among Christians of diverse church affiliations as well as among non-Christians. Mormons believe that the kingdom of God shall center in Independence, Missouri, led by the vanguard of Mormons. They also believe that their church has a peculiar mission in establishing a theocracy in America.

Views within Christianity and churches toward the Church of Jesus Christ of Latter-day Saints vary. Historically, the Christian churches and the Mormon churches have often related to one another with suspicion and hostility. Some Christian leaders and theologians have ridiculed the Mormon church as peculiar, antiquated, quasi-Christian, and/or heretical. Christian scholars for the most part have not given serious research to the sacred texts, theology, and church practices of the Mormon church. Christian laypersons, in individual relations with Mormons, have cultivated friendships often oblivious of the differences between each other's faith and practice.

In recent times, with the rapid growth of the Mormon church from a Western United States people to a global mission movement, both Christianity and Mormonism have found themselves competing for new members in the religious marketplace of mass media, unchurched populations, world religions, and urban masses. Both bodies have become world conscious and world present, and both encounter and often confront each other in their various ministries and missions. Since there has been so little official contact between the Christian churches and the Mormon church, the future only offers expanding possibilities for such engagements as space shrinks between the two and more information and relationships become available.

A Christian Posture Toward Mormons

The Church of Jesus Christ of Latter-day Saints is a monolithic and hierarchical institution. Its General Authorities and exclusive temples seem some distance from daily activities; however, persons who claim and practice the Mormon faith abound in local settings. Most towns and cities across America have ward and stake buildings, and a beehive of activities occurs in and from those places.

One Christian posture sees Mormons as persons who need community, church, temple, home fellowship, promises of eternity, discipline, stewardship of time and talent, and a religious vision. Mormons are homemakers, providers, citizens, dreamers, and neighbors. As persons, then, they are not peculiar, quasi-anything, heretical, or ridiculous. They—as do Christians—have worth as persons, commonality as humans, and a present promise and a future destiny with God. This posture is based on integrity, openness, and honesty in both verbal and nonverbal communication. The Mormon has a story to tell, and a very personal one at that. I do, too.

The Mormon story may revolve around feelings about the veracity of Joseph Smith, his visions, revelations, and teachings; the truth of the *Book of Mormon* and other sacred scriptures; and the Savior. The Mormon story may include biblical references. Given time in relationships, it will include the following: focus on the family, keeping the family together for eternity, concern and care for the dead, clean and moral living, tithing one's income, and going on mission as a missionary.

The story may speak of voluntarism and sacrificial work in the church, of the emphasis on the laity, of paying for the temple before construction, and of planning to send one's son as a missionary to a faraway land.

Some Mormons will know the story of their church more deeply and intricately than others and will be able to communicate it most effectively. Especially the young missionaries who have trained for several months will be able to communicate a well-memorized outline of their belief and faith. Other Mormons will know less theology, and many will not be aware of the meanings of the temple ceremonies.

A Christian attitude toward Mormons will recognize the diversity of knowledge, commitment, and active obedience among them. They will be accepted as they are. Christians need to be prepared before communicating with a Mormon and continue to prepare for forthcoming encounters. A Christian posture does not survive on feelings, as Mormons might encourage a person to believe. Rather, a Christian posture stands on revelation and reason with roots in the Bible; some two thousand years of Christian church, community, scholarship, and service; and one's own religious experience. Christianity and Mormonism differ greatly on

- major theological interpretations of the Bible
- principles of hermeneutics
- church practices
- the historical interpretation of Christianity.

Both Christians and Mormons will recite Scriptures to explicate their points of belief and practice, although their explications and pointings are quite dissimilar in content and meaning. Also, both point to Jesus Christ as Savior.

These differences do not mean that a Christian cannot appreciate much in the life-style and commitment of Mormons. They stress a high moral code. They emphasize close family life. Their stewardship of money, time, and talent is a grand ideal to follow. Their voluntary efforts in youth and retirement to serve their church around the world are most admirable. Their rapid growth both in America and other lands demonstrates hard work, organizational structure, and appeal to the religious needs of diverse peoples.

In conclusion, a Christian posture toward Mormons might include the following considerations:

1. Mormons are persons with religious needs that Mormonism may or may not fulfill. Their church appeals to authoritarian and structured religious life-styles, cohesive family relations, and eternal security for the family.

2. A Christian posture does not view Joseph Smith as prophet, seer, and revelator, nor does it accept the validity of his priesthood. If Mormonism stands or falls on the validity and legitimacy of prophet Joseph Smith, as many Mormon leaders have stated, then it falls. A Christian posture rests in the lordship and saviorhood of Jesus Christ, who is above prophethood and priesthood and who judges both.

3. The Bible is the authoritative and trustworthy sacred written tradition. A Christian posture includes no other sacred and revelatory written traditions alongside the Bible. Other Christian writings have helped interpret and illuminate the Bible, but none is equal to or supersedes the Bible. A Christian posture does not accept the *Book of Mormon, Doctrine and Covenants,* and *The Pearl of Great Price* as divine revelations and authoritative for belief and practices.

4. A Christian posture voices the oneness and unity of God as He is revealed and experienced in the Father, Son, and Holy Spirit. Doctrinally, the Trinity speaks to the beliefs in monotheism, the biblical witness about God, and the church's theology and experience since New Testament times. God is worshiped in spirit and truth. Mormonism does not accept the Trinity, although the *Book of Mormon* affirms it. For Mormons, God is viewed anthropomorphically, that is, materially with flesh and bones. Mormons recognize little distinction between God and man.

5. Christians affirm Jesus Christ as the Messiah, the Word become flesh, the Son of God born of the virgin Mary, all in the context of the understanding of the Trinity. Jesus Christ is true God and true man. He is both Savior and Lord. A Christian posture does not accept the Mormon view that

Jesus was Jehovah, that he was a god alongside other gods, that he was a preexistent spirit little different from other pre-existent spirits, or that Jesus was involved in polygamous marriages, as some Mormon authorities have stated.

6. A Christian posture views salvation in the context of the grace, love, mercy, righteousness, and judgment of God and the acceptance of and participation in salvation by the person through faith and obedience. The patterns and means of salvation are seen in the life and teachings, the ministry, the crucifixion, and the resurrection of Jesus Christ in the context of the Trinity. Salvation is by grace through faith. A Christian posture does not accept the Mormon distinction between salvation and exaltation. Neither does it accept the ideas of exaltation in which an individual may become a god and inhabit and have dominion over a kingdom for eternity or of the exclusivism of temple rights and privileges to enable a person to attain exaltation.

7. Temple works including baptism for the dead, endowments, and marriage for eternity are not acceptable by a Christian posture. The temple complex has roots in Egyptology, the occult, and Masonism, mixed with biblical references. It represents an authoritarian, exclusivistic, and gnostic approach to salvation/exaltation and churchmanship. Such a view of temple and works has no prominence in the biblical tradition nor is it taught, practiced, or in any way emphasized by Jesus Christ and New Testament writers.

8. A Christian posture sees the Mormon storehouse as a vital and functional ministry to provide for emergency and critical needs of people. The Mormon storehouse is, however, exclusivistic in that it is for Mormons only, with exceptions being made for the "Gentiles" on recommendation by the bishop.

9. A Christian posture encourages Mormons to be open and up front with their missionary and church messages. Where there may be contradictions, discrepancies, and gaps in Mormon literature and teachings, they are encouraged to examine them. They are also encouraged in claiming the name of Jesus Christ in the title of their church, as well as Saints, to seek with others the communication of the gospel.

10. A Christian posture affirms those Mormons who talk of the Sermon on the Mount, the teachings of Jesus Christ on the good Samaritan and the woman at the well, His death on the cross and His words from the cross, and His resurrection from the tomb. Mormons are affirmed in their spiritual search for God through Jesus Christ, in their serious concern for ethics and morality based in the biblical revelation, and in their commitments to make the world a safe and sane abode.

11. Religious freedoms and separation of church and state are fostered by a Christian posture that claims for Mormons their rights and freedoms as guaranteed in the Constitution of the United States of America.

2

JEHOVAH'S WITNESSES
■   ■

Publishers and Kingdom Hall Builders

The doorbell rings. Standing on the porch are a middle-aged mother and her seven-year-old daughter. They have *The Watchtower* magazine to extend to me for a donation, and they would also like to talk with me about Jehovah and the Scriptures. If I invite them in, they are ready to discuss their scriptural understandings with me; or they will return if I will see them at another time. They evoke some sympathy toward themselves, especially toward the purchase of the reading material. I notice across the street another woman and child on the porch of a neighbor. They, together with millions of "publishers," have come from the Kingdom Hall and are canvassing the globe.

The television nightly news focuses on a religious community nearby building a church structure. Jehovah's Witnesses, the publishers, are constructing their Kingdom Hall. They have come from across the state and from adjoining states. With a concrete foundation already in place, they will build the building over the weekend with voluntary labor and multiple skills of carpentry, plumbing, electrical work, and carpeting. They will be ready for their worship and theocratic ministry classes by the first of next week. The publishers will be ready to hit the streets.

Assorted clippings from national magazines over the past decade paint an enlarged picture of Jehovah's Witnesses. They refuse blood transfusions; do not salute the American flag; anticipate the end of the world and sell their possessions in preparation for the coming of Armageddon; comprise a solid community of over four million followers around the world; call Christmas and Easter celebrations pagan and refuse to participate in them; and have a highly organized and hierarchical elite group of leaders at their Bethel headquarters in Brooklyn, New York.

These leaders hand down all printed matter with their interpretations. A large and growing number of publishers, disenchanted with Jehovah's Witnesses' theology and practice, speak out; and many have been disfellowshipped. What does one make of these constant visits to homes? What is the reality behind these printed stories in the mass media about this substantial and pervasive religious community?

The stories of Jehovah's Witnesses are told by publishers and at the Kingdom Hall. The Kingdom Hall is the training ground and launching pad of the Witnesses and where the theocratic ministry studies are held. Everyone is being equipped with Bible knowledge, trained in public speaking, and motivated to leave the Kingdom Hall to enter the world with a supply of published materials such as *The Watchtower* and *Awake*. All of the Kingdom Hall teaching and training activities are under close supervision of Bethel headquarters. The governing board at Bethel, numbering some fourteen members, discusses and writes the theology and biblical interpretations and strategy for every Kingdom Hall in the world.

Publishers are Jehovah's Witnesses who disseminate the teachings through published materials. They are (1) door knockers, (2) book distributors, (3) witnesses to the doctrines of their fellowship, (4) inviters to the Bible studies they lead and to the Kingdom Hall, and (5) warners of the coming judgment, Armageddon, and the millennium. Every Witness is trained to be a publisher. Each publisher is expected to spend at least ten hours a month knocking on doors and distributing literature. Some Witnesses spend ninety or more hours monthly doing their publishing and carry special names like *pioneer* or *special pioneer*.

Jehovah's Witnesses have grown rapidly since World War II. Their statistics show that through their 1990-1991 service year there were 4,278,820 publishers (members) working out of 66,207 Kingdom Halls (congregations) in 211 countries. Publishers logged some 951,870,021 hours in their work. At their annual memorial attendance (Lord's Supper observance), there were 10,650,158 attenders, indicating many more than their membership.[1]

Jehovah's Witnesses are a nineteenth-century native American religion. Charles Taze Russell (1852-1916) founded and organized the corporation in 1874. Thus, Jehovah's Witnesses have a history of more than a hundred years. Their growth has mushroomed since the 1940s, including a world wide mission emphasis. They have caught the attention and often the allegiance of those willing to place power and authority in a governing select few; of those looking to the end time in their own generation and making religious and often material plans for the end of the world; of those who like voluntarism in religious community, since the Witnesses are mostly a layperson's movement; of those who at least theoretically and to a certain extent theologically have deep suspicion and distrust of the worldly powers and values; and of those who are willing to work together interracially and interethnically in the Kingdom Hall to publish the tidings of Jehovah.

Rumors and facts of dissenters and excommunication within and from Kingdom Halls are publicized. Witnesses face similar challenges that other religious communities face. What, if any, accommodations will they make in the midst of change? How will they continue to relate to government and certain laws of the land? Will they continue to view Roman

Catholics and Protestants as the whores of Babylon and themselves as the only true Christians? How will they handle their highly authoritarian patterns of leadership, the place of women in their ministries, and their historic view on blood transfusions?

Jehovah's Witnesses exclude members of the churches as being Christians. They view church members as apostates. They do not accept the doctrine of the Trinity, and they have their own translation of the Bible. Thus, they exclude themselves from historical and traditional Christianity. The following study will examine their major doctrines and practices, their historical development, and the contrasts between the Witnesses and traditional Christian teachings and practices.

The Four Presidents: A Brief History

The Jehovah's Witnesses have had four presidents since their inception in the 1870s. They and their years of leadership are (1) Charles Taze Russell (1874-1916), (2) Judge Joseph F. Rutherford (1916-1942), (3) Nathan H. Knorr (1942-1977), and (4) Frederick W. Franz (1977-present). These four men have provided the major biblical and theological interpretations, the style of organization, the life-style of the Kingdom Hall, and the flavor of the published materials used by all publishers.

Charles Taze Russell (1852-1916), founder and first president, grew up with a background in Presbyterian and Congregational churches. He was familiar with the YMCA, and he attended lectures and read widely in Adventism. He became a close student of the Bible. In his studies and experiences, he reacted against certain doctrines of the churches and against the churches themselves. Russell denied the existence of hell, the Trinity, the physical return of Jesus Christ, people's possession of a soul, and the validity of the churches. He became fascinated with the study of Bible chronology and turned much of his energies toward prophecies in the Bible.

Russell was a voluminous writer, and his major works included *Studies in the Scriptures*. In this writing he stated,

> Not only do we find that people cannot see the divine plan in studying the Bible by itself, but we see, also, that if anyone lays the "Scripture Studies" aside, even after he has used them, after he has become familiar with them, after he has read them for ten years—if he then lays them aside and ignores them and goes to the Bible alone, though he has understood his Bible for ten years, our experiences show that within two years he goes into darkness. On the other hand, if he had merely read the "Scripture Studies" with their references and had not read a page of the Bible as such, he would be in the light at the end of two years, because he would have the light of the Scriptures.[2]

Russell's statement indicates the direction that he and other leaders would take in terms of the value of their own writings as authoritative in comparison to the Bible. He began Zion's Watch Tower and Tract Society, *The Watchtower* magazine, and founded the world headquarters at Bethel in Brooklyn, New York. His teachings at Bethel focused on prophecies and dates. He (1) prophesied dates for the invisible return of Jesus Christ in 1914 and the beginnings of the end time; (2) had much to say about Armageddon, the millennium, and the elect (3) wrote of the 144,000 elect persons from his studies of Revelation 20 who would reign with Jehovah; and (4) advocated the doctrine that humans will have a chance to be saved during the millennium.

Russell claimed to have been a world traveler, delivering sermons in many lands. He faced several crises in both domestic and personal matters. Once he lost a lawsuit when it was discovered that he was marketing a falsely advertised brand of miracle wheat. He sued a Christian minister for libel and lost the case. He was proven to be a perjurer in court upon his false claims that he knew the Greek language and that he had been ordained. His wife divorced him on several grounds, including his improper conduct with other women.

Bible teaching, theological interpretations, and public relations appeared to be Russell's forte. His early followers, often called Russellites, observed him as a charismatic figure, controversial to be sure; and they viewed him as tenacious in his vision and pursuit to herald a world already judged, about to enter Armageddon and judgment.

When Russell died in 1916, Judge *Joseph Franklin Rutherford* preached the funeral sermon. Rutherford (1869-1942) had been Russell's legal advisor and had defended him at one of his trials. Rutherford, a native of Missouri and a former Baptist, became president in 1916. The transition from Russell to Rutherford was not calm, and some challenged his assumption of the presidency. Rutherford began controlling various committees at Bethel headquarters and *The Watchtower* magazine. He forced some leaders out. About four thousand members (approximately 20 percent of the organization's membership) left.

In 1917 Judge Rutherford published a tract entitled "The Fall of Babylon," describing Roman Catholic and Protestant churches as Babylon. In 1918 he and other leaders were imprisoned by the United States government on charges of insubordination and refusal to serve in the armed forces during World War I. They were released in 1919.

Rutherford inherited much from Russell, including his Bible chronology. He projected Armageddon into the future, forecasting it for 1919, then 1920, then 1925. His publication of "Millions Now Living Will Never Die" in 1920 spoke of 1925 as the year of Armageddon. His publication helped elicit a 44 percent increase in membership. His leadership was both theological and organizational. He wrote more prolifically than Russell, but he was not considered as charismatic in appeal. He placed great emphasis upon the distribution and selling of Bethel headquarters literature, visitation, and the meticulous reporting and bookkeeping of all sales and visits.

The board of directors at Bethel became more prominent in its authority, changing, as one scholar states, from a stage of "mystification to deification."[3] He castigated all those who knew Hebrew or Greek and lumped those of other religions as "of the devil." Under his leadership he began the magazine *Awake*, and in 1931 he assigned the name Jehovah's Witnesses to the membership, basing the name on Isaiah 43:10. After his death in 1942 he was followed quietly by Knorr.

Nathan H. Knorr (1905-1977) had become a member of the organization at age sixteen, and at eighteen he began work at Bethel headquarters, working his way up the system and becoming vice president in 1935. Heather and Gary Botting state, "The most important feature of Knorr's tenure was the complete transfer from individual to corporate leadership: the society became in effect a collective oligarchy."[4] After 1942 none of the Witnesses' publications admits an individual author. Knorr emphasized that Jehovah speaks through the "organization," through the governing board, and not through an individual.

Knorr was an administrator. He founded Gilead Missionary Training School in New York City, emphasized biblical and doctrinal studies, improved techniques for door-to-door witnessing, and held mass rallies. *Make Sure of All Things* (1953), a collection of Scripture passages on specific subjects, and *The New World Translation of the Holy Scriptures* (1961), written incorporating Witnesses' theology, were under Knorr's supervision. He promoted the mass gatherings of Witnesses in 1958 at Yankee Stadium and the Polo Grounds, when a quarter of a million attended and mass baptisms were held. International missions were emphasized under his leadership; and from 1942 until 1977, membership increased from 113,000 to 2,000,000 and countries increased from 54 to 210.

Frederick William Franz (1893-present) had served as vice president under Knorr, and at Knorr's death in 1977 he assumed the presidency. Franz had been the behind-the-scenes theologian at Bethel headquarters for decades. He chaired the committee which produced the Witnesses' Bible, *The New World Translation of the Holy Scriptures*. Franz is credited with the application of Bible chronology to the date of 1975 as the significant year for something to happen in Jehovah's Witnesses' expectations. As early as 1966 he asked the assemblies, "What is it going to mean, dear friends? . . . Does it mean that Armageddon is going to be finished, with Satan bound by 1975? It could! It could!"[5] In response to this preachment, many Witnesses prepared for the coming of 1975 with postponements of marriages, withdrawal of bank funds, selling of homes, and with a period of waiting. The year 1975 passed without Armageddon and the end.

By the time Franz became president, rumblings and dissent were across the Kingdom Halls of the heartland and within Bethel headquarters. The yearbook of 1979 reported,

> The Lord Jesus Christ, who knows the spiritual condition of each one who professes to be his follower, does not tolerate lukewarmness. He advises any who are in that state now to rectify their condition if they are to please him. And just as some deviated from the truth in the first century, it is not surprising that the same thing happens today. Jehovah knows those who belong to him. Warning examples of what befell the Israelites as they were about to enter the Promised Land should keep us individually from becoming overconfident. The seriousness of this matter is emphasized in the fact that 29,893 were disfellowshipped last year. There is no question that our faith is being tested today.[6]

Under both the Knorr and Franz eras of leadership, there had been great "apostasy." A tightening of control ensued at Bethel. Members of the board of directors became suspect, were interrogated, and dismissed. Included among those disfellowshipped was Raymond Franz, the nephew of the president. Raymond Franz had served in the top leadership positions at Bethel, including the board of directors. He said after his dismissal, "By one stroke they eliminated all my years of service. . . . I frankly do not believe there is another organization more insistent on 100 percent conformity."[7]

Throughout the tenures of the four presidents, their leadership has provided strength and firmness. Russell and Rutherford operated in the public arena, while Knorr and Franz led in a quieter style. The Witnesses, for the most part, have obediently accepted the style of leadership from the headquarters in Brooklyn.

The Theocratic Society: The Leaders and the Led

From the publication *Make Sure of All Things* (1953), Jehovah's Witnesses are described as,

> Servants of Jehovah, the Almighty God, and active witnesses to his sovereign supremacy. Since the time of Christ Jesus they are Christian ministers, doing the will of God by following the course exemplified by Christ their leader. The name Jehovah meaning "The Purposer," his witnesses declare him as the only true God, who is working out his purpose of vindicating his name and sovereignty and blessing all faithful mankind through his kingdom. Not a sect or cult that follows or adulates human leaders or rites and ceremonies.[8]

Since Russell's time, when the followers were called Russellites, the leaders have focused not on individuals but on the leadership at headquarters. Leaders and followers among the Witnesses function in an hierarchical arrangement. Jesus Christ is the chief witness of Jehovah, and each witness is a minister. Witnesses have been known by many names, including Russellites, Watch Tower Bible and Tract Society, People's Pulpit Association, International Bible Students Association, and since 1931, Jehovah's Witnesses.

The Governing Board, known as "The Society," is composed of some fourteen to eighteen men who preside over all matters of the organization. They operate out of the

Bethel headquarters in Brooklyn, New York, with about two thousand Witnesses carrying various work loads. The board's responsibilities include,

> taking the lead in actual preaching work . . ., making decisions, issuing counsel on doctrinal matters, reproving, correcting, settling disputes on organizational matters, directing conduct of (the) organization, making appointments to special service positions in congregations, dividing territory, making territory and missionary assignments, directing defense of the good news before courts and legal bodies, directing relief work to benefit the needy among the entire Christian congregation, supervising cleanness of the organization.[9]

Bethel tends toward being a self-sufficient community, raising its food on farms outside New York City. Members of the community are provided room and board and a very modest monthly allowance. The largest printing press among more than thirty-five in the world is located at Bethel.

Members of the Governing Board claim to be included in the 144,000 elect who will live with Jehovah and King Jesus. The elect are given various names, including the "little flock," the "Heavenly Class," "the faithful and discreet slave," and "the Remnant of the Bride Class." Other Witnesses not included in the 144,000 elect are referred to as the "other sheep," "the Multitude," and the "Jonadabs." Thus, there are two classes of Jehovah's Witnesses—the elect, who will live and reign with King Jesus, and the others, who will live on a cleansed earth.

The Governing Board is viewed as the voice of Jehovah in communicating doctrine and practice to the Witnesses.

> The record that the "faithful and discreet slave" organization has made for the past more than 100 years forces us to the conclusion that Peter expressed when Jesus asked if his apostles also wanted to leave him, namely, "Whom shall we go away to?" (John 6:66-69). No question about it. We all need help to understand the Bible, and we cannot find the Scriptural guidance

we need outside the "faithful and discreet slave" organization.[10]

Witnesses have been discouraged by the Governing Board from doing Bible study independent of the Board's interpretations in their publications. Their view of the Bible is as follows:

> The Bible is an organizational book and belongs to the Christian organization as an organization, not to individuals, regardless of how sincerely they may believe that they can interpret the Bible. For this reason the Bible cannot be properly understood without Jehovah's visible organization in mind.[11]

> In view of its unbreakable connection with the Christian Theocratic Organization, the Bible is organization-minded and it cannot be fully understood without our having the Theocratic organization in mind . . . All the sheep in God's flock must be organization-minded, like the Bible.[12]

The organizational framework of Jehovah's Witnesses centers on Jehovah, his chief minister Jesus Christ, "the faithful and discreet slave" organization or the Governing Board, and the millions of publishers in the Kingdom Halls. The Governing Board is led by the president and has various committees.

Appointments are made by the board for national and local posts. A branch overseer may supervise the work in a nation or an aggregate of several lands. Regional servants are appointed by the board to oversee the work in various countries. There are six regional servants in the United States. Zone servants oversee a number of circuits. There are zone servants in the United States. A circuit servant has supervision for some fifteen congregations or Kingdom Halls. Kingdom Hall is where the company meets and is usually limited to some two hundred publishers.

Kingdom Hall is the preparation center for each Witness to worship, to study materials, to train for door-to-door visitation, and to receive literature. The building is usually small, meeting the needs of some two-hundred members. It is simple in decor, and is kept very clean. When a new Kingdom Hall is constructed, Witnesses come from hundreds of miles to voluntarily build it over a weekend. Each congregation has a particular territory to serve, and each house in that territory is pinpointed on a map for door-to-door visitation.

Elders, or overseers, supervise the various ministries of the Kingdom Hall.[13] The presiding overseer is appointed by the Governing Board. He serves without salary and has responsibility for the entire congregation. He has several assistants. The field overseer supervises the distribution of the literature, which originates from Bethel headquarters, including *The Watchtower* and *Awake*. He administers the visitation program and the reporting records of all visits and sales. The Bible study overseer helps Witnesses plan for home Bible studies either in their homes or in the homes of interested non-Witnesses. The Theocratic Ministry School overseer has the primary responsibility of training the Witnesses in skills of teaching and public speaking. In addition to supervising the library, he may drill members in techniques of speaking, give counsel in the preparation of their lessons, and say who is ready at what time to go door-to-door.

The Watchtower Study conductor leads the weekly study of this magazine. The congregation book study conductor teaches the approved doctrines of the Governing Board. These leaders usually serve in these capacities for one year.

Five meetings are held each week to train Witnesses. Four of these meetings are conducted in the Kingdom Hall, and the other one is held in a home. It is a congregation book study of some Watchtower Society book. The four meetings, usually held for one hour each week in the Kingdom Hall, are the Public Talk, *The Watchtower* Study, The Kingdom Ministry School, and The Service Meeting.[14] The Public Talk is designed for the general public to help "those who are studying the Bible in their homes with Jehovah's Witnesses to become acquainted with Jehovah's great purpose for mankind and to associate with God's Organization regularly."

The Watchtower Study uses the format of question-answer concerning *The Watchtower*. This study offers spiritual truths to keep participants abreast of the application and fulfillment of Bible prophecy. During these studies men, women, and children learn their Christian roles. The Kingdom Ministry School is a weekly "clinic" for men, women, and children in preparation and training for speaking and debating concerning the doctrines and message of the Witnesses. The Theocratic Ministry School is designed for the purpose of teaching and equipping Jehovah's Witnesses to preach the good news. Unlike most schools, there are no graduates, and the course is a lifelong one.

The Service Meeting prepares members for effective dissemination of their literature and doctrines and gives "Jehovah's Witnesses practical instructions to help them to become better qualified ministers and more efficient in carrying on their house-to-house ministry. This is done through talks, demonstrations, question and answer parts, interviews and discussions between two or more persons."

The format for the meetings in the Kingdom Hall is simple and direct. An opening and closing song and a prayer are always included. The major part of the meeting concerns Bible study, using the materials of the Watchtower Society and training and discussions on doctrine, methods of presentation of doctrines to non-Witnesses, and better ways to distribute the literature. Visitors are welcomed at the entrance. At the entrance is a literature distribution office where Witnesses receive literature and make their reports on sales.

One of the main goals of hours spent in the Kingdom Hall is to prepare the Witnesses to go on the streets in door-to-door visitation. They make over two hundred million visits each year. A faithful Witness will spend at least ten hours each month in publishing door-to-door. He or she will also attempt to sell twelve magazines subscriptions and hold a Bible study every month. An auxiliary pioneer will work at least sixty hours each month and a regular pioneer will work at least ninety hours a month.

Although most of the work of Witnesses is voluntary, salaries are given to certain full-time overseers. Pioneers are remunerated with the volume of distribution of literature. Missionaries, who have taken the six-month course at the School of Gilead, are sent out to over two-hundred countries.

From the Governing Board to the Kingdom Hall, Jehovah's Witnesses are arranged in a tightly-knit, hierarchical organization. Although they have experienced tens of thousands of "excommunications" and have lost both members of "the Little Flock" as well as the "other sheep," they have continued to make their appeal through publishing and door-to-door visitations and have continued to grow. By 1991, their membership had reached over four million and the circulation of *The Watchtower* had soared to some 10,000,000 copies bimonthly. The Governing Body had made its explanations of the "failure" of 1975, tightened its reigns on those led, the Witnesses, and looked to the future.

Jehovah, King Jesus, and the Holy Spirit

What Jehovah's Witnesses believe and what they practice are found in the teachings and writings of the leadership at Bethel headquarters. Witnesses say that the Bible is the authoritative source for their life. "Everything it says is true. . . . The Bible is true about history, science, and especially in foretelling the future."[15] The Witnesses have their own translation of the Bible, *The New World Translation of the Holy Scriptures*. This translation serves their theological purposes in defining their doctrine of God, Jesus Christ, the Holy Spirit, and salvation. The Bible is studied in the light of their translation together with the writings of Russell, Rutherford, and the myriad of literature which comes from the Governing Board.

Since their inception, Jehovah's Witnesses have been antitrinitarian. "Jehovah is no Babylonish triad of Gods, no

God of three Persons in one individual. Jehovah is only one God, one Person."[16] They assert that the doctrine of the Trinity is a false doctrine originated by Satan and foisted by Emperor Constantine in the Council of Nicea in 325 B.C.

The name of God is "Jehovah" for Witnesses. In their translation, they insert the name "Jehovah" for "God" or "Lord." They argue that the use of "God" is like a title of President, whereas Jehovah is the true name used some seven thousand times in the Bible. Jehovah is one whose major characteristics are justice, wisdom, power, and love. Jehovah is a person, and man was created in his image. Jehovah is "the Greatest Personality in the universe, distinguished by that exclusive name. The Great Theocrat, the Unfailing Purposer, the True and Living God, Creator and Supreme Sovereign of the universe."[17] God is one and can have no equal, and no one can claim title to His name. In the publications of the Witnesses, Jehovah is portrayed with pictorials of a hand or a pair of hands extending from heaven. Recently, Jehovah has been shown as the Great Shepherd.

Jesus Christ is viewed in three stages in Witnesses' thought: (1) He spent an unknown number of years with Jehovah in heaven before He became human; (2) He spent thirty-three-and-one-half years on earth, and (3) His return to heaven as a spirit son.[18] Anthony Hoekema, in his book *Jehovah's Witnesses*, describes these stages as prehuman, human, and posthuman. Jesus was created as the first creation by Jehovah and given the name Archangel Michael. All things were created through Jesus, for He was Jehovah's firstborn heir; however, He was not equal with Jehovah, nor was he cocreator with Jehovah.

The New World Translation of the Holy Scriptures translates Colossians 1:16-17 as Jesus' creating "all other things," the word "other" being added to the text to indicate that Jesus was created by Jehovah and then became Jehovah's creating Agent. In the unknown years in heaven, Jesus existed as a spirit son of Jehovah, the first and only creation of Jehovah. *The New World Translation of the Holy Scriptures* states that there was a time when Jesus did not exist.

Jesus was born in the human stage to the virgin Mary. "Jehovah transferred the life of his mighty spirit Son from heaven to the womb of the virgin Mary."[19] It appears that the Witnesses believe there was a process of genetic transfer of Christ to the womb of Mary. "God's 'firstborn Son' disappeared from heaven. His life-force was transferred down to the virgin body of Mary."[20] They believe that Jesus was born about October 2, 2 B.C. and died on Friday afternoon the fourteenth of the month of Nisan (March-April), A.D. 33.

Jesus is not seen as God in the flesh, as God incarnate, or as God-Man. In the human stage, Jesus was a perfect human creature.[21] He may be called a god according to *The New World Translation of the Holy Scriptures* in John 1:1, "In the beginning the Word was, and the Word was with God, and the Word was a god." They believe that Jehovah is greater than Jesus, and although Jesus was a mighty god, He was not Almighty God. He is not Jehovah or a part of Jehovah.

Witnesses believe that the baptism of Jesus means that He has become Jehovah's High Priest, the Messiah, and the Heir of the Heavenly Kingdom. "After being anointed with God's holy spirit at the Jordan River, Jesus could have attached to his name the title Messiah or Jesus Christ."[22] Through this baptism Jehovah was appointing Jesus "to be the King of His coming kingdom. . . . he became, in fact, Jesus Christ, or Jesus the Anointed."[23]

What was the basic meaning of the human stage in the life of Jesus? Witnesses use the words *atonement* and *ransom*. Jesus atoned and paid a ransom for the sin of Adam. Because of Adam's sin and since his time, all humans have sin and have suffered physical death. Adam lived a perfect life before sin, and Jesus lived a perfect life without sin. The "human life that Jesus Christ laid down in sacrifice must be exactly equal to that life which Adam forfeited for all his offspring; it must be a perfect human life, no more, no less."[24] Jesus paid the ransom for sin by dying on a "torture stake," not a cross, which Witnesses assert is a pagan symbol. Adam's sin, for which Jesus paid the penalty, was not to end in physical pain in hell. It was to end in annihilation. Adam was to be excluded from the atonement made by Jesus; the atonement was valid for the children of Adam.

In the posthuman stage after the resurrection, Jehovah raised Jesus from the dead as a "spirit Son." There was no physical resurrection of Jesus, but "Jehovah saw fit to remove Jesus' body, even as he had done before with Moses' body (Deut. 34:5, 6)."[25] Jesus was then raised "not as a human Son, but as a mighty spirit Son."[26] His appearances after the resurrection were not visible, physical ones but similar to the appearance of angels. Jehovah elevated Jesus to be the head of creation and gave Him the name Michael, which Jesus had in his prehuman stage. It appears that Jesus began as the first creation of Jehovah, named Michael; then He became the perfect human man separate from His prehuman existence but as a god; and He returned after His death and resurrection to be the spirit Son named Michael.

Bruce M. Metzger, a biblical scholar, wrote that the Witnesses' belief of Jesus

> is a modern form of the ancient heresy of Arianism. According to the Jehovah's Witnesses, Christ before his earthly life was a spirit-creature named Michael, the first of God's creation, through whom God made the other created things. As a consequence of his birth on earth, which was not an incarnation, Jesus became a perfect human being, the equal of Adam prior to the fall. In his death Jesus' human nature, being sacrificed, was annihilated. As a reward for his sacrificial obedience God gave him a divine, spirit nature. Throughout his existence, therefore, Jesus Christ has never been co-equal with God. He is not eternal, for there was a time when he was not. While he was on earth he was nothing

more than a man, and therefore the atoning effect of his death can have no more significance than that of a perfect human being. Throughout there is an ill-concealed discontinuity between the pre-existent spirit creature, the earthly man Jesus, and the present spirit existence of Christ Jesus.[27]

Anthony Hoekema, a Protestant theologian, also writes of the Witnesses' view of Jesus:

The individual who laid down his life at Calvary was not the individual who existed previously in heaven and was God's agent in creation; the individual who is now ruling over his heavenly Kingdom is not the individual who died on the cross for us. Really, Jehovah's Witnesses have three Christs, none of whom is equal to Jehovah and none of whom is the Christ of the Scriptures.[28]

The posthuman state of Jesus includes His defeat of Satan in heaven, His return to earth to cleanse it at the Battle of Armageddon, and his reign for a thousand years before the kingdom is turned over to Jehovah. Jehovah and King Jesus will be with the elect while the "other sheep" inherit the Satan-free earth.

In Witness teaching the idea of the Holy Spirit is one of an invisible active force in the world. The words *Holy Spirit* are not capitalized in the writings of Witnesses, including *The New World Translation of the Holy Scriptures*. The Holy Spirit is not a person in keeping with their view of Jehovah as God, Jesus as the first of the creation, and the Holy Spirit as an impersonal force.

The Witnesses' understanding of man is based on creation of man in the image of Jehovah, on man as a soul, and on the fall of mankind under Adam. Mankind was created in the image of Jehovah with the characteristics of wisdom, justice, love, and power, "the same attributes as his Creator."[29] Witnesses believe that "God did not create man with a soul. Man is a soul. So as we expect, when man dies, his soul dies."[30] Spirit is distinct from soul. At death, Jehovah takes back the spirit while the soul ceases to exist, and there is no conscious existence after death. At the time of resurrection the spirit is returned by Jehovah to form with a new body a living soul. Witnesses explain, "When a person is in a very deep sleep, he remembers nothing. It is similar with the dead. They have no feelings at all. They no longer exist. But, in God's due time, the dead who are ransomed by God will be raised to life."[31]

Armageddon, a New Heaven, a New Earth

Much doctrine, time, and energy among the Witnesses have been directed toward proclaiming and preparing for the end of the present world, its judgment, and a new heaven and a new earth. The leaders have provided specific chronologies from Bible research to indicate eras of the reign of Jesus Christ, the defeat of Satan in the Battle of Armageddon, the presence of the 144,000 elect forever with Jehovah and King Jesus, the paradise earth for the other faithful Witnesses, and the annihilation of the damned.

Several key dates in Witnesses' interpretation have provided a world view of Jehovah's dealings with the world. Witnesses have desired to know what year Jesus Christ began rule as king of Jehovah's government. They established the year 607 B.C.E. (Before Christian Era) as the year God's rulership was "cut down," leaving no government to represent Jehovah on the earth. They arrived at this date from interpretations of Daniel 4:10-37, Ezekiel 21:25-27, and 1 Chronicles 29:23. "Thus, in 607 B.C.E. a period of time began that Jesus Christ later referred to as 'the appointed times of the nations,' or, 'the times of the Gentiles' (Luke 21:24). During these 'appointed times' God did not have a government to represent his rulership in the earth."[32]

The "appointed times" of which Jesus spoke are interpreted to mean the "seven times" mentioned in Daniel. What do the "seven times" mean?

In Revelation chapter 12, verses 6 and 14, we learn that 1,260 days are equal to "a time (that is, 1 time) and times (that is, 2 times) and half a time." That is a total of 3 1/2 times. So "a time" would be equal to 360 days. Therefore, "seven times" would be 7 times 360, or 2,520 days. Now if we count a day for a year, according to a Bible rule, the "seven times" equal 2,520 years.—Numbers 14:34; Ezekiel 4:6.

We have already learned that "the appointed times of the nations" began in the year 607 B.C.E. So by counting 2,520 years from that date, we come down to 1914 C.E. That is the year these "appointed times" ended.[33]

Witnesses believe that the Kingdom of Jehovah was restored in 1914 with Jesus' reign in heaven and with the casting out of Satan, "a mighty spirit creature," to the earth. Satan has control over the earth, including world governments and religions. Jehovah's Kingdom will include the earth after Satan is defeated at the Battle of Armageddon. Witnesses expect this battle to begin momentarily, and they have forecast dates for its beginning. Signs of the impending battle include wars, pestilences, earthquakes, starvation, and false worship. After the battle, witnesses believe that Jesus Christ will rule over the world for a thousand years before handing over the keys of the Kingdom to Jehovah, His father.

An important component of the Kingdom of Jehovah is the reign of King Jesus with the 144,000 elect. These 144,000 persons "will rule with Christ in this kingdom" (Rev. 14:1-4; 20:6). So the Bible also refers to it as "their kingdom"—Daniel 7:27."[34] These persons will no longer be subjects to Christ, but then will be kings with Him in the Kingdom. The process of choosing these persons began with the apostles. "It seems evident that the heavenly calling in general was completed by about the year 1935 C.E. . . . Does this mean that none are now being called by God for heavenly life? Until the final sealing is done, it is possible that some few who have that hope may prove unfaithful, and others will have to be chosen to take their place."[35]

Each year on Nisan 14 (Jewish Passover evening), Jehovah's Witnesses gather at local places around the world to observe the Lord's Supper or memorial. Those in attendance include Witnesses as well as interested seekers. Unleavened bread is served, followed by wine. However, only those of the elect or "little flock" or anointed may take the bread and the wine. The "other sheep" are forbidden to take the symbolic elements of the flesh and blood of Christ. Attendance figures for the 1991 memorial service were 10,650,158, many more than membership in the congregations. Only 8,850, however, actually took the bread and the wine, which meant they considered themselves as part of the elect, the 144,000.

The description of the 144,000 elect includes their being named "the bride, the Lamb's wife," "the body of the Christ," "the temple of God," "the Israel of God," and the "New Jerusalem."[36]

> In the vision of Revelation 20:11-13 those whom the apostle John saw "standing before the throne" to be judged do not include the congregation of Christ's 144,000 faithful followers. This congregation takes part in the "first resurrection," and concerning them Revelation 20:4-6 says: "I saw thrones, and there were those who sat down on them, and power of judging was given them . . . they will be priests of God and of the Christ, and will rule as kings with him for the thousand years." Through the "first resurrection" they come to life in heaven as spirit persons and so do not stand with mankind on earth before God's judgment throne.
>
> Instead of coming under judgment with mankind, they are given "power of judging" and for this reason they sit down on heavenly thrones. So they serve, not only as heavenly kings and priests with Jesus Christ, but also as associate judges with him over mankind. Their term of office as judges with Jesus Christ is the same as their reign, namely, a thousand years long. Hence the judgment day of mankind under the "new heavens" will be a thousand years long.[37]

Only the elect will be with Jehovah and King Jesus in heaven. After the Battle of Armageddon and before the beginning of the millennium, there will be two resurrections. The first will be of the "other sheep" or Jonadabs, those Jehovah's Witnesses who were faithful in life. The second will be those ignorant of Jehovah in their lifetime, and they will be given the opportunity through correct teaching by the resurrected Witnesses to prove themselves worthy Witnesses. All of these Witnesses will inherit the paradise earth. It is believed that Satan will have one final chance at the conclusion of the millennium to test the worthiness of those of the second resurrection. Satan, then, will be destroyed along with all the unworthy ones.

Witnesses do not include a doctrine of hell or eternal punishment in their teachings. They reject the doctrine of hell as unscriptural, unreasonable, contrary to God's love, and repugnant to justice.[38] They interpret hades and sheol as the grave, and they interpret Gehenna as meaning extinction or annihilation.

There are three final possibilities for persons. First, there are those few who reign forever with Jehovah and Jesus Christ in heaven. Second, there are those who reside in a paradise earth forever. Third, there are those who are annihilated.

Literature, Theology, and Missions

If there is one constant characteristic of Witnesses both in their Kingdom Halls and in their door-to-door visits, it is the omnipresent literature—mass-produced, simple to read, pictorial, and inexpensive. The literature is used for the continuing indoctrination of the members and for potential converts. About 90 percent of the recorded time of Witnesses' publishing activities concerns the distribution of literature.[39]

Among the many tracts, booklets, and magazines authored and published by the Governing Board, there are several of significant importance. The Watchtower is one of the most widely published religious magazines in the world, having a bimonthly circulation of over ten million. Sunday's *Watchtower* Study is one of the more popular meetings in the Kingdom Halls with its question and answer format. "It is at the *Watchtower* Study where doctrinal points are established and timely spiritual truths are provided—keeping one abreast with the application and fulfillment of Bible prophecy."[40]

Awake magazine is published bimonthly with a circulation of over nine million. It appeals to and addresses family matters. *The New World Translation of the Holy Scriptures* was published in 1961 to become the official scriptures of the Witnesses. Before that time, they had used the *King James Version* of the Bible, but their translation reflects their particular theological doctrines.

You Can Live Forever in Paradise on Earth, published in 1982, has become the best-selling book. More than 15,000,000 copies had been published in over fifty-five languages. It, too, is projected to youth and the family. It has been described as "putting all the Society's literature into one small volume." It contains 256 pages with many pictures and illustrations.

Each year the *Yearbook of Jehovah's Witnesses*, which provides the statistics of all the accomplishments for the year (baptisms, hours of visitation, numbers of Bible studies, and distribution of publications) is published. Brief summaries of the work in each country, as well as a Bible verse and commentary for each day of the coming year, are included.

Watchtower literature has served as the indispensable guide for the doctrines and practices of the Jehovah's Witnesses. Even before *The New World Translation of the Holy Scriptures*, Witnesses used Society literature as the aid to understand the King James Bible. Concerning the dating of the coming of the Kingdom, Armageddon, and the Millennium, *The Watchtower* magazine has provided the prophecies, the suggested dates, and commentaries on old dates gone by and new dates to come. They prophesied that

Armageddon was to end in 1914, but later admitted it was not to take place as calculated. Judge Rutherford stated that Abraham and others were to be resurrected in 1925. Later, the magazine admitted that it might not have happened. At another time it was said that Armageddon was near in 1940, and *The Watchtower* printed its arrival in a matter of months. The year 1975 was projected as a special year in Bible chronology. Witnesses were encouraged to sell homes and other possessions and give much time to publishing. Later, *The Watchtower* stated that it was uncertain as to whether the time frame was weeks, months, or years.

The 1974-75 period saw an influx of new members into the Kingdom halls in larger numbers than before that time or since. The literature of that period projected the frightening aspects of the impending end of the world. In recent times, with some controversy, thousands have been disfellowshipped, membership has declined, and it has been suggested that another date may be projected in the literature for the great battle and end of time.

Perhaps *The New World Translation of the Holy Scriptures* (NWT) provides a more specific and clear insight into how Witness theology is worked into the Bible. With regard to their interpretation of the Holy Spirit as impersonal, they translate Genesis 1:2, ". . . and God's active force was moving to and fro over the surface of the waters." Because they interpret the use of the word *cross* as a pagan derivative, they translate Matthew 27:40, "If you are a son of God, come down off the torture stake."

Because they do not teach the Trinity and the incarnation of God in Jesus Christ, they translate various passages of Scripture concerning Jesus Christ to fit their particular interpretations. They translate John 1:1, "In the beginning the Word was, and the Word was with God, and the Word was a god." With the words "a god" they insert the indefinite article and leave out the capital G. Witnesses claim that although the Word (Christ) was godlike, Christ was not actually God Himself. The word *God* (*Theos* or *Theon*) appears six times in John 1:1-18; however, John 1:1 is the only time their translation uses the indefinite article before God. Both *Theos* and *Theon* are translated as God. NWT is inconsistent in its translation, and the Witnesses' translation opens members up to the idea of a belief in several gods. Witnesses interpret Isaiah 9:6 in referring to Jesus as a "Mighty God" and to Jehovah as "Almighty God."

In Colossians 1:16-20 the word "other" has been added five times with the translators using parentheses around the word. In verse 16 NWT reads, "Because by means of Him all (other) things were created. . . ." It appears that "other" is added to the text to determine that Jesus created all things except Himself. He, Himself, according to Witnesses' teachings was the first creation of Jehovah. The question may be raised why the translators did not add "(other)" to John 1:3 to be consistent with their theology.[41]

Other additions of commas, parentheses, and the indefinite article in the NWT demonstrate Witnesses' theology injected into biblical translation. For example, in NWT, Luke 23:24 reads, "And he said to him: 'Truly I tell you today, you will be with me in Paradise.'" With the comma placed after "today" instead of before it, the translators interpret into the passage their doctrine that the earthly resurrection is a future event. They would argue that the thief on the torture stake could not have been promised paradise with Jesus that very day.

In Revelation 20:5, NWT reads, "(The rest of the dead did not come to life until the thousand years were ended.) This is the first resurrection." Their theology states that Revelation 20 is literal except for the part of verse 5 which they place in parenthesis. They believe that what is stated after verse 5 will happen during the millennium and not after it as verse 5 implies. In other words, they teach the resurrection coming after Armageddon and before the thousand-year reign of Christ. Whereas, if chapter 20 is read entirely in its context, the early resurrection comes after the end of the thousand-year reign of Christ, not after Armageddon.

A final example of NWT which demonstrates the Governing Board's strong reign over Witnesses occurs in Ephesians 6:4.[42]

Version	Text
King James (1942)	And ye, fathers, provoke not your children to wrath: but bring them up in the nurture and admonition of the Lord.
NWT (1950 and 1961)	And you fathers, do not be irritating your children, but go on bringing them up in the discipline and authoritative advice of Jehovah.
NWT (1981)	And you, fathers, do not be irritating your children, but go on bringing them up in the discipline and mental-regulating of Jehovah.

Note the changes from "nurture and admonition" to "discipline and authoritative advice" to "discipline and mental-regulating." If the Governing Board, which interprets and translates the Bible according to the theologies developed through Russell, Rutherford, Knorr, Franz, and anonymous members of the Board, views itself and is looked upon by Witnesses as "The Theocracy" (Voice of Jehovah), then Witnesses in the Kingdom Halls are "mentally regulated" through the question and answer format to expound the teaching of the Board.

Although Jehovah's Witnesses are future-oriented in terms of their eschatology and expectations of the momentary end of the world, they are serious about their obligations in the present time to proclaim and publish the "good news." Witnesses' children are trained early in learning about the literature as well as in door-to-door visitation. Their major emphasis in missions among non-Witnesses is to introduce them to the formal study of *Watchtower* literature and to lead them to join the "Organization" through water baptism.

Witnesses have a carefully planned and straightforward strategy in their missionary work, sometimes called the "seven step" program.[43] The program includes:

1. Door-to-door visit and street contact, in which literature is placed with the prospect. Tracts, magazines, or books may be used, and a small contribution is sought.

2. The return visit or "back-call." This visit is used to discuss some Bible concern and to encourage the prospect to read the literature.

3. Encouraging the interested one to have a "Home Bible Study" led by a Witness and to subscribe to *The Watchtower* and *Awake* magazines. In this study, Witness literature is used.

4. Invitation with interested persons to attend a Bible study led by a Witness in the area.

5. Invitation to attend a *Watchtower* Study at the Kingdom Hall.

6. When the Witness feels that the prospect is sufficiently grounded in Witness doctrine, one is encouraged to go with the Witness door-to-door as a publisher.

7. New member is led to seek water baptism through counsel with the overseer and to affiliate with a local Kingdom Hall.

Witnesses are careful in step six as they prepare to invite a prospect with them to publish from door-to-door.

> Do the person's expressions show that he believes the Bible is the inspired Word of God? (2 Tim. 3:16) Does he know and believe the basic teachings of the Scriptures so that, when asked questions, he will answer in harmony with the Bible and not according to his own ideas or false religious teachings? (2 Tim. 2:15; Matt. 7:21-23) Is he heeding the Bible's command to associate with Jehovah's people in congregation meetings (if he physically and circumstantially can)? (Heb. 10:24-25; Ps. 122:1). Does he know what the Bible says about fornication, adultery, polygamy and homosexuality, and is he living in harmony with such teachings? If

the person is living with one of the opposite sex, are they properly married? (Matt. 19:9; 1 Cor. 6:9-10; 1 Tim. 3:2,12; Heb. 13:4) Does he heed the Bible's prohibition of drunkenness? (Eph. 5:18; 1 Pet. 4:3-4) Does he keep himself clean from the defilement of tobacco, betel nut, and other things that contaminate the body? Is he free from nonmedical use of addictive drugs? (2 Cor. 7:1) Has he definitely broken off membership in all false religious organizations with which he may have been affiliated, and has he ceased attending meetings and supporting or sharing in their activities? (2 Cor. 6:14-18; Rev. 18:4) Is he free from all involvement in the political affairs of the world? (John 6:15; 15:19; Jas. 1:27) Does he believe and live in harmony with what the Bible says about the affairs of the nations at Isaiah 2:4? Does he really want to be one of Jehovah's Witnesses? (Ps. 110:3)[44]

Based on their theology of the impending end of the world and the urgency to proclaim and win converts, the thrust of Witnesses' work is to place literature in the hands of as many persons as possible and to seek their baptism into "The Organization." Each one must keep detailed and exact records of visits, literature distribution, Bible studies, and hours of publishing. Every member of a Kingdom Hall is a missionary.

However, there are special categories for missionary service beyond the every member status. There are auxiliary, regular, and special pioneer service. The auxiliary pioneer may be approved by the local Kingdom Hall. Service is for sixty hours a month and may be done during special months of the year, such as holiday seasons or the visit of the circuit overseer or the memorial observance (Lord's Supper).

Regular and special pioneers are appointed by the Governing Board. A regular pioneer works some ninety hours a month and may choose the specific territory in counsel with the Kingdom Hall. One must have been baptized within at least six months and a good publisher. The special pioneer is chosen from among regular pioneers and must be willing to go wherever the Governing Board chooses. Often, the assignment is to begin work in a new place to result in a new congregation. The special pioneer is aided financially by the Government Board.

Missionaries are also sent internationally, and they are trained at the Gilead school in New York. One must be between the ages of twenty-one and forty with good health credentials. Missionaries may also serve at Bethel headquarters in Brooklyn, as well as other Bethel facilities (factories, farms, offices) around the world. Bethel means "House of God." Bethel service may mean running printing presses, farming, and doing general clerical work. There may be over six thousand Bethel workers at any given time, assisting in producing Bibles, books, magazines, besides many other millions of printed matter. These publications are sent out in some two hundred languages.

Publishing and missionary work involves persons and finances. Local congregations in the Kingdom Hall are responsible for all local expenses, including the building and maintenance of the Kingdom Hall. Much of the local work of the congregation is voluntary, from the congregational overseer to the cutting of grass. Members give voluntarily of their monies in a collection box in the building. Members also return monies to the congregation through the distribution of literature. Local congregations make decisions on the amounts of money sent to Bethel headquarters. Certain overseers and missionaries are provided for financially when their duties call for more full-time work. From time to time members leave estate gifts to the congregation.

Through their service year of 1990-91, there were a total of 4,278,820 publishers located in 211 countries. The number of congregations was 66,207 with 951,870,021 hours of visitation. For the year there were 300,945 baptisms. Of the over four million world wide, in the United States there were 901,028 publishers.[45]

Statistics indicate the intensive and extensive work load of the faithful Jehovah's Witnesses. To be a member of the congregation is to be a publisher and a missionary; to be less is not to be a Witness. To be more only enables most to be members of "the other sheep," to inherit paradise earth, and not to be a member of the elect 144,000 to reign with King Jesus in the presence of Jehovah forever.

Witness Life-style

In talking with Jehovah's Witnesses and in reviewing the mass of literature, several key symbols and practices emerge which may generally describe their religious life-style. Time is a quality and a quantity for them. Literature is filled with pictures and words about the imminent end of the world. Included are Gentile times, the time of the beginning of the Kingdom, the time of Armageddon, and the millennium. Time must be spent in the Kingdom Hall in weekly meetings, visitations, assemblies, and in voluntary work on building and grounds. Time is work and publishing, and work and publishing is time registered on report cards turned into millions of hours. One's "witness" is measured by time. One's eternity is the quality of time spent in heaven or on paradise earth.

Another symbol is Satan and a decadent, evil, and deteriorating world. Satan is in control of the present world in his cunning, craftiness, deception, materialism, spiritism, sexual temptation, and "independent thinking." Witnesses are warned against false religions, political movements, and oppressive commercial systems which are a part of Satan's world. One is to withdraw from the world of Satan and to be active in the congregation.[46]

Witnesses believe they must submit themselves to the authority of government and pay taxes. They believe they must obey Jehovah over any worldly peers. In wartime they are conscientious objectors. They do not salute the flag of any nation, pledge allegiance, or sing patriotic songs. They remain out of politics and do not hold political office.

Participation in the celebration of religious occasions such as Christmas and Easter is considered a part of false religion.

They claim that the Lord's Memorial (Lord's Supper) is the only scriptural observance mentioned by Jesus, and they deny the validity of Christmas and Easter celebrations as handed down through tradition. They believe that Jesus was born about October 1 in 2 B.C., and they claim that neither Jesus nor the early Christians encouraged the celebration of His birth. They also state that December 25 was chosen as the date because the Romans observed that date as the birthday of the sun. Likewise, they say that Easter was not celebrated by early Christians and has its origins in non-Christian celebrations. They believe that Jesus died on Nisan 14, and they commemorate His death according to the Jewish calendar.

Witnesses condone the drinking of alcoholic beverages in moderation, but drunkenness is against Jehovah's law. Addictive drugs such as marijuana, heroin, cocaine, and tobacco are to be shunned, for they are against Jehovah's injunctions. Other evils of Satan are homosexuality and adultery.

> Through various means, including television, movies, certain forms of dancing and immoral literature, Satan encourages sexual relations between unmarried persons, as well as adultery. . . . this is against God's law.[47]

Blood transfusions are rejected.

> Another common practice in various parts of the world is the eating of blood. Thus, animals not properly bled are eaten or the blood may be drained out and used as food in a meal. Yet God's Word forbids the eating of blood. (Gen. 9:3,4; Leviticus 17:10). What, then, about taking blood transfusions? Some persons may reason that getting a blood transfusion is not actually "eating." But is it not true that when a patient is unable to take food through his mouth, the doctor often recommends feeding him by the same method in which a blood transfusion is given? The Bible tells us to "abstain from . . . blood." (Acts 15:20,29). What does this mean? If

a doctor were to tell you to abstain from alcohol, would that simply mean that you should not take it through your mouth but that you could transfuse it directly into your veins? Of course not! So, too, "abstaining from blood" means not taking it into your body at all.[48]

Witnesses view blood as sacred, and it is not to be manipulated from body to body. They point out that transfusions may bring malaria, syphilis, and hepatitis and that anyone having transfusions stands under judgment of Jehovah.

Another symbol of Witness life-style is high boundary maintenance. There tends to be a dualism or dichotomy in their thinking and in their activities. Choices are clear cut and obvious in theological beliefs and in moral behavior.- They tend to think in terms of either/or, right/wrong, and my/our as opposed to theirs. One is either friend or foe and is either a part of Jehovah's organization or a part of Satan's world. One is a member of the 144,000 or "the other sheep" or "the whore of Babylon." One either knows "the Truth" or one does not. One either lives separate from the world or in the world.

Their boundary maintenance fosters unity, unanimity, and uniformity. Security and "at homeness" or "at-one-ment" is found in a hierarchical and authoritarian structuring of life together. The Governing Board is the apex of the hierarchy, and its authority is not to be questioned. Theological patterns for belief and practice, which are to be submitted to by the members are given by the Board. The Board speaks and writes in the name of Jehovah, and consequently, no one has to sign any of the millions of pieces of literature. No one is supposed to question Jehovah.

The Kingdom Hall is like a beehive. Time is filled. Hours are spent. Members are called "brother" and "sister." A stranger is called Mr., Mrs., or Miss. The streets are a part of the world, and the workplace is a part of the world. Churches are a part of the world. School is a part of the world. The secure and safe places are the family gathered in the home and the family gathered in the Kingdom Hall and engaged in publishing.

Boundaries are highly obvious in the life-style of Witnesses. The home, the Kingdom Hall, Bethel headquarters, and the individual and group activities of the Witnesses are the primary places and experiences. Elsewhere, there are possibilities of risk, harm, and destruction. Jehovah's Witnesses do not own or operate hospitals, homes for senior citizens, or educational institutions, because they believe each family has the obligation to take care of its own. The family is the teaching institution, even prior to the school systems, and Witnesses' literature should supersede that of the public. They feel obligations to help other Witnesses in need and distress, and appeals are made in the local congregations to assist one another.

Life-style in the Kingdom Hall includes acceptance of ethnic and racial backgrounds. Women publishers are most active in door-to-door visitation, but in the Kingdom Hall they do not preside over the meetings. Women participate freely in the question-and-answer periods in the general meetings.

Perhaps one final description befits the life-style of Witnesses. They demonstrate devout and deep commitment to belief and practice, and they exhibit a tenacity to long hours of labor in their ministry. They exude an energy of a burden to tell the truth as they know it to the world around them.

Issues and Challenges
Among Contemporary Jehovah's Witnesses

Since its inception, there has been conflict within the organization of Witnesses and conflict between the Witnesses and the "World." There have been purges from within, notably under the leadership of Rutherford and Franz; there have been the organization's and individual's entanglements with the law, notably under Russell and Rutherford. Some have suggested that there is a crisis at the top as well as within the Kingdom Halls. About one million Witnesses have voluntarily or involuntarily left the organization since 1970.[49]

The authoritarian structure of the Governing Board is one of the reasons given for dissatisfaction. Witnesses in the past have been encouraged not to attend colleges and not to read literature aside from their own. Their literature has been written unsigned by a select few at Bethel headquarters. Dissent has surfaced toward the assumed authority of the organization and toward those individuals who allow no questioning and independent study of the Bible.[50]

Since the sixties, Witnesses have been influenced by the themes current in American culture—autonomy, individual freedoms, protest, liberation movements, and success. Also, increasingly there has become a generation gap in the leadership. The current president, Frederick Franz, continues a lineage back to the days of the founder, Charles Russell. Younger staff people have sought to express their ideas and have been ignored or silenced.

Resentment and outright rebellion have continued to occur. The rank and file have become more rigid in their theocratic posture. In a culture with increasing emphasis on education, technology, and pluralism, the question faces the Jehovah's Witnesses on the extent of their adaptability to cultural demands. Family crisis, marital failures, and an educated youth involves the Witnesses in the same challenges of change and accommodation as non-Witnesses. Witnesses' coping ability in a rapidly changing and mobile age is being tested.

Perhaps one of the most obvious issues within the organization and in the public arena is their advocacy of prophetic announcements of Armageddon, Judgment, and the Millennium. Members attest to some disillusionment with the forecasts of the end of the world. Leadership explains away or retracts references to dates of the beginning or the ending of the age. These "apologies" bring further questions.

Announcements of the impending end have spurred interest in their organization in the past, and membership roles have increased. Segments of the population are always ready to respond to speculation about the ultimate end to "bad times" and the beginning of an eternity of "good times" for those so prepared. Prior to the 1975 date as the beginning of the end, there was an increase in membership. Suggestions were made in the literature that the late eighties might be the new target date. Trends, however, indicate that though there were new baptisms, there have been hundreds of thousands of Witnesses unaccounted for, especially in the last several years.

Witnesses' leadership is faced with the embarrassment of failed prophetic utterances as well as a published record of retractions, reinterpretations, and apologies. Rutherford revised the chronology of Russell. The unsigned literature of late has suggested certain revisions in Bible chronology. The challenge to the Witnesses is how they will continue to view Bible chronology for contemporary times and how they will reinterpret their findings not only to the membership but to the public at large. Will they become so generalized in their eschatology that they lose one of their distinctives of faith and practice? This issue may affect not only membership decline or growth but may also affect the very nature of the organization.

Another challenge among Witnesses is the issue of discrepancies in faith and practice. Ex-witnesses who have served at Bethel headquarters and who have been in close contact with the leadership report the inequities of the living standards between the leaders (faithful and discreet slave class) and the followers (the other sheep). Others report that some Witnesses observe birthdays and some do not. Reports show that some accept blood transfusions, and that Witnesses handle the church-state question with differences. Thus, the question of hypocrisy emerges. How will they continue to respond to a rigid socialization process that has demanded unity and uniformity on social issues?

With Witnesses seeking more independence in Bible study and interpretation, the blood transfusion issue becomes prominent. What does the Bible really say about the issue of blood sacrifice and usage? What are the continuing health and legal procedures which confront the Witnesses and the public? Other issues which are swirling around the Witnesses are the role of women in the religious structures, war and peace and the nuclear age, alcoholism and drug addiction, and abortion.

A key to whatever challenges and issues come to Witnesses is the next generation of leadership at Bethel. Will a leader emerge who will tone down specific, dated prophecies, and consider changes and accommodations in such matters as blood transfusions? Or will it be a leader tied rigidly to the past? Perhaps there is something positive in the unsigned literature. One may emerge from that "anonymous" leadership unblemished by notoriety and with freedom to pursue a different future. From indications from the grass-roots Witnesses, they are continuing to project and build Kingdom Halls without too specific a regard for dates such as 1975 or 1984.

Jehovah's Witnesses and Christian Belief and Practice

As already noted, Jehovah's Witnesses claim the name "Christian" and the appelation "Christianity," and they view Christendom as composed of those churches of the false religions. Consequently, they have the truth. They are the theocratic organization through whom God reveals wisdom and commandments. They have little if anything to learn from the false religions; thus, they tend to be monological rather than dialogical people.

Although they claim the Bible as authoritative for their belief and practice, the Bible is only authoritative as it is interpreted and translated by their theocratic organization at Bethel headquarters. Each Witness, therefore, theoretically and practically assigns his or her interpretive ability over to the Governing Board and accepts its authority.

Witnesses, thus, disassociate themselves from more traditional views within Christianity of revelation and authority. Orthodox Christian understandings have been rooted in the Bible as the authoritative revelation of God, in the people of God as the locus for interpretation and application of the revelation, and in the individual under the leadership of God's presence in the Holy Spirit together with the Bible and the church. Christianity has its councils, creeds, commentaries, and theologians, both cleric and lay. However, it has constantly refused to grant an anonymous few supreme power and authority for control of God's revelation to the world.

The major doctrines of Jehovah's Witnesses were founded on anti-Trinitarianism, Arianism, and prophetic chronology. As previously presented, they believe that Jehovah is God; that Jesus is "a god," as well as the created son of God, as well as the angel Michael; and that the Holy Spirit is not personal, but is an active force of Jehovah. Orthodox Christian understandings have held to the doctrine of the Trinity, believing that God is one, yet revealing Himself in three persons or personal dimensions. Included in that understanding is that Jesus Christ is the Word of God in human flesh, fully God and fully man, in the beginning and uncreated. Also, the Holy Spirit is personal, and is God revealing selfhood to the world. Orthodox Christian understandings have taken the prophets of the Bible seriously and the prophetic ministry of the church seriously, but not to the point of speculating upon and announcing specific dates for kingdom, and Armageddon, and millennial scenarios.

Witnesses and orthodox Christians both believe in the premises and practices of faith and works. The Witness position, however, is certainly oriented to works with its overwhelming emphasis upon visits, hours, reports, selling literature, and pioneer status. They believe that Jesus paid the ransom in death to make it possible for the individual to earn the right to faith and works. Also, they believe that salvation is given and/or earned in two different ways by two different groups. The 144,000 "faithful and discreet slave class" is favored through its election/faith/works to live with Jehovah and Jesus Christ, and "the other sheep" are favored through their election/faith/works to live on paradise earth. Others who are not Witnesses may be granted paradise earth after the resurrection, or they may be annihilated.

Orthodox Christian understandings have placed emphasis upon grace and faith, while at the same time holding that works will proceed from the prior relationships of grace and faith. By grace is one saved through one's faith and not of works lest anyone should boast. Works are important, but of more importance is the grace of God through Jesus Christ and one's faith response to that grace in the life, teachings, death, and resurrection of Jesus Christ.

In conclusion, the Witnesses believe that their organization, their translation of the Bible, their literature, their doctrines, and their Kingdom Halls are the only and absolute expressions of true religion in the world. If one is not a Witness, one is not included in the benevolences of the organization. Missions is only garnering new members for the organization. Orthodox Christian understandings do not include absolute organizations, institutions, or methods. The kingdom of God is a dynamic and mysterious concept and experience, including both present and future realities. The world is a mission field where the naked, imprisoned, sick, alienated, starving, and the lost are to be met where they are, have their needs met, and invited to respond to the grace of God through Jesus Christ in faith and willingness to serve.

A Christian Posture Toward Jehovah's Witnesses

Jehovah's Witnesses, like Mormons, represent a religion born and developed in America with mission enterprises around the world. This religion has appealed to Americans with a basic mind-set for authority and with a basic life-style of religious works. A Christian posture toward them would include acceptance of them as persons created in the image of God whom God loves; a knowledge of their doctrines and practices in order to better communicate with them; and willingness to take time with them at work, in school, and especially as they visit one's home to share one's knowledge of the Bible and one's faith in God through Jesus Christ would be included.

The following considerations for the Christian may be helpful when encountering a Jehovah's Witness:

1. A Christian should be prepared with portions of the Bible which speak to the love and grace of God in salvation through Jesus Christ and which speak to the meaning of faith and works in a life-style of discipleship. A Christian should know that Witnesses do not accept the doctrine of the Trinity or the understanding of the Holy Spirit as a personal quality of God, and be prepared with one's own faith story of how God speaks to one in Father, Son, and Holy Spirit.

2. Witnesses are persons with felt religious needs. They have responded to belief and commitment, often in very loyal and tenacious patterns. All Witnesses, however, are not the same in terms of the depth, strength, and quality of their beliefs and practices. Some who go door-to-door are possible initiants into the organization. Others whom one may greet at the door may be new Witnesses, borderline Witnesses, or confused and tired Witnesses. A Christian must be careful in stereotyping all Witnesses as identical in their religious condition. One Witness may be much more open to what a Christian has to say than his or her companion. Be sensitive to a person, not a stereotype.

3. Christians and Christendom are looked upon by Witnesses as a part of false religion; therefore, there may be suspicion and distrust. A Christian needs to understand this attitude and be prepared not to reinforce it but to change it.

4. Christians need to be aware of, and sensitive to, their use of the Bible and Watchtower literature. Witnesses have studied the Bible, doctrines, and practices from the translations, interpretations, and writings of the several men on the Gov-

erning Board at Bethel headquarters. Witnesses do not read the Bible in independent Bible study and with the inspiration of the Holy Spirit. A Christian needs to be prepared with Bible in hand to discuss biblical texts with Witnesses. A Christian needs to exercise care in the use of Witness literature in utilizing it to be better trained to talk with a Witness about one's faith. Witnesses have their own translation of the Bible with emphatic and clear additions to the biblical texts which highlight their own peculiar beliefs.

5. Keep in mind that Witnesses have a definite and straightforward strategy for witnessing or "publishing." Their seven steps, or stages, have already been described. By receiving literature from a Witness at the door, one may, by that action, lead the Witness on a "back-call" visit, since he or she assumes that one has interest in the literature and in the organization. A Christian may assume a witness posture when a Witness comes to the door.[51] One may be courteous and invite the Witness in. One need not receive the literature, argue, or respond to any probing questions by the Witness.

Often, the Witness attempts to find out one's fears of world events or one's possible loneliness by asking leading questions. Let the Witness finish the presentation without responding to the questions. Afterwards, briefly give your testimony of grace and faith in Jesus Christ. Ask if the Witness could share his or her testimony of faith and grace. The Witness may not be able to do this, and may leave. If there is opportunity then or on a back-call visit when the Witness returns, take the Bible and for every passage the Witness desires to discuss, read it in context from your Bible. In this way you do not argue or belittle the Witness. You exercise your own faith and practice in a positive and sharing way. The Witness is used to a set method, and once he or she is off the track, it may be difficult or confusing, and the Witness may leave. The Christian has, however, taken the opportunity to discuss faith, and has taken the initiative in the conversation.

6. A Christian remembers that America is a land and a society which cherishes religious freedom, religious liberty, and the

separation of church and state. Jehovah's Witnesses have their right under the laws of the land to believe and practice their religion. A Christian affirms that right and privilege and is vigilant for its safeguarding for Witnesses as well as for other religious communities.

7. Jehovah's Witnesses have affected millions of Americans as well as peoples of the globe. They have had their days of increase and of decrease. They are to be taken seriously as a religious community. Christians may do well not only to understand them but to communicate to them biblical truths and the good news and glad publishings of Jesus Christ.

3

The Unification Church
■ ■

Reverend Sun Myung Moon
and the Moonies

Who are the young people selling flowers at the street intersections and the shopping malls? Who is the man from Korea who speaks through a translator to crowds and the press of his idea of The Holy Spirit Association for the Unification of World Christianity (the name of his unification movement)? What is behind the rumors and reports of young people being "brainwashed" as Moonies? Why does the Unification Church purchase the New Yorker Hotel or operate a newspaper, *The Washington Times,* in the nation's capital, or invite ministers and scholars at little expense to conferences around the nation and across the world? During the 1970s the Reverend Sun Myung Moon came to America from Korea to build the base for his church, and his followers were called Moonies. Since those initial days, members of the church, sometimes called Unificationists, have become missionaries to some 120 countries. They herald the message of Moon, founded on the written source, *Divine Principle*. Who are Moon and the Moonies?

Sun Myung Moon was born on January 6, 1920, in what is now known as North Korea. As a young child, it is reported that he was sensitive to God and nature. One time he prayed, "Father, give me greater wisdom than Solomon, greater faith than the apostle Paul and greater love than even Jesus."[1] His parents had been introduced to Christianity under the influence of Presbyterian missionaries. On Easter 1936, Moon had a mystical encounter with Jesus, the first of many revelatory experiences. The sixteen-year-old Moon was inspired to "take up Jesus' unfinished work and establish the Kingdom of God on earth."[2]

From 1936 to 1944, Moon studied the Bible, received revelations, and reflected upon the ideas which later became the framework for *Divine Principle*. During this period he also assisted his family and studied engineering at a university in Japan. At the conclusion of World War II, Korea was freed from Japanese occupation, but the country was soon divided into north and south with Moon's North Korea coming under Communist influence. Moon was imprisoned by the Communists because of his preaching in the city of Pyongyang during 1948 through 1950. He was liberated in 1950 by United Nations' forces, barely escaping execution. He journeyed south to Pusan; and in 1951, in a small hut in a refugee camp, Moon began teaching *Divine Principle*. Gathering a following, he moved to Seoul in 1953 and in 1954 officially established his church.

Reverend Joseph McCabe, an Australian missionary, visited Moon's church in Seoul in its infancy and reported the following:

> The group of Christians to whom I have come are not Pentecostal or Apostolic as we know it, and yet the Spirit of the Lord is manifest among them, as some have visions, others have tongues and interpretations, while a spirit of prophecy is exercised by others in private. The fervor and sincerity of the worship, the soul-stirring preaching of Mr. Moon, a born orator who stirs his congregation to response both in praying and preaching, is wonderful. Almost without exception the members are there because they longed for something

deeper. The meeting place is an old hall in an out of the way spot. . . . To this hall come between three hundred and four hundred people. . . . There are no seats as in other churches; everyone sits on the floor. Half an hour before the service is due to begin we have a time of singing, and the place is packed. . . . Mr. Yoo, the lecturer, gives lectures on the Principles, as they term their beliefs, for four or five hours each day.[3]

He also wrote that there were eight centers of Moon's movement from Seoul to Pusan with possibly twelve hundred members.

Neil Salonen, a former president of the Unification Church in America, observes that in the formative years of Moon's theological development, Moon believed that God was attempting to find someone to restore the human family's relationship to God. Moon found in the Old Testament that Jacob served as a model for restoration. Jacob spent twenty-one years in Haran after he regained the birthright. Those twenty-one years were divided into three seven-year periods of growth and maturity. Likewise, Moon believed that from 1945 to 1966, a twenty-one-year period, a foundation for restoration to God was a distinct possibility. Events, however, prevented its happening, including the division of Korea and the persecution of Christians. Moon was still to continue to form the foundation for restoring Jacob's mission and eventually Adam's family.[4]

In 1960, Moon married Hak-Ja Han. Three elders of his church and their wives, together with Moon and his new wife, provided the foundation for the restoration of Adam's family. The holy marriage Blessing for restoration was begun. That twenty-one-year period lasted from 1960 to 1981 and saw the foundation of his church laid in America as well as its worldwide mission to some 120 countries. Hak-Ja Han was eighteen at the time of the marriage and was not schooled in the "Principle." During the first seven years Moon taught her, and through the next cycles of seven-year periods, she matured to become equal with him as members of the family. God, thus, worked through them as a couple.[5] It is known that Moon married in the 1940s and that the marriage failed. There are rumors that he had other marriages. The Moons now have thirteen children.[6]

Four years after the founding of the church, Moon sent his first missionaries from Korea. Sang Ik Choi went to Japan. In 1959, Dr. Young Oon Kim came to the United States to Oregon as a missionary of Moon's teachings. In 1961, she took a small group to the San Francisco Bay area where she began the first Unification Church of America. Kim, known as Miss Kim, had been a Methodist and had taught in a Methodist university in Seoul. She had lived and studied with Moon's group from 1954 to 1959, and had written the English version of *Divine Principle*.

The Christian community was upset with Miss Kim's decision to join Moon's church, and there was much friction between the two. Salonen reports that the Methodist Church attempted to discredit Moon and his followers, including Miss Kim. It was at this time, 1955, that Moon was imprisoned "on the trumped-up charge of draft evasion. He was held for three months, but he was released without trial and declared innocent. . . . It was cooperation between the Christians in the government and the Methodist hierarchy that sought to suppress the Unification Church movement at that time."[7]

Around 1959, David Sang Chul Kim came to the West Coast as a missionary of the church. He has since served as president of the Unification Theological Seminary in Barrytown, New York. Colonel Bo Hi Pak, one of the early members of the Korean church, came to America as a military attache in the Korean embassy in Washington, D.C. On his retirement, he formed the Korean Cultural and Freedom Foundation, which sponsors the Little Angels and the National Folk Ballet of Korea. They tour worldwide under the auspices of the United Nations, the Korean government, and in association with the church. Colonel Pak is a close associate of Moon and has been involved in many church activities, including the launching of the newspaper, *The Washington Times.*

Choi, with converts from his missionary service in Japan, came to America in 1965 to settle on the West Coast. By the late sixties, there were four rather independent groups of Moon's followers on the West Coast and in Washington, D.C. These groups began to send missionaries from the United States to Germany, Austria, and Italy.

In 1965 Moon made his first visit to America. He visited every state, blessed a particular holy ground in each place, and launched his worldwide movement. He toured the world and blessed 120 holy grounds. In 1966, Miss Kim joined with Colonel Pak in Washington, D.C., to form the National Headquarters of the Unification Church. Moon moved his family to America in 1972. Since 1960, he and Mrs. Moon have "Blessed" thousands of couples in marriage in multiples of 36, 72, 124, 430, 777, and 1,800. On July 1, 1982, the Blessing of 2,075 couples at Madison Square Garden in New York City was the first large wedding to take place outside Korea. On October 16, 1982, Moon and his wife officiated at the Blessing of 5,800 couples in Seoul, Korea.

Moon launched his "God Bless America" rallies in 1976. The purpose of these rallies was to remind America of its responsibility before the world of renewing its Christian roots and of challenging atheistic communism. The first rally was held June 1 in Yankee Stadium, and the second was held September 18 at the Washington Monument. It is reported that Moon concluded his public ministry with his appearance at the Washington rally. Since 1976, the church has sought two objectives: (1) "deepening its roots in the community and (2) attending to the support of the world missions."[8]

Salonen observed that after 1981, which signaled the end of the twenty-one-year period Moon began in 1960, each member of the church began his or her own twenty-one-year period which offered much diversity in the expansion of the church. It will:

become the responsibility of the individual members to decide how their lives should be an offering to God and how they can make a twenty-one year offering center-ing on faithfulness and on willingness to sacrifice to accomplish substantial achievements. Jacob didn't just go and endure twenty-one years to Haran. He earned his wife, he earned a great deal of goods and he used those things as an offering when he went back to the promised land in order to be accepted."[9]

As the Unification Church has moved into the 1990s, it has sought acceptance from churches, world religion com-munities, and the general public. The church has diversified its approach. It has sought to be involved in ecumenicity at the grassroots in conferences and coalitions with other churches on political and social issues. It has invested heavily in operating newspapers, producing a movie, sponsoring conferences, mailing out videocassettes, and in various industries and real estate. The church has its own seminary and sends its select students with full scholarships to the best graduate schools of the nation.

Moon has launched a church with a vision for world impact. The church reports some three million members worldwide. Joy Garratt, who handles public relations for the church, stated that there are eight thousand missionaries in the states spreading its word and raising funds. Another thirty-seven thousand Americans are members with various levels of commitment. The annual operating budget is between $20 million and $24 million. The church has spent about $500 million on humanitarian and educational projects in the United States.[10]

Although Reverend Sun Myung Moon ended his public appearances in 1976, he has remained in the public eye. In July 1984, he began serving an eighteen-month federal prison sentence for income tax evasion. Much publicity sur-rounded the trial. Many Christian communities protested the legality and the methods that the government used against Moon.

In the spring of 1985, the church had a mass mailing of three videocassettes to select clergy and others. Estimates of the cost of the mailing ran into the millions. Moon's message from prison, in a book entitled *God's Warning to the World*, was included. On May 11, 1985, Shaw University Divinity School in Raleigh, North Carolina, conferred an honorary doctor of divinity degree on Moon. Moon's wife, Hak-Ja Han, received the degree because Moon was in prison. She was accompanied by Dr. Bo Hi Pak, Moon's special assistant, and by Dr. Durst Mose, who was president of the Unification Church of America.

Authority in the Church
Reverend Moon, Divine Principle, Bible

Three primary sources of authority for the Unification Church are found in the religious experiences of Moon, in the *Divine Principle*, and in the Bible. A leading theologian of the Unification Church places the "new revelation" of Moon in the stages of "primordial revelations," when God spoke to Abraham, Moses, Samuel, Jesus, and Paul.

> In Moses' cases, he spoke with God on Mt. Sinai, received the Torah, and was commissioned to unify his people for their occupation of the Promised Land. In Jesus' case, once he heard God's words, "Thou art my beloved son," he was challenged to proclaim the coming of the kingdom. Reverend Moon's revelation should be interpreted in that light. As he explains, while still a teenager, he received a vision of Jesus who asked him to complete the task of establishing the kingdom of God on earth. Thus, his revelatory experience involved a mission of the utmost significance.[12]

Dr. Young Oon Kim compares the background for Moon's revelation with that of Jesus. After Moon's initial vision,

> The next several years were spent pondering the full implications of his response. As Jesus grew up in a land permeated with eschatological expectancy, so did Rev-

erend Moon. The north Korean milieu at that time greatly resembled the environment of first century Palestine. As Roman soldiers occupied Palestine, Japanese soldiers occupied Korea. As the pious Jews meditated on the apocalyptic prophecies of the Old Testament, the oppressed Korean Christians longed for the dawn of the messianic age. During Reverend Moon's youth and early manhood, little groups of Christians studied the book of Revelation and tearfully prayed for the advent of the long-awaited Messiah. Several who possessed unusual psychic gifts predicted that these were the Last Days and Korea would have a special role to play in the coming of God's New Age. More than one of these Christian seers announced that Christ would appear in their own land. We should not overlook the charged charismatic atmosphere which stimulated, supported and encouraged Reverend Moon's growth in spiritual maturity. As Jesus' message and mission cannot be fully understood apart from the time in which he lived, neither can one understand Reverend Moon apart from his Korean environment.[13]

Kim further states that within the biblical tradition, when someone chosen by God fails to carry out His will, the role is given to another. Moses failed to enter the Promised Land, and his mission was turned over to Joshua. King Saul failed, and his throne was given to David. Jesus was rejected by the religious authorities, and Paul was selected to carry the faith to the Gentile world. Kim concludes that it is the purpose of God to appear in a new place and "anoint a different individual to the messianic office once occupied by Jesus."[14] While Kim did not explicitly state who the messiah may be from Korea, she did write that the new revelation expressed in *Divine Principle* is a reaffirmation and clarification of the biblical revelation.

Who does Moon say that he is? A further question is, Who do Moonies say that he is? Moon has not stated that he is the Messiah or the Lord of the Second Advent. In an interview with Frederick Sontag, Moon responded to the question of his own role compared to that of Jesus. He said that Jesus established spiritual salvation. Complete salvation, which is both spiritual and physical, is the intent of the will of God; and Jesus' mission was not totally accomplished. Moon answered that a messianic crusade is to begin on the earth to consummate God's will. "The work of the Unification Church and my mission is to proclaim the coming of the Messianic Age."[15]

In his message from prison, Moon said,

> I am telling you many unusual things, and you may ask by what authority I am speaking. It is the authority of the Bible, with the authority of revelation.[16] . . . I spoke with Jesus Christ in the spirit world. And I also spoke with John the Baptist. This is my authority. If you cannot at this time determine that my words are the truth, you will surely discover that they are in the course of time. These are hidden truths presented to you as new revelations. You have heard me speak from the Bible. If you believe the Bible you must believe what I am saying.[17] . . . The major criticism Christians have is their contention that I pose as the Lord of the Second Advent. But I never said that. They created rumors like that. Christians have been waiting all these years for the second coming, so they should have had the courtesy to come and find out for themselves whether our members have valid reason to spread such a rumor.[18] . . . The end of the world is at hand, not only for Christians but for all people throughout the world. The new history of God will begin with the arrival of the Lord. Blessed are those who see him and accept him.[19]

What do members of the Unification Church say about Moon? Frederick Sontag traveled around the world, including Korea, Japan, Europe, and America, interviewing Moonies. He interviewed those who began with Moon in the early days and those more recently involved. He found the answers quite diverse.

They varied all the way from "a mirror in which I see myself truly" to "teacher" to "revealer" to "God's instrument" and "messiah" to the straightforward declaration that "he is the Lord of the Second Advent, the expected messiah returned." From all this it is clear that Moonies follow no consistent, prescribed public teaching on this matter and that each is allowed some latitude to make out his or her own opinions on the topic. Of course, all is not relaxed. Given the claims of the doctrine, one must determine Moon's role and the follower's relationship to it.[20]

In interviewing two pastors of the Unification Church in Washington, D.C., in 1983 and 1984, I learned that both viewed Moon as Lord of the Second Advent and as Messiah. In an interview in one of my classes, the public relations officer of the Unification Church in Raleigh, N.C., stated her view of Moon as the Messiah and the Lord of the Second Advent. Perhaps since Sontag's interviews of the mid-seventies, Moonies are more certain and/or bold to state their view of the role of Moon. Sontag observed that the idea of the messianic secret might be used by Moonies. Perhaps only the inner circle knew the secret and would announce it at the right time. Moonies sing, "The Lord of Love has come to us . . . and we want to pass it on." There is a feeling among Moonies that the messianic age has arrived, that the "Principle" is being announced, and the one who boldly does it in the tradition of Jesus is Reverend Sun Myung Moon. It appears that in the nineties more Moonies are arriving at the conclusion that Moon is the Messiah.

What is the relationship of *Divine Principle* to the Bible? According to Moon and his early disciples, Moon spent much time in Bible study. From this study, together with prayer and meditation, the ideas of *Divine Principle* were preached.

Two texts, titled Wol-li Hae-sul (Explanation of The Principle) (Seoul, Korea: Segye Kidokyo Tongil Shilly-ong Hyophwe, 1957; untranslated) and Wol-li Kangron (Discourse on The Principle) (Seoul, Korea: Segye Kidokyo Tongil Shillyong Hyophwe, 1966; published in English as *Divine Principle*, Washington, D.C.: HSA-UWC, 1973) have been used as the official doctrine of the Unification Church. They were written by Hyo Won Eu, the first president of the Korean Unification Church, who served Reverend Moon in the early years of his ministry and was taught directly by him.[21]

The church states that much of "The Principle" received by Moon is still unpublished but that it will be published as the dispensation progresses and the foundation is laid.

In the general introduction to *Divine Principle*, it is reported,

It may be displeasing to religious believers, especially to Christians, to learn that a new expression of truth must appear. They believe that the Bible, which they now have, is perfect and absolute in itself. Truth, of course, is unique, eternal, unchangeable, and absolute. The Bible, however, is not the truth itself, but a textbook teaching the truth. Naturally, the quality of teaching and the method and extent of giving the truth must vary according to each age, for the truth is given to people of different spiritual and intellectual levels. Therefore, we must not regard the textbook as absolute in every detail.[22]

In the text of the *Divine Principle*, it is written,

We must realize that Biblical words are a means of expressing the truth and are not the truth itself. Seeing matters from this point of view, we can understand that the New Testament was given as a textbook for the teaching of truth to people of 2,000 years ago, people whose spiritual and intellectual standard was very low, compared to that of today. It is thus impossible to satisfy completely man's desire for truth, in this modern scientific civilization, by using the same method of expressing the truth, in parables and symbols, which was used to awaken the people of an earlier age. In consequence, today the truth must appear with a higher standard and with a scientific method of expression in order to enable intelligent modern man to understand it.[23]

The Unification Church, thus, is founded on "three testaments." There is the (1) Old Testament, (2) the New Testament, and (3) the Completed Testament (*Divine Principle*). The *Divine Principle* has been referred to as the "fullest explanation" of the Scriptures of Old Testament and New Testament. It has also been referred to as "a metaphysical reality," as an attribute of God which cannot be expressed fully.[24]

It would appear, therefore, that the primary source of authority for members of the Unification Church is the "primordial revelation" given to Reverend Moon, like that revelation given to Moses and Jesus. *Divine Principle* enunciates the outlines of the revelatory experience of Moon, utilizing his interpretations of the texts of the Bible. Those interpretations would include "progressive revelation," the origin of sin as an illicit sexual act between Satan and Eve, the failure of Jesus to bring physical restoration or salvation, and the second coming of Christ or Messiah or Lord of the Second Advent arising out of Korea after World War I. A key teaching by Moon is the restoration of the "Four Foundation" (God-Man-Woman-Children) as it was intended to be with Adam and Eve. Since Jesus' mission was terminated before he could marry, the Lord of the Second Advent will marry, become the "True Parent," and begin the process of perfect restoration of God-Man-Woman-Children. The *Divine Principle* not only heralds the new messianic age but outlines the contours for its completion.

Unification Theology—Creation, Fall, Jesus Christ, Lord of the Second Advent

Theology in the Unification Church is a young science. Its source book is *Divine Principle*; Reverend Moon's living witness is its prime interpreter; and emerging leaders in the church are neophyte theologians. The theology is rooted in Asian concepts including backgrounds in animism, shamanism, tribalism, Confucianism, and Buddhism. Christian concepts and biblical data are meshed together with Korean religious traditions in particular.

The nature of God may be discussed in terms of polarity, utilizing the concepts of *yang* and *ying*. Numerology is prominent in *Divine Principle*, in theological premises, and in mass-marriage ceremonies. The Eastern traditions of ancestor emphasis, the importance of family, and the respect for one's superiors are evident in the church's theology of the ideal family and true parents. The data for theological reflection are complex. One needs to read *Divine Principle* with recently-published study guides to grapple with key doctrines. Even Moonies admit its complexity and their own wrestling with the theological concepts.

For our purposes, and simply stated, Unification theology holds that God created Adam and Eve to realize His ideal of love. They failed because of an illicit sexual encounter between Eve and Satan. Eve transmitted this pollution in her sexual relations with Adam. Sin, or the fall, was handed down through the blood. God has sought restoration or indemnity through the various ages and peoples, including Abraham, Jacob, Moses, and Jesus Christ.

Jesus' mission as the second Adam was to restore true parentage or family (God-Man-Woman-Children). His mission, or messiahship, failed because He was prevented from marriage by premature death and nonacceptance of His messiahship. Through the cross and spiritual resurrection, Jesus brought spiritual salvation. But He failed to bring physical salvation through His lack of marriage and the restoration of the true family. A new Messiah was promised. He would marry, restore the true family, and complete physical salvation. The new messianic age has begun with Korea as its birthplace, Reverend Moon and his wife as True Parents and the proclaimer of the new age, and America as the Land of Promise.

There are many theological concepts to be explored in Unification thought. What is the nature of God and man? What is the meaning of creation, the fall, salvation, and kingdom and the new age? Who is Jesus Christ? Who is the Lord of the Second Advent? When and where will he come? Perhaps these topics may best be explored in our limited space by focusing on four key concepts: creation, fall, Jesus Christ, and Lord of the Second Advent.

Creation

The theology of creation includes two major patterns of God's creative activity. There is the pattern of origin-division-union action which is closely associated with the stages of formation, growth, and completion. To achieve union, action, or completion, Adam and Eve should have experienced in their polarities of masculinity and femininity the fullness of "give and take" with God, with each other, and with others in this pattern and these stages.

A second pattern is "The Four Position Foundation." Adam and Eve were supposed to become the embodiment of God's spirit. As *Divine Principle* states, "This means that man attains deity."[25] This pattern means that there was to be perfect harmony and unity within the family of God-Man-Woman-Children.

In creation, Adam and Eve were given three blessings. They were 1) to be fruitful; 2) to multiply; and 3) to have dominion. "To be fruitful" means to perfect one's own individuality and humanity. It is unrestricted "give and take" with God and one another. It enables God to have perfect joy. "To multiply" means that marriage is sanctified. Since God exists in polarity, a husband and wife can reflect more fully God's dual essentialities."[26] "To have dominion" means the kind of God-centered family which could expand into a clan, tribe, nation, and global community.

If Adam and Eve had become complete, they would have become True Parents of humankind and would have served as prophet, high priest, and king. "If God's plan had worked out as intended, starting with the primal couple, all subsequent men and women would have served as vehicles for God's continuing incarnation. Consequently, the goal for humankind is to become a visible manifestation of God and therefore the proper lord of all creation."[27]

Divine Principle does not have a specific doctrine of God outlined as it does of creation. God's nature is seen from the fact of polarity; He has both masculine and feminine qualities. Unification theology views the Trinity concept as flexible and fluid; it sees Jesus Christ as masculine and the Holy Spirit as feminine. God desires to be in a reciprocal or "give and take" relationship with man. Because God is love, He created humans. "God sought to experience for Himself what it means to live at the physical level. Thus, we could say that God created man to be His body."[28] God is a God of heart, of feeling above all else. God feels at least as deeply as man. God is not omnipotent or omniscient, for He is limited by His own nature, His cosmic laws, and by man's free will. God has created man to achieve "The Four Position Foundation." Thus, Unification theology places great value upon God as parent, upon man as family, and upon the ideal of the perfect family and the perfect world.

Fall

Unification theology views the fall, or origin of sin, as the instigation of Lucifer, the immaturity of Adam and Eve in the growth stage, and fornication between Lucifer and Eve. Lucifer, a spirit, was jealous of God's love to Adam. He became desirous of the love of Eve. "It was not merely adultery in Eve's heart but actual sexual intercourse which affected her in both spirit and body. Their union is called a spiritual fall because the male partner was a spirit rather than a human being."[29]

Divine Principle states,

> We have come to understand that the root of sin is not that the first human ancestors ate a fruit, but that they had an illicit blood relationship with an angel symbol-

ized by a serpent. Consequently, they could not multiply the good lineage of God, but rather multiplied the evil lineage of Satan. . . . It is because the root of sin began by a blood relationship that the original sin is transmitted from generation to generation[30]. . . . The fall through the blood relationship between the angel and Eve was the spiritual fall, while that through the blood relationship between Eve and Adam was the physical fall.[31]

Eve, thus, polluted Adam as Lucifer had polluted her. They lost their status as God's children and became servants of Satan. Original sin was transmitted to all their descendants. This sin can only be removed when the Messiah comes and restores man's original intent before the fall of "The Four Position Foundation." "Accordingly, the Lord of the Second Advent must be able to solve this problem completely. All these facts prove that the root of sin lies in adultery."[32]

Jesus Christ

The Christological view of Unification thought is influenced by Asian concepts as well as biblical data and Western ideas. For example, Jesus is seen as the masculine polarity in the "give and take" while the Holy Spirit is seen as feminine. Both are seen as True Parents. Jesus is viewed as the second Adam, God's representative on earth. Jesus is not God though "one body with God . . . and may well be called God. . . . He can by no means be God Himself."[33] Jesus is seen as man and somehow as God. "In the spirit world he lives as a spirit person just as his disciples do, the only difference being that his spirit self is without original sin and shines brilliantly."[34] The *Divine Principle* states:

The Principle does not deny the attitude of faith held by many Christians that Jesus is God, since it is true that a perfected man is one body with God. Furthermore, when the Principle asserts that Jesus is a man having attained the purpose of creation, this does not in the least diminish his value. However, the principle of creation sees the original value of perfected man as being equal to that of Jesus.[35]

In dealing with the virgin birth, Kim indicates that Mary may have had sexual intercourse with the priest, Zacharias, who gave validity to holy marriage rites, spiritual dedication, and a divine incarnation sanctified by the Eastern tradition.[36]

The first reference to Jesus occurs in *Divine Principle* on page 53 in a listing of the ways God has worked to restore the number three. Jesus had "thirty years of private life and three years of public ministry." There were "three major disciples," "three temptations," and "three prayers at Gethsemane." Peter denied Jesus three times. There were three hours of darkness during the crucifixion, and Jesus was raised after three days. This is a typical example of the use of numbers.

The purpose of the advent of Jesus was "to accomplish the providence of restoration" and to fulfill "the salvation of both spirit and body."[37] Jesus was to restore "The Four Position Foundation" by becoming the True Parent in marriage and defeating Satan. Kim writes,

> Jesus was appointed God's earthly representative in order to subjugate Satan, cleanse men of original sin and free them from the power of evil. Christ's mission involved liberation from sin and raising mankind to the perfection stage. His purpose was to bring about the kingdom of heaven in our world with the help of men filled with divine truth and love. Jesus' goal was to restore the garden of Eden, a place of joy and beauty in which true families of perfected parents would dwell with God in a full relationship of reciprocal love. To use the terminology of *Divine Principle*, the kingdom of God on earth refers to individuals, couples, families and nations built upon the four position foundation centered in God.[38]

According to Unification theology, as much good as Jesus was able to do, He could not do enough to accomplish His mission; He failed. There were many reasons for failure: (a) John the Baptist had failed to lay the proper foundation for Jesus' messiahship; (b) the Jewish authorities inhibited Jesus; (c) people refused to believe Him; (d) Satan was most active against Him; (e) although Jesus' mission was not to die on the cross, He was crucified. Concerning the crucifixion, *Divine Principle* states,

> We, therefore, must realize that Jesus did not come to die on the cross.[39] . . . we can see that Jesus' crucifixion was the result of the ignorance and disbelief of the Jewish people and was not God's predestination to fulfill the whole purpose of Jesus' coming as the Messiah.[40] . . . Because the Jewish people disbelieved Jesus and delivered Him up for crucifixion, His body was invaded by Satan, and He was killed. Therefore, even when Christians believe in and become one body with Jesus, whose body was invaded by Satan, their bodies still remain subject to Satan's invasion. In this manner, however devout a man of faith may be, he cannot fulfill physical salvation by redemption through Jesus' crucifixion alone. . . . Salvation through redemption by the cross is spiritual only. . . . Thus, Christ must come again on the earth to accomplish the purpose of the providence of the physical, as well as the spiritual salvation, by redeeming the original sin which has not been liquidated even through the cross.[41]

Unificationists further explain the crucifixion,

> Since Jesus is the root of life for all mankind, Satan's invasion of Jesus' physical body means that even saints who believe in Jesus and become one with Him cannot avoid satanic invasion of their physical bodies (Rom. 7:22,23). No matter how faithful believers may be, their bodies are still within the realm of Satan's invasion. . . . Because of the crucifixion, mankind lost the physical body of the savior and thus lost its physical object of faith and could not receive physical salvation. . . . Although God let Satan take Jesus' body so that man's faithlessness could be redeemed, the foundation

for spiritual salvation was established when God, using Jesus' absolute obedience as a foundation, resurrected Jesus' spirit self and placed Him in a position where Satan could not invade. . . . He stood as the spiritual Messiah. . . . The most fundamental role of the Messiah is the role of the True Father. The resurrected Jesus became the spiritual True Father by restoring the Holy Spirit. The arrival of the Holy Spirit recorded in the second chapter of Acts is the arrival of the spiritual True Mother. The resurrected Jesus, as the spiritual True Father, and the Holy Spirit, as the spiritual True Mother, work together to give spiritual rebirth to believers.[42]

In some sense it appears that the crucifixion became the indemnity of Jesus in paying the ransom for sin. Unification literature points out the necessity for establishing the foundation for faith in every age. Jesus had to build upon the failure of John the Baptist to prepare the people for faith in the messianic age. Jesus' forty days in the wilderness and the three temptations are seen as His experience in indemnity. He had to "rework" the plan and pay the price for past failures. Of course, in the final analysis, Moonies believe that Jesus' mission was only partially successful. In summary form Kim says of Jesus and the messianic age,

God's original aim for man was to bestow three blessings: Be fruitful, multiply and have dominion over creation (Genesis 1:28). Having achieved individual perfection (being fruitful), Adam was with God's blessing to marry Eve and produce offspring (multiply), creating a quadruple base on the family level. On that foundation Adam and Eve could receive the third blessing (have dominion), becoming lord of all creation and true parents of mankind. As the Second Adam, Jesus was supposed to carry out these responsibilities. The Messiah must inaugurate a new family of God.

Because of Adam's fall, Jesus had to subjugate Satan by eradicating the root of original sin prior to receiving the second blessing. However, conditions beyond His control made it impossible for him to complete His mission. As Jews have always pointed out, the messianic age never came. Or as conservative Protestants believe, the kingdom will arrive when the Second Advent takes place. Nevertheless through His ministry and resurrection, Jesus laid a spiritual foundation for the continuing work of God through the Christian Church.[43]

The first Adam failed in the restoration plan. Jesus, the second Adam, failed in the restoration plan. Who will complete the restoration? Who will bring the perfect spiritual and physical salvation? Who will be the third Adam, the returned Christ, the new Messiah, the Lord of the Second Advent? The preparation period for the coming of the new Messiah is believed to have been the four-hundred-year time from the Reformation of 1517 until the conclusion of World War I in 1918. As to who may know the time of the coming of the Messiah, *Divine Principle* states,

> By examining the words of Jesus, "Only the Father knows" (Matt. 24:36), and the verse, "Surely the Lord God does nothing without revealing His secret to his servants the prophets" (Amos 3:7), we can understand that God, who knows of the day and hour, will surely let His prophets know all the secrets concerning the Second Advent of the Lord before actualizing it.[44]

The Second Advent

When will the Messiah, or Christ, return? He must be born in the flesh according to Unificationist thought. There are six major periods of dispensational history from Jesus to the second coming which number 1,930 years. Thus, 1930 is the approximate time for the birth of the Messiah, give or take ten years. So Christ or the Messiah should have been born between 1918 and 1930. Where will he be born? *Divine Principle* reviews certain texts in the Book of Revelation.

We read the record of the Lamb having opened the sixth seal (Rev. 6:12). . . . The Bible goes on to say in Revelation 7:2-4 that another angel ascended from the rising of the sun with the seal of the living God and sealed the chosen servants of God on their foreheads. . . . The Bible teaches us that the nation is in the East.[45]

Divine Principle reasons that from ancient times the phrase "Eastern nations" has referred to Korea, Japan, and China. "The nation of the East where Christ will come again would be none other than Korea," it states.[46] It justifies this conclusion with five considerations.

1. New Israel, or land of the Messiah, must have paid an indemnity for providing the foundations for restoration. Korea lay for forty years under the bondage of Japan like Israel did for 400 years under Egypt. Korea has earned the right.

2. The nation must be God's front line and also the front line of Satan. The thirty-eighth parallel divides the forces for good from those for evil, democracy from communism, so Korea is the bulwark against godless communism and Satan's forces.

3. The nation must be the object of God's heart.

4. The nation must have prophetic testimonies to the coming of a new messianic age.

5. The nation's culture must bear fruit.

These five conditions have been met in Korea, according to the *Divine Principle*.[47]

On July 20, 1984, as Reverend Sun Myung Moon departed for imprisonment in Danbury, Connecticut, he spoke to his followers. The following are some excerpts from his talk:[48]

What is the path I am walking? My ultimate mission as a son of God is to bring about the unity of the entire world.

God has worked so hard to bring unity on the levels of family, clan, nation, and world. But if Adam and Eve had not fallen, they would have automatically created that unified family, clan, tribe, nation and world. If that was the reality, then God would be free to travel everywhere, joyfully experiencing unity. Wherever He would go, He would be with His people. Therefore, a godly man must appear who has the power to bring unity and overcome the power of divisiveness. How much joy that would bring God!

There have been many saints throughout history and they were always unifiers. . . . Among such people, the greatest of all was Jesus Christ. . . . When Jesus was bearing the cross he was a single, solitary person. His disciples were not supporting Jesus; the chosen nation was not supporting Him. He was absolutely alone. But today, what is Reverend Moon doing? Reverend Moon came to this modern age to bring unity. He is a unifier—he is casting fire to bring about unity. Thus, no matter what we face, we will succeed. The forces of Satan are trying to divide the Moonies and they are trying to divide Christianity, but they cannot do it.

The entire world is watching the Unification Church and Reverend and Mrs. Moon.

Even though Reverend Moon is opposed by the entire United States, I will never be defeated.

Today I am going the road of incarceration and I am asking God, "What is Your next chapter for me? Let Your will be done and bring the unity of all humankind, centering upon the True Parents."

When Jesus was crucified, He went into hell first and opened the doors there. Today I am bearing my cross, but I will not die; I will open the doors of hell as a living person. From that point on, resurrection and Pentecost will come. That is the way I understand the meaning of this day.

The living God never dies. Therefore, my cross will only bring unification and victory. The doors to 120 nations shall be opened from today forward, depending on how you act.

I want you to understand that I am going to prison on the worldwide level at this time. I have already gone to prison on the individual level, the family and the national level. This is my destiny. Jesus told his people, if you want to follow me follow me with your cross. Therefore, if you want to follow Reverend Moon, you must bear the worldwide cross. Once you are victorious with the worldwide cross, you can come to visit me. After you have been victorious in carrying your own cross, then I will be able to come out of prison. I want you to understand that.

When I was in the North Korean prison, my mother came to visit me. She had walked many hundreds of miles, all the way across the peninsula, and the moment she saw me, she began to cry very strongly. At that point, I shouted out to my own mother, calling her by her given name, not mother, "I am not just your son. I have only come to this world through you. I am a son of God—you gave birth to me, so you should be as great as your son. You cannot be cowardly or weak. You must walk forward courageously and encourage me."

Today I am saying the same thing to you . . . go out to the battlefield. Go out and bring unity to the world. Do not waste your time visiting me at the prison but bring the victory for God in the world.

Now show me your determination by standing and giving three cheers.

Salvation

Divine Principle, unification theology, and conversations with Moonies center on the words, *indemnity, restoration,* and *salvation. Indemnity* means setting up the proper conditions by paying what is owed to God in order for restoration and salvation to occur.[49] One separates oneself from Satan through cleansing and purification, through devotional and prayer life, through various activities commissioned by the Unification Church. Indemnity is paying off a debt or penalty. *Restoration* is setting up the foundation and then participating in the original intention of God for True Parents and "The Four Position Foundation" of God-Man-Woman-Children. A key in restoration is the marriage "Blessing" given by Reverend and Mrs. Moon at the mass wedding ceremonies with its accompanying regulations of the purity and consummation of the marriage.

Salvation is viewed in two stages—spiritual salvation which comes through Jesus, the second Adam, and physical salvation which comes by the new Messiah or third Adam, called Lord of the Second Advent. Physical salvation is dependent upon the marriage of the new Messiah, who becomes the True Parent and passes on the "Blessed Marriage" to the followers. Salvation is achieved; indemnity is paid; and the restoration occurs with good works.

Kim interprets salvation not by grace alone but by the partnership of God and man, in synergism. "God cannot redeem man without man's cooperation and man cannot be restored to his original status without God's constant help."[50] A man must set up the conditions which assist God in realizing the purpose of creation. She refers to the concept of indemnity as rooted in cause and effect, in the Hindu principle of karma, one reaps what one sows. Man can only repair the damage done to God in the fall "through penitential discipline, conscientious obedience to the divine will and painstaking restoration of his original nature as God's loving child. As Jesus taught in His parable, once the prodigal son recognizes the folly of his ways, he must work his way back to his Father's home."[51] In other words, one must work out one's own salvation.

Unity is a key term throughout unification literature. Moon teaches and preaches the unification of all religions and the unification of the world. As peoples become one, so do languages. The world will be unified politically as well, with democracy and America playing their roles in overcoming communism. With Unification thought and practice in place in the world, all will then be saved, as hell will no longer be. The new Messiah will be a fleshly one. The new Kingdom will be a social, political, economic, and religious one. Unity means indemnity has been paid, both spiritual and physical salvation are complete, and restoration of the perfect Garden of Eden is accomplished.

Life-style of Moonies and Their Movement—Mass Marriages to Mobile Fund-raising to Mass Media

Reverend Moon affectionately calls his followers Moonies, and that is the term used by mass media. Moonies have been in the news and highly visible for over twenty-five years. Stories have circulated, especially by former Moonies, of the brainwashing techniques of recruitment by the Unification Church. These stories have pointed especially to methods by the church on the West Coast. During the 1970s, Moonies appeared to be omnipresent in shopping malls and at street intersections, selling their wares of flowers, tea, and other commodities in fund-raising for the church. Often they were accused of "heavenly deception" and receiving monies or inviting people to meetings without revealing their affiliation with the church.

A strategical change in the methods of Moonies has occurred. They tend to be more open and up front of who they are and what they desire. While they continue to sell flowers, they also sell newspapers which they own and print. They have pastors of churches as well as fishing fleet captains. More Moonies are quicker to state their belief in Moon as Messiah. They live communally in house centers, have mobile fund-raising teams and evangelistic rallies, as well as families living in single-family housing. They operate their own seminary, a 250-acre campus of the former Christian Brothers Monastery, with a pluralistic faculty. They also send their students to Harvard and Princeton for theological education. Moonies appear to be settling into the more normal patterns of church life.[52]

Devotional Practices

Moonie spirituality and piety cluster around personal and corporate prayer and the study of the Bible and *Divine Principle*. Prayers are frequently "punctuated" with the word *father*. A "prayer in action" is a prayer based on conditions to accomplish a goal. For example, Moonies do a seven-day fast. One sets a goal to witness to so many persons a day during the fast period. One may be timid to meet strangers, but that condition may be alleviated with the goal of meeting specific people.

Informal worship is held once or twice each day in the center with the rotation of leadership. Worship includes singing, prayer, scripture, and a message. One church tradition is the pledge, which is recited every Sunday at 5:00 A.M.; the first day of every month; and on holy days such as Parents' Day, Children's Day, Day of All Things, and God's Day. It is a time of rededication to God and recommitment to the mission of the church. During the pledge ceremony, men and women sit separately. They bow three times in respect to God and as a sign of humility. The pledge is recited in unison, and songs and prayers are a part of the service. At large church gatherings for socializing and entertainment, sometimes with Reverend Moon present, there is much singing and some spontaneous dancing.

Spiritual or mystical experiences tend to be common among Moonies. They believe in the spirit world and that people and angels in the spirit world can help them. Moonies refer to dreams about Reverend and Mrs. Moon, Jesus Christ, and dead relatives.

Unification Centers

Unification centers are in cities across the nation and the world, as well as several large churches. The Unification

Church of Washington, D.C., formerly a Mormon church, is of Gothic architecture and has a full-time pastor. Centers have directors. There are directors for states as well as regional directors for special emphases such as evangelism. In 1978, Moon initiated the concept of "home church." He asked each Moonie to assume responsibility for an area of 360 homes in which to serve, witness, and love the people of those homes. The number 360 represents a complete circle.

Raising money has been a prominent part of Moonie life. Both selling goods and seeking contributions have brought in funds. Mobile Fund-raising Teams (MFT) have been employed, with each team having eight to ten members, a captain, and a team mother. By having a male leader and a team mother, there is the recognition of the masculine and feminine aspects of God, of Adam and Eve, and of True Parents. Goals of the amount of money to be collected are set; areas are established; and the captain leads the team. Often, the Unification center is dependent on fund-raising for the maintenance of the center as well as to send finances to national headquarters. Moonies who hold paying jobs also contribute monies toward meeting the budgetary needs.

Mass Marriage

A most distinctive life-style event for Moonies is the marriage ceremony. Someone has said that the doctrine of marriage and the family is the central concept of Unification belief and life-style. All those who have committed to marriage assemble with Reverend Moon. He is sensitive to all those who desire marriage and often interviews individuals. Moonies have filled out questionnaires, and these data are available for "the matching" of couples. Once Moon has matched the couples, the marriage or Blessing is pronounced. These vows are said in mass meetings where there have been thousands of couples united.

> What is special about marriage in the Unification Church? For Unificationists, the Blessing is a passport to heaven. Marriage has that purpose and significance.

It is conceived in relationship to God. The Blessing ceremony has sacramental qualities. . . . For example,
during the wedding ceremony, holy water is used in a
baptismal fashion and holy wine in an eucharistic manner. During the time of the Blessing ceremony, according to Unification theology, one's sins are forgiven and
new life is given.[53]

An absolute condition in the church is a waiting period
after the marriage before its consummation. In 1970 there
was a forty-day waiting period. In 1975 Moon asked the
couples to wait three years before having sexual intercourse.
Marriage is seen in the greater context of devotion, discipline, and mission. Moon often sends the recently married
couples in separate missions around the globe. Another
absolute is fidelity to one's partner. Moon encourages couples to have many children, for children are looked on as the
only thing the couple can attain that is eternal in the world.
When a child is eight days old, the parents dedicate the child
to God through a simple ceremony. Families are to have a
special place in the home set aside for prayer.

It is evident that Reverend and Mrs. Moon have a most
important role in the Blessing. One Moonie writes,

In the world today, Rev. Moon is God's primary spiritual instrument. Unification marriage is lived in accord
with the tradition that Rev. and Mrs. Moon have established through the example of their sacrificial, loving
lives. Rev. and Mrs. Moon have reached a level of spiritual maturity that makes them ideal or true as people,
as husband and wife, and most importantly, as parents.
That is to say, they are parents capable of giving uncon-
ditional love to their children and to others without
expecting anything in return. For me, Rev. Moon is not
only a leader, nor just a brother in Christ or a friend. He
is all those things, but he's more. He's a spiritual father,
Mrs. Moon is a spiritual mother in the sense that I can
inherit a spiritual tradition from them that can lead me
to God.[54]

One may ask about the role of single females or the role of women in general in Unification thought. What about the debated issues in American society over homosexuals and abortion? Moonies have begun to discuss these matters. Women in particular have pointed out the overstress of male models in *Divine Principle* and the lack of female models. Yet they see the emphasis on polarity and seek to continue examining the theological significance of masculinity and femininity. Unification theology is new as a discipline like the church is young, and Moonies claim that time and the maturing of their church will give them opportunities to deal with challenging and problematic issues.

The worldview of the Unification Church is unitive, holistic, and pragmatic. The Kingdom is to take shape in the context of social, economic, political and religious realities. There is no "pie in the sky by and by." Moonies are on mission to change the world where spiritual and physical realities become one. They are committed to uniting the polarities of God and man, of religion and science, of Adam and Eve, and of Jesus and Christ. They are concerned with the human mind as it is expressed in the sciences and humanities and as it is formed and influenced on university campuses. They are prepared to solicit food and organize its distribution to the needy, as well as clothes and proper housing. They are lobbyists to the congress in Washington, as well as on the state and local levels. They are, thus, visionaries and architects of a Unificationist world.

Unification Enterprises

Some of the Unification Church's religious, cultural, educational, political, and business organizations are:

Religious

Holy Spirit Association for the Unification of World Christianity (HSA-UWC). This is the formal title of the church which is informally called the Unification Church.

Unification Theological Seminary (UTS). The seminary is located in Barrytown, N.Y. It represents the ecumenical interest of the church with a faculty representing some ten denominations as well as the Unification Church.

Cultural

Project Volunteer (PV). This is a social service entity which has distributed millions of pounds of surplus food and materials through a network of over three hundred charitable organizations. It is involved in recycling, vocational training, and other community projects.

New Hope Singers International. It is composed of about fifty young singers from around the world. It performs at many cultural events sponsored by Moon.

Little Angels of Korea. These troups of young Korean girls have performed in the White House and before Queen Elizabeth.

New York City Symphony Orchestra. It was purchased by Moon in 1975 and performs separate from Moon activities. Others are *Sunburst*, a folk-rock band; *International Folk Ballet*; *New World Players*.

International Relief Friendship Foundation. This foundation works in over fifty countries providing emergency and long-term assistance through food and material aid, extended education projects, and medical care.

Educational

College Association for the Research of Principles (CARP). This is a campus organization which provides an alternative to communism and works toward a revitalization of morality. Members remain in school and work with recruiting and fund-raising.

The Women's Federation for World Peace. This organization was begun in April 1992, with Hak Ja Han Moon as its president.

United to Serve America (USA). USA is a cooperative project of the American Freedom Foundation and the American Freedom Coalition. Its focus is on concerns about drugs, crime, and illiteracy.

International Conference on the Unity of the Sciences (ICUS). ICUS is held annually for scientists and scholars from many cultures to explore ways toward world peace. It has included Nobel prize winners.

D. C. Striders. This is a team of young black athletes. Most are not members of the Unification Church but are encouraged toward athletic scholarships. They have numerous track records.

World Media Conference. This conference provides an international forum for publishers, broadcasters, and scholars to consider the responsibility and future of the free press.

New Ecumenical Research Association (New ERA). New ERA sponsors conferences involving scholars of religion, political science, and other disciplines in dialogue with members of the Unification Church.

International Religious Foundation, Inc. (IRF). IRF holds religious dialogue meetings with scholars, religious leaders, and ministers. Its activities are interreligious, intercultural, and interracial in composition.

Political

Freedom Leadership Foundation (FLF). It has its main offices in Washington, D.C. It sponsors lectures and forums on threats of communism and abuses of human rights. Its series of lectures has been called Victory Over Communism (VOC).

New World Forum. This forum deals with the ambassadorial and United Nations communities with a religious view of values and concern for mankind.

The Rising Tide. A bimonthly newspaper published by FLF.

Business

U.S. Master Marine deals with Mastercraft Repairs, P & H Construction Company, and seafood endeavors in Alaska, Virginia, and Massachusetts.

Diplomat's National Bank is located in Washington, D.C., with a majority of stock owned by the church.

News World, a New York daily newspaper, is run by the church to give an alternative to the *New York Times.*

The Washington Times, a Washington, D.C., daily newspaper, is run by the church to give an alternative to the *Washington Post.*

Ginseng Teahouse (USA)

Ginseng Trading Company (USA)

Fong Industries (Korea)

Il Wha Pharmaceuticals Company (Korea)

Shin Stoneworks Company (Korea)

Tong Il Enterprises (Korea and USA)

New World Cleaning Service (USA)

New Yorker Hotel

Inchon is a high-cost Hollywood movie about the Korean War.

The Unification Church also owns various farms, real estate holdings, seafood processing plants, printing, audio-visual, and other business concerns across the United States, Korea, and other places.

Publications

The church owns *News World* and *The Washington Times,* daily newspapers in New York and Washington. *World Student Times* is published by CARP. *New Hope News* and *Master Speaks* are in-house publications for members. The church publishes the proceedings of conferences and dialogue sessions as well as pamphlets, hand-outs, and small books. Of course, it publishes *Divine Principle* and supporting materials.

The Unification Church will celebrate its fortieth anniversary on May 1, 1994. Its publications state, "The Unification message has spread from one small hut on a Korean hillside to more than 120 countries."[55] As indicated above, the church, with over three million members, has wide interest and involvement through its organizations, especially in the

United States and Korea. Often it has been criticized for not being open and up front in ownership of businesses, foundations, and conferences. The church has had a pattern of involvement in political, educational, cultural, and religious matters through financial support and background presence, although not having public leadership.

Membership in the church is open to those who study *Divine Principle* and its study aids. Seminars, lectures, discussions, and question-and-answer periods are provided in church centers across the nation and at retreat centers. Seminars may range in length from one day to forty days. Membership is contingent upon the completion of a twenty-one-day program.

Hierarchy of leadership in the church begins with Reverend Moon. Elders of the church, especially the early Korean followers of Moon, are looked to for counsel and guidance by Moonies. Moon has several of the old-timers in close association. While the church has not formally ordained ministers, it designates state directors and center directors. The church in Washington, D.C., uses the nomenclature of "Pastor" for its leader.

As the church grows it adds structures. Members are involved in public relations, mass media, lobbying, education, and the planning and administering of a multitude of conferences. Neil Salonen was the first president of The Unification Church of America. The chairman of the church is Mose Durst. There appears to be much freedom given to local centers in methods of ministry and missions, although there is accountability from local to national headquarters.

The emblem of the church has a central focus of a circle with spokes extending to an outer circle.

> The circle in the center represents God, the twelve rays emanating from the center represent the twelve gates to the new Jerusalem mentioned in Revelation 21:10-14 (. . . on the gates the names of the twelve tribes of the sons of Israel were inscribed . . . and the wall of the city had twelve foundations, and on them the twelve

names of the twelve apostles of the Lamb.), and the arrows encircling the symbol represent the universal give and take among God, man and creation that is the basis for harmony and union.[56]

Issues and Challenges
Among Contemporary Moonies

The Unification Church is a recent phenomenon among religious communities in the United States. Its very newness, along with its claims to be Christian and a church, presents for it the challenge of interpretation acceptance. With new revelation, new converts, and exploding energy level, expanding resources of persons and monies, and a spirit of daring and outreach without fear, timidity, or intimidation, it is, so to speak, the new kid on the block.

Moonies have been one of the most visible religious communities in salesmanship on the streets and in mass media. The group has also been the recipient of attacks by families, churches, and other organizations. The imprisonment of Reverend Moon added another chapter in Moonie apologetics and public harassment, as well as certain group support for protection of its rights and privileges as a religious community.

Perhaps one of the greatest issues internally for the Moonies is their public relations stance. There is much suspicion and distrust toward them. A public stereotype of the Moonies includes "followers of a Korean Messiah," the use of "deception in seeking converts," "brainwashing" in recruitment and training, manipulation in religion and politics for control of church and government, "buying their way into positions of power and influence," and "a pep rally cult." The church has been embroiled with de-programmers, legal suits, court actions, and the imprisonment of its leader. Moonies have attempted recently to deal with many of these stereotypes by being straightforward with their identities, both personally and organizationally, as well as holding various conferences with different groups with open and candid discussions. Reverend Moon has visited with the leaders of Communist countries to bolster his status As a world statesman.

Another challenge for the Moonies is the routinization of their movement. Are they an "Association" as their official name states, or a church as their popular appellation expresses, or a movement as the president of their seminary suggests, or a center, or "the messianic community"? As the Moonies mature in faith and practice, what shape do they intend to become?

What will happen at the passing of Moon? Who will succeed him, if anyone? Rumors have circulated for some time of competition and tension between the Korean elders and the first-generation Americans in the church. Disagreements between leadership on the East Coast with that on the West Coast have been rumored. Some Moonies believe that a son of the Moons will someday head the church. Also, there is the challenge of having some three million members in some 120 countries, all involved in a church of the first generation with a single charismatic visionary at its head.

The church basically has been a lay movement. Recently a seminary has been established, and a theological movement has begun in the church. In the American church, the contextualization of *Divine Principle* has been raised. What are the strengths and weaknesses of the Korean cultural context of Reverend Moon's revelatory teachings as they are applied to the American cultural stream? How will *Divine Principle* and theological interpretations and sociological applications deal with issues such as the role of women, the unmarried, abortion, homosexuality, and church and state?

A primary challenge for the Moonies is in their efforts at the call and practice of ecumenical Christianity. Moonies often appear like little children desperately wanting to be accepted and affirmed by their parents, namely Christians, and by Christianity. On the other hand, they often appear like parents knowing what is best for the entire Christian communities and offering sweets in the form of expense-paid trips to faraway places to learn of what unity in Christianity is all about. They state that they are Christian and that they offer norms of authority and belief and practice which supersede those traditional Christian norms of Bible, Jesus Christ, and salvation by grace through faith in Jesus Christ. An issue presented to them is their acceptance in the ecumenical communities and councils of Christianity.

Moonies and Christian Belief and Practice

In examining the claims, teachings, and practices of Reverend Moon and the Unification Christ to be Christian, one recognizes that there is much diversity within Christianity and even disagreement over doctrine and practice. Even in ecumenical Christianity, there is an important core of Christian belief and practice which unites the various communities. That common core includes the Bible and the life, death, and resurrection of Jesus Christ as normative, superceding any other "inspired" book, theologians, theologies, and "inspired" persons. Realizing that Christian theology has a long and deep tradition and that Unification thought is complex, a brief attempt will be made to compare certain doctrines and practices of traditional Christianity and the Unification Church.

Basic presuppositions upon which Unification theology is built are the revelations claimed by Reverend Moon, the authority he asserts, and the affirmation which his followers give him. It is true that Moon has not explicitly said in public that he is the new Messiah. His testimony, however, is that he has talked with Jesus and other biblical figures in the spirit world, that he has been sent to complete the mission of Jesus, and that his book of principles supersedes the Bible. His followers increasingly claim him as "Father," as True Parent, as Lord of the Second Advent. One would, therefore, have to accept Reverend Moon as a greater authority than Jesus Christ. Traditional Christian faith and practice, though accepting theological interpretations from various individuals throughout history, would not accept the extrabiblical authority and revelation which Moon and the Moonies claim.

Divine Principle presents ideas of dualism, "trinity," Jesus' failure, a split view of salvation, and an eschatology that are contrary to traditional Christian views. Present is an embedded teaching of cosmic dualism that distorts the nature of God. God is discussed in essential nature as negative and positive, masculine and feminine, as *yang* and *ying*, and as good and evil. Man in his nature is dualistic in terms of "spirit man" and "physical man." Salvation is viewed as spiritual salvation and physical salvation. Jesus is viewed as the bearer of spiritual salvation, and Christ (new Messiah) is looked upon as the giver of physical salvation. Satan is so elevated as to become a second, rival god. Traditional Christian teachings have emphasized the eternal unity of God, His dominion over creation, and His divine reign through righteousness. Human nature has never been divided so we need two kinds of salvation, nor have two saviors been necessary—one for the spirit and one for the body.

The Unification idea of trinity is unacceptable to traditional Christian understandings. Adam and Eve as True Parents who center on God are trinity. Jesus as masculine and the Holy Spirit as feminine who center on God are trinity. Adam and Eve who are contaminated with the blood of Satan form a trinity with Satan. This thought combines principles of dualism with "trinity," and it is in conflict with Christian teachings which regard the Trinity as a unitive expression of God, not of man and God and Satan.

The Unification concept of Jesus is antithetical and contrary to the biblical witness, as well as to traditional Christian teachings on the life, crucifixion, and resurrection of Jesus. Jesus is viewed as dualistic as Jesus and Christ. He is the second Adam, of the same value as prefallen humanity. Jesus is capable of bringing spiritual salvation but not material salvation. He paid the indemnity of the failure of John the Baptist, but He failed in His mission before He was able to marry.

Traditional Christian teachings cannot accept that the saving work of Jesus Christ was only spiritual and that He could not affect the created material order in a redemptive way. Unification thought falls back into its premises of dualism. Jesus is a half-savior, one of the divisions of the cosmic polarity of spirit and matter. On one hand, Jesus is not God, not the incarnation of God in human flesh, and not the child of a virgin woman. On the other hand, Jesus, the Son of God, brings not material but spiritual salvation. Christian teachings hold that Jesus Christ is Savior, Lord, the last Adam, whose death and resurrection are sufficient for human salvation.

Unification teachings on the church are brief and sketchy. The word *church* is first used in *Divine Principle* on page 213, and little is said of church afterwards. Its teachings on eschatology are unacceptable to traditional Christian thought. Its view of history in terms of individuals and nations as good and evil, of economics and politics in terms of democracy versus communism, is simplistic and patronizing, as well as unfounded biblically. Its belief that Korea is the third Israel and that Korea plays the role of the messianic nation to bear the new Messiah is unacceptable to Christian teachings. The earthly kingdom, expected by Unificationists, appears capable of being achieved by the use of technology and a democratic society and "matched" marriages blessed by True Parents. A Christian critique of this position would suggest the overemphasis on human achievement with little regard for divine intervention and reign.

In conclusion, for Christians the biblical witness is the normative authority. God as Father, Son, and Holy Spirit, has acted in creation and salvation on behalf of the human family in saving it from sin and death. Jesus Christ as the eternal Word of God incarnate is the way of salvation for all humanity and for all creation. Man responds to the grace of God through faith and faithfulness. Unification thought uses texts of the Bible and Christian terms. Those texts and terms, however, are always interpreted in the light of *Divine Princi-*

ple. Divine Principle is seen as the "new, ultimate, final truth," that not only completes, but supplants past Christian teachings, beliefs, and practices. These premises and presuppositions are unacceptable to Christianity.

A Christian Posture Toward Moonies

The Holy Spirit Association for the Unification of World Christianity claims to be Christian. The Association wants to unite with councils of churches and to work alongside ministers and laypersons in the ecumenical Christian context. What may a Christian posture toward Moonies include?

1. A sensitivity toward the background out of which Reverend Sun Myung Moon came is needed. Evidently, Moon's parents were introduced to Christianity from a Presbyterian church mission. Consequently, Moon was brought up in a Christian family environment. Early Christianity in Korea faced crises of misunderstanding and persecution, as did Moon. In recent years, Christianity in Korea has seen revival and great growth in baptisms and churches.

   Elements of sacrifice and commitment on the part of early Korean Christians can be appreciated as well as the growth of Christianity in the country. At the same time, one needs to be sensitive to the indigenization and contextualization of Christian belief and practice in the Korean context. Christianity must be allowed to take root in the cultural context. Syncretism and accommodation of faith and practice, however, must be evaluated. Moon's teachings appear to be heavily influenced by Asian ideas and practices that contradict, distort, and compromise Christian doctrines and practices.

2. An appreciation for the mix of backgrounds and reasons why Moonies are attracted to follow Moon is appropriate. Some Moonies tell of being "born again" into the evangelical Christian faith prior to embracing *Divine Principle*. Some speak of the apathy and hypocrisy in the churches as reasons for leaving them and joining the movement. Others relate that the Moonie vision, zeal, love, and discipline attracted them. According to data released by the Unification

Church in the 1980s on the past religious affiliations of its members, 40 percent come from Protestantism and 36 percent come from Roman Catholicism. Of Protestants, Baptists are 7.9 percent and Methodists are 7.7 percent. Jewish are 5.6 percent. The average age of a full-time member is twenty-eight years old. The educational level is 38.5 percent with some college and 25.9 percent with a college degree or graduate work.

One can understand the appeal of Moon's movement to youth in the turbulent sixties and early seventies, and one can appreciate the diversity of backgrounds and reasons of those attracted to the movement. We need to observe that all Moonies are not the same in their understanding of and commitment to Reverend Moon, *Divine Principle*, and the Unification Church. Consequently, personal conversations and group discussions with Moonies should consider the diversity of the persons and their backgrounds and commitments.

3. The movement centering around Moon reflects a myriad of challenges within American society, including social, political, religious, and psychological problems. Christians may be aware of these challenges as the Moonies attempt to address them and respond in constructive ways. Moonies stress the deterioration of family structures and marriage vows and emphasize a strong love ethic and marital relation. They point out the apathy of many religious institutions, and seek ways to meet the needs for world peace, hunger, and adequate housing.

The Unification Church also mirrors the issue of intruding its philosophy and goals into politics, government, and the church and state relationship. The church has raised once again the challenge of the church's usage and control of money and power. Christians need to observe the Moonie stress on traditional values of peace, love, and family as well as assistance to meet humanitarian needs. Christians also need to be aware and evaluative of Moonie attempts at using church resources for manipulation and power in politics and government. Christian churches and individual Christians need to decide in what ways, if any, they may work with the Unification Church.

4. The Unification Church and its theology and practice are young and still in the formative stages. The Unification Church of America, especially, will face transitions as leadership may change more from Korean influences to American. How will Moon be viewed beyond his lifetime? Will the movement become more "church"? What will be the theology and practice of second-generation Moonies? Christians need to be watchful for the shape of Unificationism in the future and for the contours of faith and practice in the lives of Moonies.

5. For some fifteen years there have been the issues of the deprogramming of Moonies and testimonies of former Moonies of coercion and brainwashing. There have been court cases involving Moonies, parents, and their children which have deeply affected the relationships between the Unification Church and Christian churches and Christians. Moonies have had divided views on how their zeal together with the interest of possible converts might have bordered on excessive "love," "acceptance," "training," "nurturing," and "family acceptance." Christians have called for Moonies to be up front, open, and honest in their identity, propaganda, and solicitation.

6. Christians may dialogue with Moonies, join Moonies in humanitarian projects, and be called on to love them and share their faith. At the center of a Christian posture toward Moonies and their church's theology and practice is the question of Jesus Christ and His mission, of how the Triune God acts in history for the salvation of humankind, and of the scriptural norm for revelation and the authority of faith and practice. As discussed above, Unification theology is often incompatible with and contrary to Christian traditional teachings. Christian teachings on the nature of God, Christology, salvation, the role and authority of Scripture, and the nature of revelation are among those doctrines in disagreement with Unification thought. A Christian posture does not accept the teachings and practices of Reverend Moon, his

self-claimed authority from Jesus Christ, or the *Divine Principle* as normative for faith and practice.

7. A Christian posture will affirm and support the rights of the Unification Church under the First Amendment of the Constitution of the United States, as it does for all religions. Christians continually need to be vigilant for the protection of religious freedom and religious liberty as well as the separation of church and state.

4

CHRISTIAN SCIENCE, UNITY, AND SCIENTOLOGY
■   ■

Christian Science

A neat, manicured lawn sets off the well-architectured building known as the Church of Christ, Scientist. There are more than three thousand churches in over fifty countries. A Christian Science reading room may be adjacent to the church or located in the busy block of an urban corridor. The Christian Science Practitioner may advertise his/her service of healing in the daily newspaper. *The Christian Science Monitor* is read by Wall Street brokers, members of Congress, and internationals across the globe. Who are Christian Scientists? Who was Mary Baker Eddy? What is *Science and Health with Key to the Scriptures?*

Origins of Christian Science

Christian Science began as a religious movement and a church in the latter half of the nineteenth century, a century which witnessed the birth of several other American nativistic religious movements, including the Mormons and the Jehovah's Witnesses. Christian Science was founded by Mary Baker Eddy, a woman of much sickness, but great leadership ability. Gottschalk has written that "Mrs. Eddy

located the loss of true Biblical Christianity in the abandon-
ment of healing as practiced in the early Christian church."[1]
Her sickness led to her search for healing and for answers in
the Bible. She found her clues based upon the healing of
Christ (Christian) and the knowledge (Science) thereof.

Mary Morse Baker (1821-1910) was born on a farm in
Bow, New Hampshire, on July 16, 1821.[2] She grew up in
the Congregational Church of her parents, and at age seventeen she joined the church. She refused to agree with the
view of predestination held by the church. However, after
deliberation they admitted her. She remained a member of
the church until she founded her own in 1879. Her brother,
Albert, went off to Dartmouth College, and encouraged her
on her own to study Greek and Hebrew as well as natural
philosophy and moral science. When she was twenty-two,
she married Major George Washington Glover of Charles-
ton, South Carolina. He contracted yellow fever and died in
seven months. She returned to New Hampshire, where she
gave birth to their son. She was in poor health and unable to
raise him. Her marriage in 1853 to Dr. Daniel Patterson, a
dentist, gave her some financial and domestic security. However, she remained bedridden much of the time.

During those years she tried various methods of therapy.
She received treatment under Phineas P. Quimby, a healer
in Portland, Maine. With the help she received from him,
she became enthusiastic about his therapeutic methods and
began to treat people. Non-Christian Science scholars have
indicated from their research that there is a close similarity
between the teachings and writings of Quimby and Eddy and
that Eddy was most probably heavily dependent on Quimby.
Eddy denied these accusations, however, even in her lifetime; and Christian Scientists deny them today. Certainly,
Eddy went far beyond Quimby in her biblical interpretations
and in establishing her church.

By 1866, Dr. Patterson had left his wife, and seven years
later she obtained a divorce on the grounds of desertion.
That same year her therapist and teacher Quimby died, and

Mary was painfully injured through a fall on an icy pavement in Lynn, Massachusetts. She was unconscious for some time, bedridden, and was feared paralyzed. She refused medical attention. On a February Sunday in 1866, she read the story of the paralytic in Matthew 9:2-8 in which he was told by Jesus to take up his bed and walk. Through her reading of Scripture and prayer, she describes the following:

> As I read, the healing Truth dawned upon my sense; and the result was that I rose, dressed myself, and ever after was in better health than I had before enjoyed. That short experience included a glimpse of the great fact that I have since tried to make plain to others, namely Life in and of Spirit; this life being the sole reality of existence.[3]

> For three years after my discovery, I sought the solution of this problem of Mind-healing, searched the Scriptures and read little else, kept aloof from society, and devoted time and energies to discovering a positive rule. The search was sweet, calm, and buoyant with hope, not selfish nor depressing. I know the Principle of all harmonious Mind-action to be in God, and that cures were produced in primitive Christian healing by holy, uplifting faith; but I must know the Science of this healing, and I won my way to absolute conclusions through divine revelation, reason, and demonstration. The revelation of Truth in the understanding came to me gradually and apparently through divine power.[4]

For nine years Mary studied the Bible, engaged in prayer, and made her research notes. She became a teacher and healer, gathered a small following, and claimed the title "Christian Science Teacher." By 1875, she had published the first edition of *Science and Health*. In 1877, she married Asa Gilbert Eddy, who had become a follower of her teachings. He organized the first Christian Science Sunday School and helped his wife gain the proper copyright protection. They were married for five years before his sudden death. In 1879, she founded the Church of Christ, Scientist in Boston which is the famous Mother Church. By 1883, the sixth edition of her book had been published with the new title *Science and Health with Key to the Scriptures*. She continued to teach, write, and organize her church until her death in 1910 at eighty-nine years old.

How did Mary Baker Eddy view her own role and authority in her church? She wrote:

> In the year 1866, I discovered the Christ Science or divine laws of Life, Truth, and Love, named my discovery Christian Science. God had been graciously preparing me during many years for the reception of this final revelation of the divine Principle of scientific mental healing.[5]

> No human pen nor tongue taught me the Science contained in this book, *Science and Health*; and neither tongue nor pen can overthrow it.[6]

Eddy claimed the Bible as her authority. "The Bible has been my only authority. I have had no other guide in 'the straight and narrow way' of Truth."[7] "In following these leanings of scientific revelation, the Bible was my only Textbook."[8]

Christian Scientists view Eddy as the discoverer and founder of Christian Science. Officially, they write to the question of why she is called their leader:

> For the same reason the children of Israel looked on Moses as their leader. He led them out of captivity in Egypt. Mrs. Eddy's writings are leading thousands of people out of bondage to materialism and into spiritual freedom. As they follow her leadership, they find themselves becoming deeper and truer disciples of Christ Jesus. Mrs. Eddy herself has written, "Follow your leader only so far as she follows Christ."[9]

Eddy's followers view her writing *Science and Health with Key to the Scriptures* as divine revelation. However, they state that her book does not replace the Bible.

No, it provides us with a "key" to the Scriptures—and a key doesn't replace the door it opens. Christian Scientists study the Bible more than most people do, because *Science and Health* has made it so wonderfully alive and practical to them. The first tenet of Christian Science reads: "As adherents of Truth, we take the inspired Word of the Bible as our sufficient guide to eternal life."[10]

Christian Scientists point out that Eddy returned to the Bible again and again for inspiration, healing, and enlightenment. "No honest observer can overlook the fact that the Christianly scientific rule which she established and interpreted for mankind had not been previously discovered by any of the countless students of these same Scriptures in the centuries that had passed since they were recorded."[11] They have two fundamental textbooks, the Bible and *Science and Health*. In fact, Eddy ordained the Bible and *Science and Health* to be the pastor of the Church of Christ, Scientist. She ruled that there would be no other pastors of the church.

Teachings of Christian Science

Christian Science has no creed, although Eddy listed six religious tenets as significant.

1. As adherents of Truth, we take the inspired Word of the Bible as our sufficient guide to eternal Life.

2. We acknowledge and adore one supreme and infinite God. We acknowledge His Son, one Christ; the Holy Ghost or divine Comforter; and man in God's image and likeness.

3. We acknowledge God's forgiveness of sin in the destruction of sin and the spiritual understanding that casts out evil as unreal. But the belief in sin is punished so long as the belief lasts.

4. We acknowledge Jesus' atonement as the evidence of divine, efficacious love, unfolding man's unity with God

through Christ Jesus the Way Shower; and we acknowledge that man is saved through Christ, through Truth, Life, and Love as demonstrated by the Galilean Prophet in healing the sick and overcoming sin and death.

5. We acknowledge that the crucifixion of Jesus and his resurrection served to uplift faith to understand eternal Life, even the allness of Soul, Spirit, and the nothingness of matter.

6. And we solemnly promise to watch, and to pray for that Mind to be in us which was also in Christ Jesus; to do unto others as we would have them do unto us; and to be merciful, just, and pure.[12]

What are the teachings of Christian Science about God, Jesus Christ, Holy Spirit, Trinity, man, sin, and salvation? In the glossary of *Science and Health,* God is described as follows: "The Great I Am; the all-knowing, all-seeing, all-acting, all-wise, all-loving and eternal; Principle; Mind; Soul; Spirit; Life; Truth; Love; all Substance; intelligence."[13] The key words in this definition of God are used synonymously by Eddy in describing God's nature. She also refers to God in her writings as Mother or as Father-Mother.

In the glossary Jesus is defined as "the highest human corporeal concept of the divine idea, rebuking and destroying error and bringing to light man's immortality."[14] Christ is defined as "The divine manifestation of God, which comes to the flesh to destroy incarnate error."[15] Christian Science draws a distinction between Christ and Jesus. Christ is the "Christ-idea," the Son of God, the supreme manifestation of the eternal "Mind," while Jesus is born of woman, walks the earth, and enables man to have the knowledge and understanding of God. Jesus is not affirmed as the deity. The Holy Spirit or Holy Ghost is Divine Science, the development of eternal Life, Truth, and Love.[16]

Science and Health describes the Trinity as follows:

Life, Truth, and Love constitute the triune Person called God—that is the triply divine Principle, Love. They represent a trinity in unity, three in one—the same in essence, though multiform in office: God the Father-Mother; Christ the spiritual idea of sonship; divine Science or the Holy Comforter. These three express in divine science the threefold, essential nature of the infinite. They also indicate the divine Principle of scientific being, the intelligent relation of God to man and the universe.[17]

The view of man *and* sin by Christian Science is based on the realness of the spirituality of God and the unrealness of the materiality of man. There are two accounts in Genesis of the creation of man. The first is in the image of God, and the second is that man was created from dust and sinned.

Christian Science, accepting as basic the account of man's creation given in the first chapter of Genesis, affirms and maintains man's permanent spiritual relationship to his creator, and sees in the contrasting record of the second chapter, not the fact, but the falsity of creation.[18]

It will surely be admitted that if one accepts fully (as Christian Scientists do) the premise that man was created in the image of God himself, combined with Christ Jesus' assurance that God is Spirit, he must thus conclude that man is spiritual and not material, and further that he is not a frail mortal, constantly and all but inevitably, yielding to temptation.[19]

Man in the image of God, Spirit, must be wholly spiritual and as perfect as his creator. Then it follows that the sick and sinning mortal man who appears to the physical senses is a false representation of man, a material misconception of man as he really is.[20]

Eddy wrote of man,

When speaking of God's children, not the children of men, Jesus said, "The Kingdom of God is within you";

that is, Truth and Love reign in the real man, showing that man in God's image is unfallen and eternal. Jesus beheld in Science the perfect man, who appeared to him where sinning mortal man appears to the mortals. In this perfect man the Savior saw God's own likeness, and this correct view of man healed the sick. Thus Jesus taught that the kingdom of God is in fact, universal, and that man is pure and holy. Man is not a material habitation for Soul; he is himself spiritual. Soul, being Spirit, is seen in nothing imperfect nor material.[21]

What, then, is sin in Christian Science? Eddy does not include the word "sin" in her glossary. She writes, however, concerning error and sin:

Error is a supposition that pleasure and pain, that intelligence, substance, life, are existent in matter. Error is neither Mind nor one of Mind's faculties. Error is the contradiction of Truth. Error is belief without understanding. Error is unreal because untrue. It is that which seemeth to be and is not.[22]

All reality is in God and His creation; harmonious and eternal. That which he creates is good, and it makes all that is made. Therefore, the only reality of sin, sickness, or death is the awful fact that unrealities seem real to human erring belief, until God strips off their disguise.[23]

What is salvation? "Life, Truth, and Love understood and demonstrated as supreme over all; sin, sickness, and death destroyed."[24] Salvation, thus, includes the knowledge or science of God and the practice of healing. The Greek word, *sozein*, means either "to heal" or "to save." The Bible stresses this dual aspect of salvation, which gives relief from both physical and moral infirmity. Salvation is from

every phase of evil—from all that denies the perfection of God and in his image and likeness. Thus sin, sickness, lack, sorrow, selfishness, ignorance, fear, and all material-mindedness are included within the range of mortal errors to be corrected and overcome by a scientific understanding of God. . . . Christian Science speaks of a salvation that begins here and now, releasing him into a more abundant sense of energy, purpose, identity, and joy. The word "healing" as used in Christian Science extends to the healing of family and business problems, of social injustices, intellectual limitations, psychological tensions, and moral confusions.[25]

Christian Science stresses the atonement of Christ Jesus as "at-one-ment," as the state of being at one with God. Viewing the atonement as purely vicarious, or as a type of sacrificial offering from which others are spared because of the sacrifice of Jesus, is not acceptable to Christian Scientists. Jesus gives the example as the Way Shower, and each one is called upon to do his part, individually, to overcome sin.[26] The resurrection of Jesus is looked upon as the "Spiritualization of thought, a new and higher idea of immortality, or spiritual existence, material belief yielding to spiritual understanding."[27]

Healing is a most significant function and practice in Christian Science. Eddy was healed through her Bible readings and prayer. She named her textbook *Science and Health* and stressed the art and practice of healing.[28] She established a profession in her church with primary responsibility for healing. A Christian Science Practitioner gives full time to the public practice of Christian Science healing.[29] It is both a ministry and a profession. Healing is done through prayer. It calls for systematic study of the Bible and Christian Science textbook. Prayer is both verbal as well as silent, and it relies on God's presence, power, perfect love, and control. Qualified and sanctioned Christian Science Practitioners are listed in the monthly directory of *The Christian Science Journal*. Christian Science is not combined with reliance on medical aid. A few exceptions exist. Childbirth and the setting of bones may require medical attention, but medication is not to be used. Healing is to rely on spiritual means. "Only through radical reliance on Truth can scientific healing power be realized."[30]

The Church of Christ, Scientist

Eddy established the Church of Christ, Scientist. She wrote that the Church is the structure of Truth and Love and is founded upon the Divine Principle. The church arouses "the dormant understanding from material beliefs to the apprehension of spiritual ideas and the demonstration of divine Science, thereby casting out devils, or error, and healing the sick."[31] Since she was the first and only pastor, and since she designated the Bible and *Science and Health* to be the pastor after her, the church has had no other pastors. In her *Manual of the Mother Church,* she left guidelines for church organization which have basically remained unchanged since her death. There are no clergy; it is a church of laypersons, and anyone, without distinction of sex, may serve in leadership positions based on demonstrated fitness. A Board of Directors governs the worldwide church based on the *Manual.* The Mother Church, in Boston, serves as a model for all other local churches.

The Sunday service is conducted similarly in any church.[32] There are hymns, prayers, solos, Scripture readings, and a lesson-sermon. The primary leaders are the first and second readers, usually a male and female. The lesson-sermon focuses on a topic and address written and assigned by the Mother Church to be read, not interpreted, to all the churches. There are twenty-six topics for the fifty-two Sundays, and each one is read twice during the year. The topics include God, Mind, Christ Jesus, Man, Reality, and Soul and Body. Besides the lesson-sermon, two other significant readings occur. One is the Lord's Prayer with interpretations left by Eddy, and the other is "The Scientific Statement of Being" that includes selections from *Science and Health* and the Bible and which is read at the conclusion of the service.

The Lord's Prayer, with Eddy's spiritual interpretation, is as follows:

Our father which art in heaven,

(Our Father-Mother God, all-harmonious,)

Hallowed be Thy name. (Adorable One)

Thy Kingdom come.

(Thy Kingdom is come; Thou art ever-present)

Thy will be done on earth, as it is in heaven.

(Enable us to know—as in heaven, so on earth—

God is omnipresent, supreme)

Give us this day our daily bread

(Give us grace for today; feed the famished affections)

And forgive us our debts, as we forgive our debtors

(And love is reflected in love)

And lead us not into temptation, but deliver us from evil;

(And God leadeth us not into temptation, but delivereth us from sin, disease, and death)

For Thine is the Kingdom, and the power, and the glory, forever. (For God is infinite, all powerful, all life, Truth, Love over all and All.)[33]

The Scientific Statement of Being is as follows:

There is no life, truth, intelligence, nor substance in matter. All is infinite Mind and its infinite manifestation, for God is All-in-all. Spirit is immortal Truth; matter is mortal error. Spirit is the real and eternal; matter is the unreal and temporal. Spirit is God, and man is His image and likeness. Therefore, man is not material; he is spiritual.[34]

Behold, what manner of love the Father hath bestowed upon us, that we should be called the sons of God: therefore the world knoweth us not, because it knew him not. Beloved, now we are sons of God, and it doth not yet appear what we shall be: but we know that, when we shall appear, we shall be like him, for we shall see him as he is. And every man that hath his hope in him purifieth himself, even as he is pure.[35]

Wednesday evening services focus on testimonies of healing and guidance which members have received through Christian Science. Baptism and communion are observed as meaningful inner experiences and not as outward observances with use of water, bread, and wine. There are no missionaries appointed by the church. Lecturers, however, are appointed and sent out by the Christian Science Board of Lectureship. They present lectures on topics of Christian Science in churches and public meeting halls. Lectures are free, and about four thousand are presented yearly. Christian Scientists serve as chaplains in the armed services. *The Christian Science Monitor*, founded in 1908 by Eddy, is a daily newspaper, circulated in some 120 countries and widely read by professional and government people. Its aim is to tell the news "with clarity, incisiveness, and integrity." The Christian Science Publishing Society publishes the monthly *Christian Science Journal* and the weekly *Christian Science Sentinel*. All of these publications are seen as a part of the missionary task of the church.

Christian Science and Christianity

How do Christian Scientists regard those of other faiths? They say that they feel a spiritual fellowship with all those who worship a supreme and righteous God. Although Christian Science is rooted wholly in Christianity, according to Christian Scientists, they feel a spiritual fellowship with people of any faith that reaches beyond denominational boundaries. They believe that the Christ, as distinguished from the human Jesus, has been expressed in varying degrees by good men and women throughout the ages. They state that Christianity has always reflected a generous portion of the Christ-Spirit. Christian Scientists believe that their own religion, as a revelation of the Science of Christ, is Christianity in its most practical and scientific form. Eddy wrote:

What is the cardinal point of the difference in my metaphysical system? This: that by knowing the unreality of disease, sin, and death, you demonstrate the allness of God. This difference wholly separates my system from all others. The reality of these so-called existences I deny, because they are not to be found in God, and this system is built on Him as the sole cause. It would be difficult to name any previous teachers, save Jesus and his apostles, who have thus taught.[36]

The issues within Christian Science and the challenges between Christian Science and traditional Christianity are several. Christians can appreciate the discipline and commitment asked of Christian Scientists. They forbid the use of alcohol, tobacco, and drugs, and foster a disciplined study of the Bible. They appear to have reached their zenith in membership and, in fact, have declined. It is estimated that they now number some 300,000. They have faced the issue of authoritarianism within their church. Eddy had the revelation, and she discovered the Truth and codified it in a book. Christian Scientists do not interpret the Bible; they only read from it and read the interpretations of Eddy. They have lost members and have failed to gain members because of this acceptance of Prophetess Mary Baker Eddy and her "Key to Scriptures." Christians of other churches do not accept Eddy as prophetess nor consider her peculiar teachings as valid, much less authoritative. Christians can appreciate Christian Scientists' stress on prayer and health, but not their theories and methodologies.

The theology/philosophy and the metaphysics of Eddy ring of ancient and more modern-day estrangements from orthodox Christian teachings and practices. Her teachings appear to capture some of the influences of Hinduism, Gnosticism, Docetism, Nestorianism, and Greek philosophy, although she claimed close adherence to the Bible. She allegorized and demythologized the content of the Bible and spiritualized its concepts. Her denials often sound more loudly than her affirmations. She emphasized mind over matter; the unreality of sin, sickness, death, and the fall of mankind; and the Christ-idea over the Jesus of the cross.

Traditional Christian teachings view:

- the creation as good
- the fall of man as real
- sin as rebellion and disobedience against God
- Jesus Christ as fully God and fully human
- the death of Jesus Christ on the cross as a tragic and bloody fact of history
- the resurrection as an empty tomb and a bodily raised Jesus Christ
- salvation as a grace and faith experience of the individual through the love of God in Jesus Christ, and
- the judgment of God over sin and evil powers as a present and coming event.

Traditional Christianity observes baptism and the Lord's Supper as ordinances or sacraments to be experienced historically with water and bread.

Christian Science is over a century old with its leaders, churches, and teachings. Its emphasis on the roles of laypersons, including both women and men, is admirable. Its stress on meeting the health needs of people is appreciated. Its theology, however, based on Eddy's *Science and Health,* is far removed from the teachings of orthodox Christianity. Christians are encouraged to understand Christian Science, but more importantly, to meet Christian Scientists to explore each other's biblical truths, and to share testimonies of one's relationship and experience in Jesus Christ.

Since World War II Christian Science has declined in its growth of members and churches. Its publications, however, continue to have an important impact upon mass media, especially *The Christian Science Monitor.* A controversy which affected the church has been over the issue of publication of a book, *The Destiny of the Mother Church,* written in the 1940s by Bliss Knapp, a prominent Christian Scientist and a son of one of the church's founders.

If the book had been published, the church could have inherited as much as $100 million. When the book was finished, however, the church refused to publish it. Some leaders objected that it deified Eddy by giving her a status equal to that of Jesus Christ. In the controversy over the recent attempt at publication, the chairman of the church and other top officials resigned in late 1991.

Unity School of Christianity

Who encourages millions of people through print and mass media to pick up their telephones and call a toll-free number to request prayer and counsel from a staff on duty twenty-four hours a day? Who has published the oldest magazine for children in America? Who promises sufficiency in all things including freedom from fear, health, harmony, wisdom, and fulfillment? The Unity School of Christianity in Lee's Summit, Missouri, has a hundred-year history of operation from fourteen-hundred-acre Unity Village. Its worldwide ministry offers prayers, counsel, retreats, and reading materials. It lays no claims to being a church or denomination; however, Unity churches and centers are allied with Unity School in theological and ecclesiastical training and in the ordination of ministers.

Origins

The founders and inspiration of the Unity School were Charles (1854-1948) and Myrtle (1845-1931) Fillmore. They were influenced by a movement in America late in the nineteenth century called New Thought. New Thought emphasized God-consciousness in the individual, unity between the individual and God, the practical application of spiritual power to human problems, positive thinking, and the innate goodness of the soul. The Unity School officially began in 1889 with the publication of Charles Fillmore's magazine *Modern Thought,* which is today's *Unity Maga-*

zine. Unity people say the movement really began in Kansas City in the spring of 1886 when Myrtle was healed.

Charles and Myrtle Fillmore, facing physical and financial crises that seemed insurmountable, were attending a lecture by Dr. E. B. Weeks, who was a representative of the Illinois metaphysical college, then headed by Emma Curtis Hopkins. Something strange happened to Myrtle Fillmore at this time. It was no mystical or emotional conversion. It was simply that as she left the lecture, a new, different, liberating, transforming conviction was blazing in her heart and mind. She had been raised under the belief of hereditary weakness, and was at that time living under a medical sentence of "a few months to live" due to a tubercular condition. She walked out of that meeting repeating in her mind: *I am a child of God and therefore I do not inherit sickness.*[37]

Mrs. Fillmore suffered from tuberculosis for years. From the experience in 1886, she believed that life was intelligent, and she reasoned that life can be directed by thinking and talking. She believed that she could talk to every part of her body and teach it to respond as she desired. She also sought forgiveness for misusing her body, and she promised to entertain no negative thoughts. In two years she was no longer an invalid. She began her own prayer and healing movement. Her husband was influenced by her, and he was healed after being an invalid from childhood. He wrote, "My chronic pains ceased. My hip healed and grew stronger, and my leg lengthened until in a few years I dispensed with the steel extension that I had worn since I was a child."[38]

The Fillmores began prayer and study groups in their home, known as "The Society of Silent Help." Charles brought to the movement his background of business, finances, and organizational techniques; and the movement began to grow after 1889. The couple were known as writers, lecturers, and teachers, applying practical Christianity to daily life. The Fillmores insisted that they would not become a church or a denomination. They desired to establish a school emphasizing Christian teachings which were neglected by the churches and offering counsel, prayer, and healing through classes, writing, and mass media. As their movement grew, they moved their classes from their home to downtown Kansas City. By 1950, they were established in Unity Village.

The Organization

Unity Village is a municipality outside Kansas City. The Village is beautifully designed with red-tiled buildings, formal gardens, a farm, orchards, recreational facilities, printing facilities, the Wee Wisdom School, and the 165-foot-tall Unity Tower. It is an administrative center, a prayer-counseling ministry, a retreat center, a study location, and a writing and publishing house. Central to all that occurs at the Village is the Silent Unity, a continuation of the prayer meeting once held in the Fillmore's home, and which the Unity Tower symbolizes. Some 450 employees handle the telephones and computers and letters concerning prayer and counseling. The Village continues the ministry of the Fillmores. Charles was the administrator, writer, and public figure. Myrtle founded *Wee Wisdom* and contributed much of her writing to this children's magazine. Their three sons were active in Unity. Rickett Fillmore was an architect who was responsible for designing and building Unity Village. Lowell Fillmore succeeded his father as the president of Unity School. In 1972 Charles R. Fillmore, the son of Rickett, became president. The family influence has been great, but a board of directors governs Unity's affairs, and it is not family owned.

Three primary ministries initiated at Unity Village are prayer and counseling, education and preparation for ministry, and publishing.[39] The prayer and counseling ministry is Silent Unity. Over seven thousand letters and eighteen hundred telephone calls are received daily requesting prayer, which means over three million requests yearly. Trained telephone operators are on duty around the clock, and at least one person is in the prayer chapel around the clock honoring the requests for prayer. There is a toll-free number. Unity responds to every telephone call for prayer and answers every letter request. Letters are sent out in nine languages. Prayer is looked upon by Unity as follows:

> If prayer is anything, it is high-level, creative thinking. . . . Unity teaches the prayer of affirmation. It is not begging or asking, but claiming and accepting. Not "I want," "I wish," "I hope," "I desire," but "I AM." Not . . . "Help me," "guide me," "heal me," "prosper me," but "I AM now helped and guided and healed and prospered."[40]

The educational ministry focuses on classes for laypersons, retreats, and a study program to prepare Unity ministers. The Unity School for Religious Studies (USRS) provides for continuing education programs of two weeks' duration each and for Unity retreats of one-week duration. The USRS advertises itself as "a preachy" idea for spiritual growth. It includes "committed Truth teachers and staff, convenient accommodations, vegetarian and regular meals, 1,400 acres of sweet, relaxing grounds, orchards, gardens, woodlands, golf course, nature trails, pool."[41] Courses which are offered include Bible, metaphysics (prayer, healing, prosperity), counseling, and contemporary issues. The chapel at the Village conducts services, study classes, and lectures.

Although the Unity School of Christianity states it is not a church, it provides space in the Village for the Unity Ministerial School. This school provides a two-year training curriculum which graduates over thirty yearly. The Association of Unity Churches (AUC) licenses and ordains ministers and assists in placing them in Unity churches and centers. There are over 450 churches or centers with approximately the same number of ministers. Over 60,000 members belong to Unity churches, and about one-half of the ministers are women. The AUC appears to be assuming denominational features with placement services, church growth, and religious training and ordination.

The third of the primary ministries is writing and mass communication. Three monthly publications now circulate over 3,000,000 copies annually.

> *Unity* is a respected metaphysical magazine. Its subtitle is "A Way of Life," and in its pages you will find the new, exciting, and inspiring writing of many of our leading authors in the fields of religion, education, science . . . in fact, every facet of contemporary life.[42]

Unity Magazine usually includes an article by Charles Fillmore. A second monthly publication is *Daily Word*.

> *Daily Word* is our magazine for daily prayer and meditation, each page carries a lesson for the day, a prayer, and a Scripture quotation. The magazine also features poetry, articles, and other special material.[43]

It circulates in fifteen languages and is read in some 160 countries. A third circulation is *Wee Wisdom*. Unity has announced that *Wee Wisdom* will be discontinued.

> For children, Unity has published *Wee Wisdom* for almost ninety years; it is America's oldest magazine for youngsters. Newly updated to make it interesting and meaningful to today's children, *Wee Wisdom* contains stories, poems, puzzles, pictures to color, a monthly calendar, and craft projects. It is expressly planned for children from age 5 through the 6th grade (and thousands of schoolteachers use it and love it, too).[44]

Unity School has a department for radio-television ministry. "The word from Unity" is a one-minute message which is broadcast over a thousand radio and television outlets. Unity School publishes many books, pamphlets, and cassette tapes. Thus, its outreach through its facilities and programs at Unity Village, through its wide writings and publications, and through its alliance with Unity churches and centers is worldwide in reaching millions of people with its printed and spoken words.

Unity Beliefs

What is the message of the Unity School of Christianity, and what is the substance of belief and practice behind it? Unity does not claim to be a church, to profess dogma, to have a creed, or to seek members. "Unity essentially is a technique through which you can find answers for yourself in words that are meaningful to you."[45] It classifies those who respond to its prayer and publication ministries as students or subscribers. It believes that one may benefit from its ministry and still remain a member of the church of one's choice. Often, it is difficult to get specific information about specific doctrines from the Unity School. Ministers of the Unity churches associated with AUC may, however, be quite specific in their doctrinal statements and quite diverse from minister to minister. The following statements give an overview of Unity School principles:

> Unity is a worldwide Christian organization nearly a century old. Because of similarity in names, Unity has on occasion been confused with other organizations. However there is no connection between Unity and Unitarianism or the Unification Church.

> Millions of people have been introduced to Unity through its periodicals *Daily Word, Unity Magazine* and *Wee Wisdom,* published at Unity World Headquarters in Lee's Summit, Mo. Millions of others are familiar with Unity through its prayer ministry, known as Silent Unity which has maintained a round-the-clock vigilance of prayer for more than eighty years. Thousands of people around the world call Silent Prayer via the toll free number (800-821-2935) and receive prayer help.

> Unity is an extremely positive approach to life, seeking to accept the good in people and all of life. God is seen as having many attributes, but most important that God is LOVE. Unity stresses that God is not a physical man in the sky, for this limits Him. God is Spirit, everywhere present, the one and only Spirit behind, in and through all things, visible and invisible.

Unity denies the existence of any power or presence opposed to God. It sees that there are evil appearances and suffering in the world, but ascribes these to man's ignorance and erroneous use of God's laws of life.

Unity proclaims the divinity of Jesus, but goes further and assures that you, too, are a child of God and therefore divine in nature. Jesus expressed His divine potential and sought to show us how to express ours as well. Salvation is then the expanding understanding of one's innate divinity and perfectibility through living the life demonstrated by Jesus.

Unity explains the mind as your connecting link with God or Divine Mind and shows how the action of your mind affects your body and circumstances. Much emphasis is placed on the effective power that every thought, feeling, word and act has upon your life.

Prayer is not seen as a technique for changing God, but for expanding and transforming your mind, and thus changing you.

Unity seeks to relate religion to daily needs, affirming that for every need there is God's perfect answer. Its main textbook is the Bible and it relates its lessons to your life and everyday experiences.

Unity does break from tradition some in that is has no creedal requirements, dogma, ritual or ecclesiastical garb. Unity chooses to believe that there is good in every religion. Different religions are like spokes on a wheel with the hub being God. They may be set apart by a variance of beliefs and approaches, but they are all seeking the one God as the hub of all life. Consequently, Unity does not deny anyone the right to have their own beliefs.

Unity sees worship as serving God by uplifting and glorifying God's spirit in man, in positive, joyous ways. It seeks not to emphasize one's sins of the past, but instead gives attention to the good that exists in every

person and what can be done with the now to trans-
form one's self and his life.

Its main concern is not so much with a "future life" but
with teaching people how to live fully in the present,
seeing the good in all things. Unity also believes in eternal life and views the present moment as part of eternal
life.

Unity does not impose any financial burdens or pres-
sure on its adherents. It believes the desire for giving
should be initiated from within the giver to reap the joys
of sharing. Consequently, all support is by freewill offerings.

Unity is non-denominational and welcomes in with dignity and love, people of all races, colors, religious,
social background and economic levels.

In summation, Unity emphasizes the divine potential
within every child of God and teaches that through a
practical understanding and application of what Jesus
taught, every person can realize and express his or her
divine potential for a happier, fuller and more successful
life.[46]

From these general statements, what outlines of "Christian principles" are behind the Unity School? Unity claims
the Bible as its textbook, cites its passages, uses it for devo-
tionals, and studies it in the historical-scientific context. But
it also uses the world's other sacred written traditions. It
brings its metaphysics to the Bible. Charles Fillmore wrote
that God's Word is "the agency by which God reveals Himself in some measure to all men, but to greater degree to
highly developed souls; the thought of God or the sum total
of God's creative power."[47] H. Emilie Cady of the Unity
School said in explaining Unity teaching, "I use Scriptural
terms simply because I prefer them."[48] Charles Fillmore
again wrote,

The Bible is, in its inner or spiritual meaning, a record
of the experiences and the development of the human

soul and of the whole being of man; also it is a treatise on man's relation to God, the creator and Father.[49]

There is an outer meaning and inner meaning in the Bible. Unity seeks to explore the metaphysical, spiritual meaning.

What, then, are Unity's principles about God, Jesus Christ, Trinity, mankind, salvation, and destiny? God is Mind, Spirit, Truth, and the principle of absolute good expressed in all creation; God, too, is love. "But whatever we agree God is, God is you."[50] Although God may be considered personal, God comes out to be more impersonal principle.

Who is Jesus Christ? Christ is the perfect idea of God for man. He is the divine idea. Jesus is the perfect expression of the divine idea man. He is the ideal of a perfect man. Christ is the higher self of man. Jesus is the Savior or Way Shower. Jesus placed emphasis upon man's unfoldment or achievement. Charles Fillmore wrote, "Yet He attained no more than what is expected of everyone of us."[51] Jesus was perfect, and man can be also. Jesus showed the way through his teachings, death, and resurrection. People can be taught, inspired by Jesus' example, that they, too, can attain salvation. The idea of Trinity for Unity School is that God is Infinite Mind, Idea, and Expression. God is not Father, Son, and Holy Spirit. Jesus Christ is not considered to be the second person in the traditional understanding of the Trinity.

What is salvation? Since Unity sees man's plight as ignorance, error, poor thinking, and a dimmed consciousness, it proposes that mental discipline day by day and night by night overcomes the mind's inertia and produces a consciousness of ourselves as sons of God right here and now.[52]

There is no final salvation. It is a day to day process of discipline of thought and action. Unity is "Practical Christianity," and it is practical only if it is practiced. And practice means regular and disciplined effort. Every time you make the effort to meet life with a positive thought, you are "saved" from the inevitable effect of negative thought.[53]

Heaven and hell are states of mind, and one's destiny may be related to reincarnation. Unity, however, does not have a theory of incarnation and advises one not to make it an object of study.

Unity's basic message stresses prayer, right thinking, and the abundant life. It teaches that healing will be experienced as one understands and affirms one's relationship to God in mind, truth, and love. Unity teaches that one may learn and be inspired by the example of Jesus Christ, and one must apply those teachings to everyday matters of life in order to be healed, to be successful, and to attain perfection and the abundant life.[54]

Unity and Christianity

The issues and challenges within the Unity School of Christianity and between Unity and traditional Christianity are several. The issue which faces Unity "students" who remain members of traditional Christian churches is if the two can mix. Those who regularly read *Unity Magazine, Daily Word,* and *Wee Wisdom* while also participating in other churches must raise the question of compatibility. For example, is prayer more than an affirmation of one's goodness, and is prayer more than the expressed opinion that one deserves the best because one is good? Another issue within Unity is the claim of not being a church while being closely allied with Unity churches and their ministers and ministries. Will the Unity School of Christianity face dramatic change from its historical roots if AUC grows, seeks members, finances, more training of ministers, and takes the shape of a denomination?

Within orthodox Christianity there are several challenges. How acceptable is the Unity claim to Christianity? With the development of Unity churches, how will they be viewed and related to in the wider ecumenical family of churches and denominations? Then, there are the basic differences between Unity doctrines and those of orthodox Christianity. Orthodox Christianity views God as personal, not principle; Jesus Christ as fully God and fully man, incarnate, and bodily resurrected, not as a spiritualized idea or the divine Mind and not as a Man among men; Jesus' death on the cross as atonement, sacrifice, blood spilt, God's love in suffering and in overcoming sin and evil, not just as a moral example or a pattern of life for others to spiritualize or to imitate or emulate, or as a Man demonstrating how mind may overcome matter, the higher self over the lower self; the Bible as divine revelation and authoritative for faith and practice, not an esoteric message and meaning for those of higher soul consciousness who have intuition about mind and truth.

Orthodox Christianity can appreciate the stress and importance which the Unity School of Christianity places on prayer, counseling, and healing. The responses which Unity receives to its ministry demonstrate a deep reservoir of human and spiritual searching. Orthodox Christianity can learn from Unity. Although not accepting its theology nor some of its methods, orthodox Christianity can reach out in ministry to those who seek to pray, to receive counseling and healing, and a Word from God.

Church of Scientology

The Founder

Lafayette Ron Hubbard was the founder and the force behind the Church of Scientology. Born in Tilden, Nebraska, on March 13, 1911, he spent his early childhood on his grandfather's cattle ranch in Montana. With the Navy career of his father and the wealth of his grandfather, Ron Hubbard spent his teenage years as a world traveler and adventurer. Someone said, "It was in Northern China and India, while studying with holy men, that he became vitally engrossed in the subject of the spiritual destiny of Mankind."[55]

While a student at George Washington University in Washington, D. C., Hubbard enrolled in one of the first nuclear physics courses taught in the nation. He became a science-fiction writer, and his books brought him attention from their modest sales. In fact, it is said that his "articles, stories, novels, screen plays, poems, and books have been published in as many as eight languages. His fiction sales total over 22 million."[56] In 1940 he was elected a member of the prestigious Explorer's Club of New York. He was wounded during service in World War II, and it is claimed from his previous studies of Eastern thought, physics, and psychoanalysis that he developed techniques that aided him in overcoming his injuries.

> He concluded that the results he was obtaining could help others toward greater ability and happiness, and it was during this period that some of the basic tenets of Dianetics and Scientology were first formulated.[57]

In the late 1940s Hubbard cultivated a friendship with John Campbell, editor of *Astounding Science Fiction* magazine. Hubbard, through his ideas and techniques on understanding the mind and psychological disorders, cured Campbell of a disorder. Campbell promoted Hubbard's ideas in the magazine. By 1950 Hubbard had written *Dianetics: The Modern Science of Mental Health*, which quickly made the New York Times best-seller list. He also founded the Hubbard Dianetic Research Foundation. Hubbard was popular, and his therapeutic techniques were in demand. Anyone could read his books, become instant therapists, and employ Hubbard's "auditing" or therapeutic process to attain economic gain. In 1952 Hubbard initiated Scientology, founded upon his book *Science of Survival*. "This book contained the foundations of the religion of Scientology and outlined in detail the relationship between man as a spiritual being and the physical universe."[58]

Scientology builds upon the foundations in Dianetics and presents a new therapeutic process which includes beliefs in extraterrestrial life, in reincarnation, and in a spiritual reality. In February 1954 Hubbard founded the first Church of Scientology in Washington, D. C. The Church of Scientology claims that "This was in keeping with the religious nature of the tenets dating from the earliest days of research. It was obvious that he had been exploring religious territory right along."[59] In his church, Hubbard gained greater control over who would minister and administer the therapeutic techniques and the economic ledgers. By 1955 his church had gained tax-exempt status, and he had been authorized by the United States District Court for the District of Columbia to celebrate marriages.

In 1959 Hubbard moved to Saint Hill Manor in Sussex, England, to continue his research. He gave attention to supervising his church management structure while developing and expanding the theories and techniques of Scientology.

> For more than two millenia Man had dreamed of a spiritual state, where, free of his own mental aberrations, he would be truly himself. L. Ron Hubbard called this state "Clear." And, at Saint Hill, in August of 1965, he announced the attainment of Clear.
>
> The dream of Buddha, attained by the few, was a reality. Man could be Clear.
>
> And the reality which was and is Clear was to be available to all who followed the exact route he had laid out.
>
> The explorer had reached the land he foresaw.[60]

Teaching of Scientology

The Church of Scientology rests upon the meaning of two words, *dianetics* and *scientology*. Hubbard defines dianetics as

> that branch of Scientology containing the anatomy of the human mind. From the Greek dia, through, and noos, mind, thus "through mind" or "through thought."

It is the first fully precise school of the mind. Scientology concerns itself with the rehabilitation of the spirit.[61]

He defines scientology as

an applied religious philosophy dealing with the study of Knowledge which, through the application of its technology, can bring about desirable changes in the conditions of life. The word Scientology comes from the Latin scio, knowledge, and the Greek, logos, study, and means "knowing" "how to know" or "the study of wisdom."[62]

The basic beliefs of the church are found in its creed:

We of the Church believe:

That all men of whatever race, colour or creed were created with equal rights.

That all men have inalienable rights to their own religious practices and their performance.

That all men have inalienable rights to their own lives.

That all men have inalienable rights to their sanity.

That all men have inalienable rights to their own defense.

That all men have inalienable rights to conceive, choose, assist, and support their own organizations, churches and governments.

That all men have inalienable rights to think freely, to talk freely, to write freely their own opinions and to counter or utter or write upon the opinions of others.

That all men have inalienable rights to the creation of their own kind.

That the souls of men have the rights of men.

That the study of the mind and the healing of mentally caused ills should not be alienated from religion or condoned in non-religious fields.

And that no agency less than God has the power to suspend or set aside these rights, overtly or covertly.

And we of the Church believe:

That man is basically good.

That he is seeking to survive.

That his survival depends upon himself and upon his fellows, and his attainment of brotherhood with the Universe.

And we of the Church believe that the laws of God forbid Man:

To destroy his own kind.

To destroy the sanity of another.

To destroy or enslave another's soul.

To destroy or reduce the survival of one's companions or one's group.

And we of the Church believe:

That the spirit can be saved *and*

That the spirit alone may save or heal the body.[63]

The basic ideas of the Church of Scientology center around the mind and wisdom. The analytic mind, similar to Freud's ego or consciousness, is rational. The reactive mind, similar to Freud's unconscious, causes irrational behavior. In times of stress the analytic mind breaks down and the reactive mind takes over. "Engrams" are sensory impressions stored in the reactive mind which are activated in traumatic times. Scientology's concern is to handle the "engrams" in such a way as to reduce the reactive mind and to restore the analytic mind to its healthful state.

Scientology offers a therapeutic process called "auditing." An "auditor" or counselor works with a person to rid the person of engrams. An E-meter is used. It is an apparatus used for measuring electrical impulses. From the E-meter are two sets of wires, and cans are attached to the wires. The person or "pre-clear" sits at a table holding a can in each hand, and the auditor, trained in the techniques of Scientology, sits across the table and engages the "pre-clear" in question-answer therapy. Answers are registered on the E-meter. The purpose of the counselor is to expose engrams that in turn clears up the negative aspects of the mind, and the person becomes a "clear."

With the development of Scientology and the church, Hubbard added several dimensions to the basic theory and technique of dianetics. The E-meter was one. The other was the concept of the "thetan." The "thetans" are the spiritual essences of immortal celestial beings who have lived in many forms of bodies over eons of time and have transmigrated from body to body. Over time the "thetans" have become entrapped in human bodies and have forgotten their identities. In auditing, a person must be cleared not only of the engrams accumulated during the present life but also of the engrams through many transmigrations and reincarnations. The goal is to achieve the state of clear or the clearing up of all engrams.

Auditing can be expensive and may take much time to complete the therapeutic process. One report has listed the fees and times as follows:[64]

Auditing Fees and Times			
12 1/2 hours	$ 950	100 hours	$6,600
25 hours	$1,900	125 hours	$7,700
50 hours	$3,600	150 hours	$8,900
75 hours	$5,100		

There are stages or "courses" in the auditing process which are designed to deal with the release of engrams and the final attainment of clear.

Courses in the Auditing Process	
Grade 0	Communication Release
Grade I	Problems Release
Grade II	Relief Release
Grade III	Freedom Release
Grade IV	Ability Release
Grade V	Power Release
Grade VI	Power Plus Relief
Grade VII	OT Thetan becomes more free of the body, mind, and MEST (Matter, Energy, Space, Time)

The Church of Scientology

Hubbard designed a pyramidal structure for his church with himself at the apex, his wife and a board of seven executive directors next, and various divisions and departments to supervise the vast holdings of the church and the administration of its church activities.

> The Church of Scientology holds various ceremonies for its parishioners, as do other churches. Ceremonies of the Church include marriage rites, funerals, and Naming ceremonies for infants, which are performed to welcome the child into the congregation. Ministers of the Church also hold regular Sunday Services. These activities are in addition, of course, to the pastoral counseling and training in the philosophy and use of Scientology which are offered on a daily basis.[65]

In the 1960s Hubbard, some say haunted by fears of the FBI and the IRS, took some five hundred Scientologists aboard his 330-foot converted British ferry, Apollo, and sailed the oceans. Problems continued to plague Hubbard and his church, especially with the tax authorities and with the filing of legal suits by dissident and former members. The IRS demanded some six million dollars in taxes and penalties from Scientology for the years 1970 through 1974, claiming these taxes were from income not used for church purposes. Over twenty suits were filed against the church by former members claiming to have been swindled or even kidnapped. Australia revoked the religious status of Scientology. By 1975, Hubbard had moved his headquarters to Clearwater, Florida.

Hubbard disappeared in March of 1980. *Time* reported, "A reclusive multimillionaire who preferred to work all night. A man terrified of germs who fought his growing array of ailments with a variety of drugs and massive vitamin injections. A brilliant and dominating figure who built an empire and who was both revered and feared. And now . . . the question of his fate. Even longtime intimates have not seen him in more than two years. They do not know whether he is living in seclusion by his own choice, or whether he is mentally incompetent and a captive of former underlings. Some of his old aides think he may be dead."[66]

Hubbard's son, Ronald E. DeWolf, who changed his name from L. Ron Hubbard, Jr., in 1972, believed that his father was dead or mentally incapacitated. He attempted to have his father declared legally missing so that his assets could be frozen. DeWolf petitioned a California court to name him legal recipient of the assets. DeWolf claimed that after his father's disappearance, a shakeup in the church's leadership caused the departure of some 150 staff members and brought in new leaders. "DeWolf contends the new leadership is pirating away millions of dollars in church funds and that if his father were alive and in his right mind, he would never permit such 'wholesale thefts.' DeWolf has also speculated that his father might be held incommunicado by the new guard."[67]

In 1983 Hubbard's third wife was sentenced to four years in prison, convicted along with six other church members, for bugging and burglarizing offices of the IRS, the Justice, Labor, and Treasury departments, and others in Washington, D.C. It was reported that Hubbard had an espionage system that included over five thousand covert agents.[68] In May of 1985, some two thousand Church of Scientology members picketed the courthouse in Portland, Oregon, to protest a $39 million fraud judgment against the church and Hubbard by an ex-Scientologist who underwent deprogramming.[69]

Hubbard resurfaced from his mysterious and prolonged absence in the midst of confusion and change in his organization. He had apparently lived for several years in a remote and rural section of San Luis Obispo County, California. He died in January 1986, purportedly of a stroke, according to his physician, a Scientologist. There was no autopsy, since Hubbard had forbidden it with a certificate of religious preference.

David Miscavige, in his early thirties, a high school dropout and a second generation church member, became the leader of the church. He has seen his mission as attaining credibility for Scientology in the 1990s. The church claims some seven hundred centers in sixty-five countries and some eight million members. The church's detractors assert that there may be no more than fifty thousand active members. However, it is known that Scientology affects millions with its diverse organizations and media.

The Church of Scientology presses on despite its internal struggles for leadership and its legal and tax difficulties. In 1991, *Time* reported that the organization had hired a public relations firm to help shed its fringe-group image. The church was one of three main sponsors (together with Sony and Pepsi) of Ted Turner's Goodwill Games. The church has run full-page ads in *Newsweek, Business Week,* and other major publications touting Scientology as a philosophy. It even buys massive quantities of its own books from retail stores to propel the titles onto best-seller lists. The *Time* report stated that Scientology was working under the disguise of several consulting groups in order to recruit wealthy and respectable professionals.[70]

The Church of Scientology faces many challenges. There are legal suits against it. It has filed legal suits against its detractors, including *Time*. Recent research into Hubbard's life history and his own claims raise questions of the veracity of his actual travels, studies, and war combat experience.

Scientology and Christianity

The church's relationship to Christianity is loose, as is its relationship to all religions. The Church of Scientology claims Scientology is a religion in the oldest sense of the word. It is a study of wisdom, a study of man as spirit in his relationship to life and the physical universe. Scientology is pan-denominational. By that is meant that Scientology is open to people of all religions and beliefs and in no way tries to persuade a person from his religion, but assists him to better understand that he is a spiritual being.[71]

Time described Scientology as "a sort of religion of religions, combining parts of Hindu Veda and Dharma, Taoism, Old Testament wisdom, Buddhist principles of brotherly love and compassion, the early Greeks, Lucretius, Spinoza, Nietzche, Schopenhauer, Spencer, and Freud."[72]

A Christian view of Scientology may note the following considerations:

1. Members of the Church of Scientology assigned L. Ron Hubbard authority. What kind of authority is it and what relation does that authority have to the Bible and to Jesus Christ?

2. Hubbard was concerned little with a doctrine of God and much with a doctrine of "Man" which he often capitalized in his writings. Man is also considered good. The Church of Scientology appears, then, to have no teaching on the biblical concept of sin, the nature of man, and the nature of God.

3. The Christian understanding and affirmation of the grace of God through Jesus Christ and of salvation are ignored in Scientology. One pays for auditing through

various steps to become "clear." Apparently, one places one's "faith" in Hubbard's teachings and techniques, in the E-meter, in one's own basic goodness, and in the assistance of the auditor to become free of engrams.

4. Christians may note the ethics of Hubbard and his church members in subversive activities, the unimportance of the Church of Scientology's attention to the poor and needy, and the emphasis of the church upon money and finances.

5. Christians need to be aware of the numbers of persons, some of whom have come from mainline churches, who have been attracted to the teachings of Scientology and the church. One needs to understand the needs of those persons and the organization and beliefs of the Church of Scientology, and relate to them in positive ways of Christian witness and relationship.

5

THE OCCULT

◼   ◼

Power is a word on the tip of the tongue, a dream behind one's grasp of politics, economics, or even religion. People's power! The power of the dollar! The power of Congress! The power of mass media! The power of the electronic church! The power of the ayatollah! The power of the nuclear age! In an age categorized by science, technology, the computer, the possibility of nuclear annihilation, poverty, and starvation, power tends to be sought beyond the obvious fact, the plain data, the visible world, and the established and tried institutions of science and religion. Power may be seen or projected as residing in the stars and planets, in departed spirits, in black and white magic, and in witches and churches of Satan.

The occult consists of multivarious moods and methods. People participate in occult arts and practices individually and in community. Astrology offers a mosaic of stars and planets and horoscopes to decipher their influences upon contemporary life and patterns of meanings for the future. Spiritualism provides a way of communication between the living and the dead. Seances are held, and departed spirits come in contact with the living. Various methods of divination give clues and signs of future happenings. Witchcraft involves the world of ghosts, potions, hexes on people, witches, and covens. White magic may be practiced to help people, or black magic may be used to harm others. Satanism is present. Satanism's most visible form is the Church of Satan, founded on the seven deadly sins and committed to the principles of Satan.

The occult influences millions of people through the mass media of newspaper and television. Individuals pay fees and seek the counsel of astrologers and palmists. Millions faithfully read their daily horoscopes; some attend seances; others join with covens. Some become members of churches of Satan; some participate in the occult, seeking meaning to life alongside their church and Christian experiences. Others experience the occult without having any attachment to the church or desiring any relationship. Some gravitate to the occult because of disenchantment with the church. Whatever may be the reasons, there is a belief that meaning may be found and help given in the occult experience.[1]

Astrology and Divination

Astrology appears to be alive and prosperous. In fact, it is a big business. Some twelve hundred daily newspapers carry horoscopes in the United States. There may be as many as 200,000 full and part-time astrologists. Millions of dollars are spent daily for the counsel of astrologists, horoscope materials in newspapers, magazines, and computerized editions, astrological books, college courses in astrology, and television programs with astrological content. Carroll Righter, an American astrologist, writes for over three hundred daily newspapers which enter over thirty million homes. Maurice Woodruff, a British astrologer, has sold over two million copies of his books about astrology. He, too, writes for newspapers worldwide with a circulation of over fifty million. Seekers into the mazeway of astrological meanings are global, are daily practitioners, and are willing to expend time and money to realize the secrets of the stars.[2]

Ancient Astrology

Astrology has an ancient history, and the peoples of Babylonia, Egypt, India, China, Greece, Rome, and the Americas, among others, have contributed to it. Three thousand years ago the Babylonian priests ascended the mounds called ziggurats (some were 30 stories high) to study the stars which were identified with deities. Kings were informed by the priests of their knowledge from the stars. Egyptian astrology was headquartered at Heliopolis, and priests made predictions from their findings. The Greeks and Romans offered their adaptations of astrology. The earth-centered view of Ptolemy and his writings on astrology continue to influence contemporary astrologists. The Romans offered their zodiac of twelve houses with mythological forms. Copernicus challenged Ptolemy's view by arguing that planets move about the earth in circles. Astrologists, however, continue to adhere to the earth-centered view.

What is astrology? What is a zodiac? What is a horoscope? Astrology has been described as a study of the influence which stars have upon people and things, as a study of life's reactions to planetary vibrations, and as astro (star) and logos (word), a word or message of the stars to people. Astrologists claim that planets and stars have real influence on human lives and world events. The zodiac is an imaginary belt which traces the path of the sun through the stars. Twelve constellations or patterns were named by ancient astrologists to compose the zodiac. Patterns appeared to be in the forms of animals. Zodiac means the parade of animals. A horoscope is a diagram of the zodiac's twelve divisions, with emphasis on predicting the future and with information on the position of planets at specific times, such as birth dates. A horoscope may be as simple and general as one printed in the newspaper or may be a detailed and expensive one provided by a professional astrologist.

Ancient astrology viewed the sun, moon, and other planets as deities or under the influence of deities. An individual born under the sign of the planet would be influenced by the characteristics or "personality" of the planet and/or deity. One born under the sign of Mars would be aggressive, under Mercury would be industrious, or under Venus would be romantic. Today's zodiac is complex, dealing with various symbols of planets, animals, houses, energies, rotations of sun and planets, fire/air/water/earth, and star constellations.

The twelve parts of the zodiac are listed in the following table.[3]

Zodiac	Month	Zodiac	Month
The Ram	March 21-April 19 (Aries)	The Scales	September 23-October 22 (Libra)
The Bull	April 20-May 20 (Taurus)	The Scorpion	October 23-November 21 (Scorpio)
The Twins	May 21-June 20 (Gemini)	The Archer	November 22-December 21 (Sagittarius)
The Crab	June 21-July 22 (Cancer)	The Goat	December 22-January 19 (Capricorn)
The Lion	July 23-August 22 (Leo)	The Waterman	January 20-February 18 (Aquarius)
The Virgin	August 23-September 22 (Virgo)	The Fishes	February 19-March 20 (Pisces)

Horoscopes

Interpretation of the zodiac and the charting of the horoscope may be done for an individual, a business, or a nation. Charting consists of two parts. The outer ring will demonstrate the signs of the zodiac at birth. For example, the sun rejoices during Leo (July 23-August 22), for it is summer and the time of the strength of the Lion. The sun is weaker, however, in the wintertime during Capricorn (December 22-January 19). These signs are interpreted by astrologists according to one's birth date as well as to the rising of the sun at the time of birth. An inner ring is divided into twelve houses, and each house denotes an aspect of personality or condition in life. For example, the first house represents one's personal appearance, and the second house concerns one's finances. Some astrologers relate the different signs to different parts of the human body. Aries rules the head, Cancer rules the breast, and Pisces rules the feet. Not only are the signs and houses important, but the very angles between the planets play a crucial role in interpretation. Planets which are near may indicate good influences, while planets at some distance may bring negative results.

Astrology is also founded upon the star ages. Every two thousand years the earth is supposed to begin a new star age. Recent ages have included the Age of Aries, from 2000 B.C. to the birth of Jesus Christ; the Age of Pisces, from Jesus Christ to the present; and the Age of Aquarius, which some surmise has already begun. A Broadway musical, *Hair*, featured the song "Aquarius." The lyrics herald the dawning of the Aquarian Age. The Age of Aquarius will be an age of prosperity and peace, according to astrologists, because the signs and the houses of the zodiac will be in such a state for Aquarius. Astrology has room for flexibility and variety in interpretation according to the positions and alignments and births of planets and stars and individuals and conditions.

Divination

Other moods and methods are present in the occult for which people grasp to lead them into decision-making and living in the future. Divination is the art of foretelling the future, and it has many contemporary expressions including I Ching, palmistry, Tarot cards, the Ouija board, and intuitive prophecy. Divination is, however, an ancient practice. The Babylonians were not only stargazers to the beyond, but they looked within: they read the livers of animals as predictions of the future. The liver was viewed as the locus of life. Some seven hundred archaeological tablets have been unearthed that contain prophecies based on the use of the liver. Both kings and commoners in all ages have used their priests or visited their fortune-tellers to learn what life holds in store.

I Ching is a Chinese form of divination that has migrated to America. It is based on the *Book of Changes,* which has sixty-four chapters. Simply stated, the individual tosses three coins, and the resulting combinations of coins lead an individual to one of the sixty-four chapters of the book to receive interpretations for the inquiry. Interpretations are based on the Chinese Taoist philosophy of *yang* and *ying* and on the I Ching pictograph or hexagram. The Swiss psychiatrist, Carl Jung, wrote a preface to the first Western translation of the *Book of Changes.* Tom Wolf and Bob Dylan publicized it in America. International I Ching Studies Institutes sprang up. Some have estimated that hundreds of thousands of individuals have "played" I Ching.

Palmistry also is an ancient practice. It is forecasting the future by examining the shape of the hands and their lines. Hand lines reveal character. Various shapes of hands, including the length and shortness of palms and fingers, indicate an "intellectual" hand, or a "sensitive" hand, or a "practical" hand. The "Life Line" in the palm indicates longevity, and the palmist reads one's future according to the size of palms and the length and directions of lines. Palmists, often called fortune-tellers, are found in large cities and beside rural highways, their shingles attached beside the entrance or a neon-lighted sign with arrows pointed toward the office.

Tarot cards and Ouija boards also provide ways of divining the future. The pack of Tarot cards numbers seventy-eight, with their symbols and pictures of fate. Seeker, interpreter, and cards provide the forum for divination. The seeker asks the question, the cards are shuffled, and the interpreter reads the patterns of the cards for meanings. Much is left to the interpreter because of the latitude of symbols, cards, and patterns. Death might mean physical death, failure, a negative experience, or a loss. The Ouija board consists of a marker which the questioner holds and moves across a board full of possible answers.

Psychic prophets have offered their predictions since the Greek priestesses of Delphi. Two of the better-known contemporary prophets have been Edgar Cayce and Jeane Dixon. Cayce found his Association for Research and Enlightenment, Inc. in 1931; it is now located in Virginia Beach, Virginia. Cayce was multifaceted in his psychic powers. He also forecast the future, including the disappearance of North Carolina and Georgia into the Atlantic Ocean sometime after 1960, with New York to follow in the 1970s. Jeane Dixon quickly became famous with her prediction of the death of President Kennedy in 1963. She lives and forecasts in the Washington, D.C., area, and many of her prophecies, which she credits to God, have not been fulfilled or have been incorrect.

Divination is often risky. Its seers and diviners locate answers in diverse and variable places, from the stars to the hands. As long as there is a future, it seems there will be people who will tell it like it is to be.

Spiritualism and the Psychic

In 1966, Jim Pike, the son of Episcopal Bishop James Pike, killed himself in New York City. Bishop Pike visited several mediums, including Era Twigg, Arthur Ford, and George Daisley, in order to communicate with his deceased son. The bishop appeared in an interview with Arthur Ford on television and wrote a book *The Other Side*. Bishop Pike's search for messages from his son highlighted interest in Spiritualism.

What is Spiritualism?[4] Spiritualism is a movement that believes in the existence of personality after death and that communication can occur between the dead and the living. Communication usually comes through an intermediary, called a medium, who may be aided by one or more control spirits who help establish contact with the deceased. The setting for the encounter with the spirit world is a seance in which the seeker, the medium and any other helpers employ various means of sights and sounds to foster communication.

Communication with the dead has a long history. In the Bible, Saul called on a witch to communicate with Samuel. Interest in modern Spiritualism in Europe and America began in the mid-1800s. Two sisters, Maggie and Kate Fox, claimed communication with the dead in their house in New York state. Lecturers on Spiritualism roamed the country and claimed converts to their beliefs such as William Lloyd Garrison and Horace Greeley. President Lincoln was said to accept its claims. Sir Arthur Conan Doyle, the creator of Sherlock Holmes, became a devotee. Arthur Ford, a minister of the Disciples of Christ, served as a minister and a medium for some fifty years, and carried the seance into millions of American homes through a televised encounter with Bishop Pike. Some estimate that there are over 50,000 spiritualists in Great Britain and as many as 700,000 in America. There are some eighteen spiritualist groups in America, and for over fifty years there has been a National Spiritualist Association.

The principles of the National Spiritualist Association are the following:

1. We believe in Infinite Intelligence.

2. We believe that the phenomena of Nature, both physical and spiritual, are the expression of Infinite Intelligence.

3. We affirm that correct understanding of such expressions and living in accordance therewith constitute true religion.

4. We affirm that the existence and personal identity of the individual continue after the change called death.

5. We affirm that communication with the so-called dead is a fact scientifically proven by the phenomena of Spiritualism.

6. We believe that the highest morality is contained in the Golden Rule.

7. We affirm the moral responsibility of the individual, and that he makes his own happiness or unhappiness as he obeys or disobeys Nature's physical or spiritual laws.

8. We affirm that the doorway to reformation is never closed against any human soul, here or hereafter.[5]

The seance is the primary method for communication with the dead. Various components of seances are passivity, vocal reality, trumpet revelation, lights, transfiguration, and levitation. During a seance several of these may occur. A mood of quietness and meditation may be engendered with low lights and drawn curtains. Sometimes objects on a table may move, and the medium may enter into a state of trance. The control spirit may speak through the vocal cords of the medium, as the medium's body seems to be possessed. Messages from the "other world" may also occur in the forms of facial or bodily manifestations, writings, knocks to answer questions of the medium, and the levitation of objects in the room.

In the seance which Bishop Pike had with medium Ford, Ford's control spirit, Fletcher, communicated through Ford's vocal cords. Fletcher told of many facts of the Bishop's son's life of which Bishop Pike had no knowledge. At one point Fletcher related that Jesus was just another person in the spirit world. In another seance which Bishop Pike had with medium Ena Twigg, Twigg related that his son said the spirits talk about Jesus as a mystic and a seer but not as a savior.[6]

Spiritualism has been closely related to Christianity, especially with some of its declarations of principles and with ministers such as Ford and Pike. There are Spiritualist churches which hold regular services. Many spiritualists, however, separate themselves from any Christian associations. Spiritualism is distinct from spiritism, the worship of spirits. Arguments abound among observers of the occult of the authenticity of and fraud of Spiritualism. There are examples of fakery as well as examples of unsolved explanations about seance events.

Related to Spiritualism as allied phenomena are other movements that focus on the spirit world and communication across time and space among the living. Various kinds of psychic experiences exist which contemporary science has no established criteria to evaluate. *Extrasensory perception* (ESP) has long been researched by such notables as J. B. Rhine of Duke University. ESP includes categories such as precognition, clairvoyance, and telepathy. *Precognition* is the awareness of an event before it happens. *Clairvoyance* is the interaction of an individual's mind or body with some event and knowledge received without the aid of normal sensory functions. *Telepathy* is the interaction between two minds or bodies, and knowledge is gained without the aid of known sensory functions. Research continues, and findings are tentative about these psychic happenings.

Ghosts and poltergeists are associated in the realm of spiritualism. There are *ghosts* of the living and of the dead. The ghost may haunt a house, but when the ghost departs, the house remains normal. *Poltergeists* are noisy spirits who may throw or move objects, set them on fire, and literally destroy objects. The house is never the same. *Astral projection* is the idea that the human body has two forms. One is a physical form, and one is an astral form. The astral body is composed of finer matter. It can be separated from the physical body at times of sleep and travel over time and space.

Stories have been reported by patients who apparently died on an operating table, but were restored to life. They report various stories of traveling through a tunnel and seeing at its end a bright light. *Reincarnation*, also closely allied with spiritualism, is a belief in the preexistence of souls and the reincarnation of souls into various bodies through history. The Bridey Murphy story is a famous one in America in which a girl was hypnotized and reverted to a former life in Ireland.[7]

Witchcraft and Magic

Little witches and goblins came to homes at Halloween time and play trick or treat. The ones dressed in black may play a trick, while the ones in white may be benevolent. Big witches, however, have been playing black and white magic for centuries. Witchcraft may be considered a form of magic. Archaeologists have unearthed caves with drawings of the "horned god" which date to 3,000 B.C. The witch of Endor was mentioned in the Bible. There were Greek sorcerers in Media, and the poets of Rome wrote about witches using bones to speak with the dead.

It is estimated that a half-million people were burned to death in Europe between the fifteenth and seventeenth centuries because they were convicted of witchcraft. Their witchcraft had consisted of riding broomsticks, making journeys through the air, and making pacts with the devil. The medieval church launched an inquisition against heretics and witches. In Salem, Massachusetts, in 1692, there was a craze of witchcraft with rumors, accusations, arrests, and trials. Hundreds were involved, and over twenty were executed for practicing witchcraft.

Magic and witchcraft appear to be rampant in the contemporary world. It is estimated that in Germany there are ten thousand witches, over thirty thousand in England, and possibly one hundred thousand in America, with five thousand witches in New York and ten thousand in Los Angeles. In Africa, Christian missionaries report converts of witches. Courses on witchcraft have been offered in over sixty colleges in the United States, including New York University and the University of South Carolina.[8] Some five hundred covens of witches meet in the United States.

The 1960s and 1970s brought black magic, witches, demons and Satan into public view. In 1966, Anton LaVey, known as the "Black Pope," organized his Church of Satan in San Francisco using black magic. The movie, *Rosemary's Baby*, showed the birth of a demon child. A year later, Charles Manson and his "family" entered director Roman Polanski's home in Los Angeles and ritually slaughtered his expectant wife and others. When Manson and his gang were arrested, he said that he was Satan and his female family members were witches. In 1973 the movie *The Exorcist* portrayed the demon possession of a small child. Television has played its serials of "Bewitched." Two noted witches cast their spells in America—Sybil Leek and Louise Huebner—and write their newspaper columns on witchcraft and books on the power through witchcraft.

Magic is nourished on the notion that powers exist in the universe which can be manipulated by using correct rituals. White magic is used to help people, while black magic is employed to harm, injure, or even cause the death of others. Witches may utilize various forms of magic. Through incantations and talismans, witches may chant and handle bones to affect the condition of an individual. To thrust a pin in a doll may bring harm to the named individual in the incantation. To burn a piece of an individual's clothing may affect the individual who wore it. Other forms through which magic may be attempted are the evil eye, love charms, and hypnotism. One of the most noted forms of magic used in witchcraft is the Black Mass, a featured ritual in the witch's *coven*, the primary community of witchcraft.

Coven means "to come together." Membership of the coven is usually thirteen, six men and six women and a priest or priestess. Meetings are held monthly on the evening of the full moon, with Halloween night of great significance. The monthly meeting is called an *esbat*. Eight other meetings are held, called *sabbats*, at the beginning of each season, at Halloween, on Maypole dance eve, on February eve, and on August eve.[9]

The Book of Shadows is read at coven meetings. It contains the ceremonies, incantations, and procedures for the practice of witchcraft. Some witches refer to their craft as the "Old Religion." The Old Religion superseded Christianity and was based on a horned god and a mother goddess. It was a native religion. *Witch* is derived from the Celtic word *wicca*. Covens of witches have taken a variety of organizational and ceremonial forms. Often, the initiant is inducted into the group blindfolded and naked. One is scourged and administered the fivefold kiss of the feet, knees, sexual organs, breasts, and lips. Some covens practice nudity;

some sing, dance, meet in secret places, use drugs, and perform fertility rituals. Some witches believe that clothing impedes the bodily powers of their proper functions. Witchcraft may also involve sexual intercourse among the coven members. The more ancient traditions included animal sacrifices and sexual orgies.

The Black Mass has become witchcraft's most notorious ritual.[10] It symbolizes a rebellion against Christianity in the ridicule and the misuse of the meaning and the elements in the Mass of the Roman Catholic Church. Gilles de Laval, the original Bluebeard and friend of Joan of Arc, was executed in 1440 in France for the murder of two hundred children. Laval held Black Masses in which he sacrificed children to Satan and used their blood in the masses. In the 1600s the mistress of King Louis XIV, with the aid of a priestess of Satanism, held Black Masses to gain the favor of the King. Infants were killed, and their blood together with a wafer was given to the King as a love potion. The mistress hoped through magic to maintain her relationship with the king. The priestess later admitted, when the masses were exposed, that she had buried over twenty-five hundred children in her gardens. Black Masses have included altars of coffins or naked females, various foul bodily substances in place of bread and wine, a crucifix hung upside down, black ornaments instead of white, and references to Satan. The Black Mass became a parody of the Christian mass.

Witchcraft and magic appear to be alternative and appealing practices for peoples around the globe. They still have their secret admirers and practitioners, but more recently they have come out in the open. Joan Denton of North Carolina, who claims to be a witch, was charged with causing the death of a woman through witchcraft. She placed spells on a woman and forecast her death on April 10, 1976. The woman died on that date, and her family brought charges against Denton of contributing to her death. Witchcraft has its benevolent claims, too. Sybil Leek, a well-known witch in America, claims that witchcraft may serve the religious needs of people. The witch may call on and use powers to aid people in good feelings, material benefits, and personal and professional success. Whether black or white magic is employed in witchcraft, it is the witch's craft to manipulate and control nature's forces for the benefit or the detriment of humankind.

Satanism and the Church of Satan

Devil worshipers and satanic practices are centuries old. Black Masses of the medieval ages were linked to Satanism. The medieval devil was symbolized as a goat's head, and the symbol of the devil today is one of horns and hoofs. The devil was also portrayed as the liberator for sexual urges and fleshly pursuits and against all of the teachings of the Roman Catholic Church.[11] Perhaps the one person who has brought a revival of Satanism to modern times is Aleister Crowley, who was born in Great Britain in 1875. Because of his devilish behavior, his mother considered him to be the great beast of the Book of Revelation. He referred to himself as "the wickedest man in the world." He practiced magic, wrote pornographic poems, engaged in homosexuality and heterosexual promiscuity, and gave honor to Satan. While living in poverty and injecting himself with heroin, he died in 1947. His writings are being read today and serve to popularize the moods and methods of contemporary Satanism.

Satanism burst into the headlines in the 1960s generated by three events. The movie *Rosemary's Baby* closes with the lines:

God is dead! God is dead and Satan lives!

This year is One, the first year of our Lord!

This year is One, God is done.

Charles Manson, after killing the wife of the director of *Rosemary's Baby*, proclaimed himself the devil. The Manson family was one among many groups around the nation to practice Satanic worship. The third event was the beginning of the Church of Satan by Anton Szander LaVey. Anton LaVey had played the role of the devil in *Rosemary's Baby*.

Satanism is a word used to describe various practices, symbols, and groups which claim association with Satan. The names associated with Satan are many. The word *Satan* is derived from a Greek word which suggests "adversary." The name *Devil* comes from a Greek word *diabolos*, which means a slanderer. The word *Serpent* as used in the biblical book of Revelation refers both to the devil and to Satan. Beelzebub is referred to by Jesus Christ as Satan, the ruler of demons. Anton LaVey, author of *The Satanic Bible*, includes seventy-seven names for Satan. Among them are some of the above and also Baphomet, Behemoth, Dracula, Ishtar, Kali, Marduk, Moloch, and Pan.

In the world of the occult, Satanism may be viewed in two groupings: (1) Generalized Satanism uses the associated names of Satan in music, art, symbols, and certain rituals in group settings. Generalized Satanism is expressed in popular cultural forms and in less visible institutionalized ways. (2) The Church of Satan has "ordained" leadership, public buildings, literature, budgets, a publicly announced belief system, and a tax-exempt status.

Generalized Satanism, particularly since the 1970s, has been associated with certain art forms and musical lyrics as well as certain destructive forms of behavior such as vandalism of buildings, desecration of cemeteries, and sacrificial animal remains. Often, young people attempt to imitate their favorite writers and bands in their use of Satanic symbols and rituals.

In particular, certain artists of heavy metal music emphasize and affirm lyrics, phrases and songs dealing with Satanism. Some record albums show on their covers inverted pentegrams, the symbol of Satan. Some album titles depict Satanic expressions, including "Shout at the Devil" and "Highway to Hell" with the lyric that Satan is paying one's dues and a drawing of a nude Satanic ritual with a skull and the numbers 666.

"Dungeons and Dragons," a fantasy role game, deals with the casting of spells, evil spirits, monsters, assassinations, and poisoning. Some twenty-two types of satanic demons are used in the role-playing game. Players can be cursed with twenty different kinds of insanity.

Generalized forms of satanic association also include reading literature on Satanism, including *The Satanic Bible*; drawing satanic symbols on notebooks, walls, buildings, and cemetery stones; greeting peers with the "horned hand" sign and talking to peers about Satanism; and keeping a journal composed of lyrics from heavy metal music, of chants from *The Satanic Bible*, and of accounts of real and fantasized rituals.

Besides generalized Satanism, there is the more formal, organizational expression of Satanism, often called religious Satanism. The best known example is the Church of Satan. There is another side to this expression, however, namely, "Satanic cults."

There is little "official" evidence of these cults; most information comes from ex-members who have been victims of the cults and hide for their lives, and from media and police investigative reports. Reports indicate that these cults are involved in criminal activities such as drug trafficking, pornography, kidnapping, and animal and human sacrifices.

Reports also indicate that children and teenagers are especially manipulated and controlled by the cults. They may be introduced at a very young age to practices of Satanism by family and close friends of family. Drugs, physical torture, and psychological conditioning are often used on the youth. Bibles may be burned, churches desecrated, and cemeteries vandalized to impress satanic teachings on youth.

Law enforcement agencies indicate that satanic cults are involved in crime—trespassing on and vandalism of church and cemetery properties, including grave robbing; child abuse; murder; drugs; and cruelty to animals.

Different levels of involvement are present in generalized Satanism—fun and games level; dabbler's level with half belief in Satanism; serious level of involvement based on a belief in the supernatural reality of Satan; and the level of criminal involvement. All levels utilize some expression of Satan.

Since the late 1960s the Church of Satan has popularized Satanism in America. Its founder, Anton LaVey, made it a religion using the United States Constitution's guarantee of religious freedom and the separation of church and state. LaVey has been featured on national television talk shows and in newspaper spreads depicting him and his church.

LaVey was something of a child prodigy.[12] Born in 1930 of Alsatian ancestry, he inherited the love of witchcraft from his gypsy grandmother. In high school he studied music and the occult. He dropped out of school at age sixteen. He played second oboist in the San Francisco Ballet Symphony Orchestra and later worked for the Clyde Beaty Circus as a lion feeder, assistant trainer, and a pianist. He played for the high wire acts of Zacchini and the Wallendas. At age eighteen he joined a carnival and became the assistant to the magician, which deepened his study into the occult. During these teenage years, LaVey noted:

> On Saturday night I would see men lusting after half-naked girls dancing at the carnival, and on Sunday morning when I was playing the organ for tent-show evangelists at the other end of the carnival lot, I would see these same men sitting in the pews with their wives and children, asking God to forgive them and purge them of carnal desires. And the next Saturday night they'd be back at the carnival or some other place of indulgence. I knew then that the Christian church thrives on hypocrisy, and that men's carnal nature will win out no matter how much it is purged or scourged by any white light religion.[13]

After his marriage, he studied criminology at City College at San Francisco and became a photographer with the police department. He said of that experience:

> I saw the bloodiest, grimiest side of human nature . . . People shot by nuts, knifed by friends, little kids spattered in the gutter by hit and run drivers. It was disgusting and depressing. I asked myself, "Where is God?" I came to detest the sanctimonious attitude of people toward violence, always saying it's God's will.[14]

LaVey began holding classes in magic at his home. He was well on the way to forming a religion that was to be the antithesis of Christianity.

On the last night of April 1966 was one of the most important festivals in witchcraft. LaVey shaved his head, left his beard intact, donned a clerical collar, and announced the beginning of the Church of Satan in San Francisco. He explained:

> For one thing calling it a church enabled me to follow the magic formula of one part outrage to nine parts social respectability that is needed for success. But the main purpose was to gather a group of like-minded individuals together for the use of their combined energies in calling up the dark force in nature that is called Satan.[15]

He became known as the "Black Pope," and by 1969 he had written *The Satanic Bible*. LaVey adapted the Black Mass to his own style for the modernization of satanic practice. Instead of mocking church practices, he initiated positive rituals for celebration. Satanic baptisms, weddings, and funerals were held in the Church of Satan, all dedicated to the devil. Lust rituals were launched to aid his members to attain their sexual desires. Destruction rituals were held to help members triumph over their enemies and gain success. Often, naked women were used as altars at wedding and funeral ceremonies.

The Satanic Bible was dedicated to many persons, including Friederich Nietzche, Howard Hughes, Marilyn Monroe, Jayne Mansfield, Horatio Alger, George Orwell, H. G. Wells, and Harry Houdini. In it, LaVey explains the philosophy of Satanism and describes the black magic rituals. LaVey writes, "Here is satanic thought from a truly Satanic point of view." *The Satanic Bible* begins with "The Nine Satanic Statements."

1. Satan represents indulgence, instead of abstinence!

2. Satan represents vital existence, instead of spiritual pipe dreams!

3. Satan represents undefiled wisdom, instead of hypocritical self-deceit!

4. Satan represents kindness to those who deserve it, instead of love wasted on ingrates!

5. Satan represents vengeance, instead of turning the other cheek!

6. Satan represents responsibility to the responsible, instead of concern for psychic vampires.

7. Satan represents man as just another animal, sometimes better, more often worse than those that walk on all-fours, who because of his "divine spiritual and intellectual development," has become the most vicious animal of all!

8. Satan represents all of the so-called sins, as they all lead to physical, mental, or emotional gratification!

9. Satan has been the best friend the church has ever had, as he kept it in business all these years![16]

LaVey points out that the seven deadly sins of the Christian church are: "greed, pride, envy, anger, gluttony, lust, and sloth. Satanism advocates indulging in each of these 'sins' as they all lead to physical, mental, or emotional gratification."[17] LaVey has built his church on the antithesis of Christian teachings and practices and on the art and practice of witchcraft and black magic.

Groups affiliated with or spin-offs of the Church of Satan are located across America and in England, France, Germany, Africa, and Australia. In 1975, Michael Aquino, one of LaVey's followers, organized the Temple of Set. Aquino, a former Lt. Colonel in the United States Army, took over half of LaVey's followers with him. He has appeared on national television talk shows to promote Satanism. The Church of Satan estimates its followers may number as high as two hundred thousand. LaVey once said that the film *Rosemary's Baby* was "the best paid commercial for Satanism since the Inquisition." He appeared on the Johnny Carson Show wearing a horned hood, carrying a magic sword and exposed his movement to a viewing public. LaVey's Satanism demonstrates a weaving together of the occult in its magical practices and its witchcraft art forms.

Issues and Challenges Between the Occult and Christian Faith and Practice

The occult is attractive to millions of persons globally. Direction and answers are sought from the pathways of the planets and the stars. Spirits and demons from "other worlds" are called upon to intervene in daily activities and in relationships among peoples. Magic employed in witchcraft and Satanism is utilized to manipulate and control events and peoples. There is a need to know the future and to predict the future. Billions of dollars and untold quantities of time and energies are expended on the occult. Certainly for many, the occult has become an alternate religion. Christians and church members are numbered among those who participate in some functions of the occult, especially in astrology, palmistry, and the like. What are some of the issues and challenges between the occult and Christians?

1. Astrology is an interesting study to observe, but how serious can one be about its methods and conclusions? The sun and moon influence the tides of the ocean and the agriculture of the fields. The science of astronomy is a noted critic of astrology. New planets have been discovered, and the

Copernican revolution has been accepted, but astrology has not changed. These new discoveries have not been admitted by astrologists to affect their presuppositions or methods. Why are there so many interpretations by various astrologists of the constellations of one's horoscope? The Bible cautions us against being drawn to the moon, sun, and stars and about worshiping and serving them (Deut. 4:19). Paul's letters to the Galatians and the Ephesians counseled them to beware of counterreligions which focused on planet gods and elementary spirits and vain philosophies. Christians are faced with the issues of moral freedom and responsibility, escapism, sin, and fatalism in relation to the assumptions of astrology. Planets determine one's fate, therefore, one may not be responsible for one's deeds. Astrology as a secular movement is not concerned with God, the biblical revelation, and the teachings of the Scriptures. People may have a casual interest in reading the horoscope; however, they need to beware of astrology's becoming a religion or a religious pursuit.

2. Spiritualism and related psychic phenomena have become a fascination with people and a disciplined study with scholars. Many of the assumptions of these movements are closely allied to Christian understandings. For example, Spiritualism places its prerogatives upon information allegedly obtained from the dead, not from God; on survival after life, not on eternal life with God; on a human intermediary, not on the mediator Jesus Christ; on communication with alleged spirits often unknown, not through the Holy Spirit of God; and in faith and practice bordering on skepticism, suspicion, and superstition, not on a faith and faithfulness based on God's voice saying of Jesus, "This is my beloved Son; hear ye him." There are many unknowns in psychic phenomena. Research continues in the field of extrasensory perception. Christian faith gives witness to principalities and powers and evil in the world and cautions one to test the spirits to see if they are from God. The biblical witness counsels against consulting mediums, wizards, and necromancers (Lev. 20:6,27; Deut. 18:10,11).

3. Witchcraft and Satanism have experienced a revival in recent decades. Explanations for their rise have included a functional outlet for deep anxieties and repressed hostilities. They have functioned as a counterreligion based on magical practices, the manipulation and control of the "spirit" world, the satisfaction and celebration of self-interest, and demonic and Satanic inspired and propagated activity. The biblical witness denies witches and sorcerers and their practices in such Scriptures as Exodus 22:18, Deuteronomy 18:10-12, Acts 13:10, Galatians 5:20, and Revelation 22:15. Satanism and the Church of Satan elevate through symbol and practice anti-God, anti-Christ, and anti-Church belief and life. Self-indulgence is their motto, and celebration of the flesh is their ritual. They distort and desecrate whatsoever things are true, and honest, and just, and pure. The biblical witness is that Jesus Christ has overcome Satanic powers with His life, message, death, and resurrection, and has brought liberation and salvation.

4. Christians need to be aware of the effects of the occult upon literally tens of millions of people. Christians need to be sensitive to the needs of people who feel the necessity of involvement in the occult. The occult appeals to the mental, emotional, physical, and spiritual needs of persons. A group experience may be offered, like a seance, a "church," a coven, or a class. Often, the individual seeker may read the occult literature, play its games, and read the horoscopes.

A search for meaning is rampant in society. Many seek a caring community. Fears, anxiety, and loneliness are vented in attachment to the occult. Many issues are within the occult, from its realness to pandering after money to its empty fulfillment from too many promises. Christians are challenged to see the occult revived in a "churchly" society where alternatives to church and Christian faith are rampant. The challenge is to the ministry and mission of the church and to understanding and outreach by Christians. There is no doubt that much of humankind is on a spiritual quest. The Christian faith is challenged to offer to humankind an immediate encounter with God through Jesus Christ who is Lord of heaven and of earth.

6

HINDUISM IN AMERICA

■ ━━━━━━━━━━━━━━━━━━━━━━━━━━━━ ■

Introduction

Religious experiences of India are rich and diverse and cover thousands of years of human history on the subcontinent. Scholars have written about these religious traditions and have called them Hinduism, Buddhism, Jainism, and other nouns. Hinduism encompasses an array of philosophies, theologies, beliefs, and practices. Among a population of about one billion Indians, most are Hindus.

Hinduism is one of the most inclusive religions. The sophisticated intellectual may find a comfortable niche in philosophical atheism or agnosticism and remain a good Hindu. A Hindu family man may divide his devotion between the gods of family and those of his wife. A Hindu merchant may exclusively give all his attention and devotion to one god. All may remain bona fide Hindus, accepted and respected by each other. There is a path in Hinduism for metaphysics and speculation. The contemplative life, fixed upon a search for the principles of truth, is followed by many. Also, there is a path in Hinduism of elaborate temples and colorful rituals and sacred altars in the home which all focus on the worship of countless gods and goddesses.[1]

197

Hinduism does not have the classic prophets which Judaism, Christianity, and Islam present. Instead, it has *Brahmins* (priests), *sannyasi* (holy persons), *gurus*, *swamis* and masters (wise persons often trained in techniques of yoga). These individuals, through heredity and/or years of intense study of sacred scriptures and practice of meditation, preside over communities of disciples who study under their tutelage, over temple ceremonies, over followers of their meditation practices, or over devotees who live together in an *ashram*.

Various scriptural traditions in Hinduism include the *Vedas*, the *Upanishads*, the *Ramayana*, and the *Mahabharata*, which contains the *Bhagavad-Gita*. The *Vedas*, in the ancient language of Sanskrit, contain diverse materials on the pantheon of deities, rituals of sacrifices to deities, and philosophical inquiry about the origins of creation. Their authors were probably *Brahmin* priests. The *Upanishad* scriptures surfaced around 500 B.C. and include parables, maxims, and dialogues. These scriptures place emphasis on unity in the midst of diversity and present the view of unity with the union of *Atman* (individual soul) with *Brahman* (world soul).

Correct knowledge becomes the key for achieving unity, and meditation becomes a proper technique. The *Ramayana* tells the story of Rama and his wife, Sita. Many Hindus are devoted to Rama. The *Bhagavad-Gita*, known as the Celestial Song, became prominent about the beginning of the Christian era. It recounts the story of Lord Krishna and the devotion of his followers. The *Gita* may be the most popular Hindu scripture among Hindus as well as outside of India.[2]

Much of Hindu thought and practice center on *karma* (activity) and transmigration of the soul. The individual through life collects good karma and bad karma. As long as there is an imbalance of bad karma, the individual continues in a series of rebirths until the good karma prevails. The transmigration cycle is ended, and the individual is united or absorbed into Braham (Absolute Soul) or joins a deity or deities, depending on one's philosophy, theology, or ritual. The caste system in India is associated with the philosophy of karma and transmigration, with the belief that individuals are born into species, socio-economic groupings, and occupations due to their quality of karma.

There is also the concept in Hinduism of *maya*, viewing the world as illusory and as a place from which to escape. There are paths (*margas*) of liberation from the world, and with each path there are teachings and techniques. The way of works or rituals (*karma marga*) may involve visits and offerings at temples with the assistance of a priest. The way of knowledge (*jnana marga*) concentrates on mastering sacred scriptures and wisdom literature and sacred oral traditions, often with the help of a guru. The way of yoga (*yoga marga*) focuses on techniques and processes of meditation with the aid of a master. And the way of devotion (*bhakti marga*) centers on personal commitment to a god like Krishna. Hindus may practice one or many of these paths in order to escape the illusory world, break the transmigration cycle of the soul, and attain ultimate freedom.

The classic stages in life are the student, householder, forest dweller, and holy stages. In the student stage one studies the sacred vedic literature and prepares oneself for living the correct life based on the eternal *dharma* (principles of universal truth). As a householder one raises a family within the dharma. The forest dweller stage is the time when one may conclude family life and enter a full-time life of study and meditation. The final stage of becoming a *sanyassin*, or holy person, is when one contemplates the responsibilities of mastering dharma and achieves the path of ultimate freedom. One then may attain *moksha,* or freedom. In contemporary Hinduism these stages are often intermeshed and not necessarily realized according to the classic way of development.

Hinduism is a complex religious tradition, composed of schools of philosophies, ancient traditions of diverse practices of meditation, and elaborate networks of temple complexes. It offers the depths of universal thought as well as the parochial and provincial act of worship to a single image. Even the sometimes parochial act may imply the complexities within a Hindu world view and ritual. By and large, Hinduism has not been known to be a missionary religious tradition, but has basically remained at home on the subcontinent. It tends to be inclusivistic, and accepting and sometimes absorbs other religious concepts and practices and places them alongside its own. Hinduism has migrated to various continents.

The American experience with Hinduism is not new, with the advent in the 1960s and 1970s of countercultural groups' fascination and gravitation to such Hindu-based concepts and practices as exemplified in Hare Krishna and Transcendental Meditation. The writings of Ralph Waldo Emerson and Henry David Thoreau, American writers in the 1800s, demonstrate the influences of Hinduism. These New England writers, sometimes referred to as "Transcendentalists," were deeply affected by India's literature. One of Emerson's famous poems, "Brahma," shows his insights into Hinduism and appears to rely on verses from the *Bhagavad-Gita*. In *Walden,* chapter 16, Thoreau reveals his enthusiasm about the philosophy of the *Bhagavad-Gita*. Their works, and even life-styles, have influenced generations of Americans. In fact, it was Thoreau's treatise on "Civil Disobedience" which Mahatma Gandhi read while fighting for the rights of Indians in South Africa. He later named his Indian movement "Civil Disobedience."

In 1893 the World Parliament of Religions was held in Chicago. Hinduism's missionary outreach to America was heralded by an address by Swami Vivekananda of India, a disciple of Ramakrishna. He advocated Hinduism to be a universal faith for all peoples. His vision gave birth to the Vedanta Society, which now has over fifty centers across the United States. In the first half of the twentieth century, Hindu spiritual masters occasionally visited the United States, lectured, and formed groups. One such lecturer was

Swami Yogananda. He was the *guru* of Swami Premananda of India, who in 1928 founded the Lotus Temple in Washington, D.C., also called the Self-Revelation Church of Absolute Monism. The church follows the spiritual tradition of Advaita Vedanta with a nonsectarian philosophy.

A proliferation of Hindu *gurus* and masters came from India to the United States after World War II, and especially in the 1960s and 1970s. They attracted men and women in the counter cultures, and they appealed to those seeking after spirituality or therapeutic measures or consciousness raising experiences. Names and movements such as Hare Krishna, Transcendental Meditation, Divine Light Mission, Sai Baba, Baba Ram Dass, and Rajneesh became popular. Hindu influences were on L. Ron Hubbard, his Church of Scientology, Edgar Cayce, and his Association for Research and Enlightenment.

The shape and practice of Hinduism across the United States is diverse. The Lotus Temple offers worship services, seminars on Hindu philosophy, and lectures and techniques on Yoga. The Hare Krishna have temples featuring elaborate images of the deities where the deities are ceremoniously cared for. In their temples they chant and dance before the deities and have lectures and discussions on the *Bhagavad-Gita*. Communal living involving families and singles may be associated with the temple. Classes in Transcendental Meditation (TM) are offered by Maharishi Mahesh Yogi and his trained disciples across the country. TM charges a fee for its classes on quiet meditation which blend ancient Hindu traditions with contemporary psychological theories and methods. An Indian *guru*, Bhagwan Shree Rajneesh, led his followers to settle in Antelope, Oregon. Rajneesh built a city based on his Hindu sectarianism. Hindu concepts of reincarnation and transmigration of the soul are evident in the thought of Hubbard and Cayce.

Spiritual traditions of India are visible and widespread across America. The distinctive temples are often located in residential districts beside churches and synagogues. The different dress of *gurus* and devotees, with their saffron robes, blend with suits and ties and dresses of other pedestrians along the sidewalks. Newspapers and magazines printed by these communities are sold or distributed through the mail or in airports or along city marketplaces. National news media present stories of these communities in America. Americans encounter a new vocabulary arising from Hinduism. *Yoga* (meditation) is practiced. A *mantra* (sacred saying) is chanted. A *swami* (leader) is ordained into a Hindu order. An *avatar* (appearance of a god) like Krishna takes up residence in a temple image. *Karma*, the idea that one's present life is a result of what happened in past lives, is closely associated with the concept of reincarnation.

Hinduism has come to America where its philosophies, worldviews, rituals, and life-styles have attracted numerous Americans. Several Hindu groups in America will now be studied in more detail.

Hare Krishna
International Society for Krishna Consciousness

In 1965 a seventy-year-old swami left his homeland of India for the first time and sailed to America. He arrived in New York City with few dollars and no patrons. At the time of his death in 1977, he had become a global figure.

> The worldwide fame of His Divine Grace A. C. Bhaktivedanta Swami, later known as Srila Prabhupada, was to come after 1965—after he arrived in America. Before leaving India he had written three books; in the next twelve years he was to write more than sixty. Before he left India he had initiated one disciple; in the next twelve years, he would initiate more than four thousand. Before he left India, hardly anyone had believed that he could fulfill his vision of a worldwide society of Krsna devotees; but in the next decade he would form and maintain the International Society for Krishna Consciousness and open more than a hundred centers. Before sailing for America, he had never been

outside India; but in the next twelve years he would travel many times around the world propagating the Krsna consciousness movement.[3]

Born to a cloth merchant in Calcutta in 1896, Abhay Charan or Prabhupada, as he is affectionately called by his devotees, was nurtured in the worship of Krishna. His father was a pure *Vaisnava* (devotee to Krishna) and had never eaten fish, eggs, tea, or coffee. He led his son to be Krishna conscious and desired that he be a servant of Krishna and a preacher of the sacred scriptures.

Prabhupada not only worshiped the deity, but he also became a student of the *Bhagavad-Gita*, which told the story of Lord Krishna. The Hare Krishna movement has its historical roots in the Bengali Saint Chaitanya (1485-1527). Lord Chaitanya gained a following on his preaching of salvation by constantly chanting the name of Hare Krishna. He taught that the deity was personal, indeed the "Supreme Personality of the Godhead." Teachers in the disciplic line of Lord Chaitanya continued. One of these teachers, Sarasvati, whom Prabhupada met in 1922, encouraged him to preach Lord Chaitanya's message throughout the world. Several challenges faced Prabhupada. Although he had completed his four-year degree program in chemical engineering at the University of Calcutta, he refused to accept his degree. He had become involved in the nationalistic movement and had become a sympathizer to Mahatma Gandhi's cause. He was married and had children. His successful business was burglarized.

Prabhupada continually reflected upon the counsel of his swami. Before Swami Sarasvati died in 1936, he wrote to Prabhupada,

> I am fully confident that you can explain in English our thoughts and arguments to the people who are not conversant with the languages [Bengali and Hindi]. . . . This will do much good to yourself as well as to your audience. I have every hope that you can turn yourself into a very good English preacher.[4]

Nearly thirty years later, Prabhupada finally resolved the dilemmas posed by his teacher's counsel and set sail for America. He had conceived, written, and typed the manuscript for the magazine *Back to Godhead* and began its publication. He had decided to leave his wife and children. He had found a patron, the owner of the *Jaladuta*, a regular cargo carrier, to give him passage from Calcutta to New York. On August 13, 1965, Prabhupada departed India with a suitcase, an umbrella, a supply of dry cereal, and a copy of his holy writings. It was a few days before the anniversary of the appearance of Lord Krishna. Prabhupada had lived for several years in the city of Vrndavana, the holy place of Krishna. Prabhupada was concerned that he might die away from Vrndavana. But as he sailed, he reflected,

> With great difficulty I got out of the country! Some way or another by Krsna's grace, I got out so I could spread the Krsna consciousness movement all over the world. Otherwise, to remain in India—it was not possible. I wanted to start a movement in India, but I was not at all encouraged.[5]

He turned seventy on August 21, and arrived in New York harbor on September 19, 1965.

The Lower East Side of the Bowery and the Village became the swami's abode and temple. From the hippie crowd to artists, from musicians and intellectuals to middle-class dropouts, young men and women came to hear his lectures, to participate in chanting and the worship of the deities, and to become devotees to this *guru* of Lord Krishna. American youth and American families faced critical challenges during the 1960s and early 1970s. John F. Kennedy, Martin Luther King, and Robert Kennedy were assassinated. The drug counterculture was emerging, and the Vietnam War generated its discontent. Youth, in particular, began seeking for symbols and values and life-styles appropriate for their own experiences. Prabhupada invited and welcomed these youth to sit at his feet and to absorb his tradition of Hinduism.

Prabhupada became more mobile and missionary. Visits to California gained new devotees. His magazine *Back to Godhead*, which was sold in airports, marketplaces, and streets, was begun. Renowned individuals were attracted to his movement—Allen Ginsberg wrote poetry of Krishna—George Harrison, a Beatle, composed a best-selling song about Krishna, "My Sweet Lord." A great grandson of Henry Ford was converted to the group. Temples sprang up in major cities. Prabhupada traveled the world preaching from the *Bhagavad-Gita* and establishing Hare Krishna temples.

In each issue of *Back to Godhead,* the purposes for which the International Society for Krishna Consciousness were established are stated:

1. To systematically propagate spiritual knowledge to society at large and to educate all peoples in the techniques of spiritual life in order to check the imbalance of values in life and to achieve real unity and peace in the world.

2. To propagate a consciousness of Krsna, as it is revealed in Bhagavad-Gita and Srimad-Bhagavatam.

3. To bring the members of the Society together with each other and nearer to Krsna, the prime entity thus developing the idea within the members, and humanity at large, that each soul is part and parcel of the quality of Godhead (Krsna).

4. To teach and encourage the sankirtana movement, congregational chanting of the holy names of God, as revealed in the teachings of Lord Sri Caitanya Mahaprabhu.

5. To erect for the members and for society at large a holy place of transcendental pastimes dedicated to the personality of Krsna.

6. To bring the members closer together for the purpose of teaching a simpler, more natural way of life.

7. With a view toward achieving the aforementioned purposes, to publish and distribute periodicals, books, and other writings.[6]

Prabhupada's purposes for the Society were etched out during his last twelve years in his teachings, writings, lifestyle, temple communities, publications, and printing processes. He died in his beloved Vrndavana, in India, in 1977, with thousands of devotees from around the continents at his bedside.

Over five million hardbound copies of his translation of *Bhagavad-Gita As It Is* have been published in over a dozen languages. Prabhupada built his doctrines and practices on its teachings, and it serves as the primary scripture for the Hare Krishna movement. The story is of Krishna and the warrior Arjuna engaged in a prolonged conversation that reports say took place over fifty centuries ago. Arjuna was to do battle against a force who, he discovered, was composed of family and friends. In this dilemma he turned to his charioteer Krishna.

The Hare Krishna movement has an authoritative guru or *swami*, an authoritative scripture, and follows a discipline with allegiance to the god Krishna. We may ask the Hare Krishna movement: What is authority? Who is Krishna? What is the human personality? What is reality? What is the goal of life? What is devotion? Why do the Hare Krishna chant?

Krishna is viewed as the supreme authority. In fact, the speaker of the *Gita* is Krishna. "He is mentioned on every page as the Supreme Personality of Godhead, or Bhagawan."[7] Hinduism has focused on many deities, including Brahma, Vishnu, and Siva, often called the trinity of the Hindu pantheon. Vishnu traditionally has had many appearances, including an appearance or avatar as Krsna. Hare Krishna believe that Krishna is the original Vishnu. "Krsna includes Brahma, Vishnu, Siva, and everyone else."[8] In the *Gita*, Arjuna "accepted Krsna as pure, free from all material contamination, as the supreme enjoyer, the foremost person, the Supreme Personality of the Godhead, who is unborn and is the greatest."[9] Krishna is eternal, full of bliss and knowledge; he has no beginning, yet he is the beginning of everyone.

Prabhupada taught that,

> one who knows Krsna science understands that Krsna is everything and therefore can appear in everything. . . . Krsna is everywhere—this is Krsna consciousness. But one must know how he can derive Krsna from the features of Krsna's form in wood or iron or metal.[10]

Thus, Krishna is not limited to the forms and appearances he may make.

> The Lord incarnates in order to show us His joyous nature and pastimes. When Krsna was at Vrndavana, His activities with His friends the cowherd boys and His girl friends, and all His other pastimes, were full of happiness. The whole population of Vrndavana was made after Him. At this time, He even restricted His father from worshiping the demigods, to show us that no one need worship the demigods.[11]

Prabhupada elaborates upon the concept of Krishna.

> You may want Krsna as your lover, or as your son; you may want Krsna as your friend, you may want Krsna as your Master, you may want Krsna as the Supreme Sublime. These five different kinds of direct relationships with Krsna are called devotion, or bhakti. They entail no material profit.[12]

If Krishna is the authority for the Hare Krishna movement, the word of authority is found in the *Bhagavad-Gita*. The Krishna Consciousness movement is preached on the authority of the *Bhagavad-Gita*.

> The conclusion is that Bhagavad-gita is a transcendental literature that should be read very carefully. If one follows the instructions, he can be freed of all fears and

sufferings in this life and attain a spiritual birth in the next life.[13]

No other literature is needed except the *Gita*.[14] Besides Krishna and the *Gita* as the authority in the movement, there is also a chain of disciples that presents the spiritual knowledge.

> In the Fourth Chapter of Bhagavad-gita, Lord Krsna says, . . . "This supreme science was thus received through the chain of disciplic succession, and the saintly Kings understood it in that way."[15]

Krishna is viewed as the original teacher in the chain of spiritual masters in an unbroken disciplic chain to the present. They deliver the spiritual knowledge of the Bhagavad-Gita. Thirty-two are listed in the disciplic succession with Krishna first, Sarasvati the teacher of Prabhupada thirty-first, and Prabhupada as thirty-second.[16]

The Hare Krishna movement teaches that human beings are spirit souls. Their consciousnesses are adulterated, and they are attached to matter or the material atmosphere. The material world is called *maya*, or illusion. "The illusion is that we are all trying to be lords of material nature, while actually we are under the grip of her stringent laws."[17]

Different stages of life include: bodily, mental, intellectual, and the spiritual concept of life. Hare Krishna are concerned with the spiritual concept. "First of all we have to learn that 'I am not this body . . . . I am spirit soul.'"[18] The spirit soul is part and parcel of Krishna, and it lives in the age of Kali-yuga, the age of quarrel and disagreement; it lives ignorantly and imperfectly because it does not seek realization of Krishna consciousness. The trends of modern civilization are devotion to the animal propensities of eating, sleeping, mating, and fearing. To get out of entanglement of the material body and to achieve Krishna consciousness, one must chant and become a devotee of Krishna.

The traditional ideas of karma and transmigration of souls are beliefs of the Hare Krishna. Living in the material world produces sinful activity which is alienation from Krishna. Prabhupada writes,

> This is our position. Therefore, it is stated that because people generally cannot control their senses, they engage in the materialistic way of life in which repeated birth and death in different specifics take place.[19]

According to one's karma, either good or bad effects, one will assume various bodies of species.

> I do not know what is my next life, but the next life will come. Before us there are many species of life; I can take birth in any one of them. I can become a demigod, I can become a cat, I can become a dog, I can become a Brahma—there are so many forms of life. In the next life, I shall have to accept one of these forms, even if I do not want to. . . . Therefore, it is our duty to prepare a body which will help us go back to Krsna. That is Krsna consciousness.[20]

The invitation by Hare Krishna, to become free from the material world and to become devoted to Krishna, is associated with chanting the name of God.

> And the beginning is to develop attachment for Krsna. The process which we have prescribed is chanting and dancing before the Deities, and offering prasadam, spiritual food. This will make you more Krsna conscious.[21]

Prabhupada also writes,

> Simply by chanting the holy name of God, one can attain that perfect self-realization which was attained by the yoga system. . . . by performance of great sacrifices . . . and by large-scale temple worship.[22]

In the issues of the magazine *Back to Godhead*, there is a description of chanting.

> Hare Krsna, Hare Krsna, Krsna Krsna, Hare Hare Hare Rama, Hare Rama, Rama Rama, Hare Hare

What is a mantra? In Sanskrit, *man* means "mind" and *tra* means "freeing." So a mantra is a combination of transcendental sounds that frees our minds from the anxieties of living in the material world.

Ancient India's Vedic literatures single out one mantra as the maha (supreme) mantra. The Kalisantarana Upanishad explains, "These sixteen words—'Hare Krsna, Hare Krsna, Krsna Krsna, Hare Hare/Hare Rama, Hare Rama, Rama Rama, Hare Hare'—are especially meant for counteracting the ill effects of the present age of quarrel and anxiety."

The Naranda-pancaratra adds, "All mantras and all processes for self-realization are compressed into the Hare Krsna maha-mantra."

Five centuries ago, while spreading the maha-mantra through the Indian subcontinent, Sri Caintanya, Mahaprabhu prayed, "O Supreme Personality of Godhead, in Your name You have invested all Your transcendental energies."

The name Krsna means "the all-attractive one," the name Rama means "the all-pleasing one," and the name Hare is an address to the Lord's devotional energy.

So the maha-mantra means, "O all-attractive, all-pleasing Lord, O energy of the Lord, please engage me in Your devotional service." Chant Hare Krsna maha-mantra and your life will be sublime.[23]

Behind chanting there is the idea of a homology between sound and reality. Sounds can function as direct links to the sacred. One may experience God directly. The role of chanting in the Hare Krishna movement follows that of Caitanya, who chanted and danced in India. Some Hare Krishna devotees describe their chanting as "tasting" the words of the mantra; others describe experiencing the presence of Krishna.[24] Chanting appears to be one way, and for many

Hare Krishna the primary way, of expressing their devotion or bhakti to Krishna and attaining Krishna consciousness.

Worship patterns in the movement have become quite standardized across America since Prabhupada began his temples. The temple is the primary facility of the community for daily chanting, Bhagavad-Gita lectures and study, worship and care of the deities, and communal eating and living. One may note the temple centers, farms, and restaurants which Hare Krishna operate on many continents in each issue of *Back to Godhead*. Included in the temple environs are a temple proper, residential buildings, administrative offices, support facilities, and farming areas or industrial shops.

The Hare Krishna life-style is distinctive and austere, and the worship and devotion to Krishna are demanding and time-consuming. One devotee of the Hare Krishna described the initiation ceremonies, the worship, the life-style, and the regulations which govern the society. He stated that the initiation is a formal time when one vows to accept the spiritual master as one's spiritual guide. The master gives the devotee a name at that ceremony. Generally, these names have to do with being a servant of God. He accepts the master as his authority and promises to follow the rules of the society.

Vows are taken to observe five basic rules, four of which are prohibitions. (1) One refrains from eating meat, fish, and eggs. Hare Krishna are vegetarians. (2) One vows to engage in no illicit sex. One does not date before marriage. In marriage, sexual intercourse is only for the procreation of children. Each month the married couple comes together for purification rituals and chanting before engaging in intercourse. As a devotee says, "It is taken as sort of a sacrament to conceive a child." (3) Hare Krishna refrain from intoxicants and stimulants such as alcohol, hard drugs, cigarettes, coffee, and tea. (4) Gambling is prohibited. Gambling produces greed. (5) Chanting the name of Hare Krishna with beads is required. Chanting is done each morning with 108 beads. The mantra is recited 108 times which is called one round. This round is chanted sixteen times. This means some 25,000 names are chanted and may take two hours to complete.

These vows result in a radical change of life-style for the devotee. Both men and women wear cotton *dhotis* and *saris*. Men shave their hair, and women wear a head covering. Sometimes men leave a lock of hair, called the *sikha*, which enables Krishna to pull the devotees out of trouble. Personal belongings are given to the temple. A devotee explains that these changes are inaugurated to help one forget old identities and to prepare to receive real identity as a spirit soul of Krishna. "Our spiritual master designs our life in such a way as to give us the practical life-style so we can cultivate this consciousness of God in myself as eternal servant of God. And eventually we want to come to a stage where there is a twenty-four-hour meditation."

Members may live in the temple compound or outside. In order to live at the temple, however, one must follow the vows and take responsibilities for temple life. Those who live outside, both singles and married, may or may not follow the vows. There are different levels of commitment. The schedule at the temple begins early. The *arti*, or worship ceremony, begins about 4:30 A.M. Before the arti, one must have bathed. Bathing oneself several times each day is necessary for cleanliness in the temple.

Chanting the holy names of God and dancing before the deities are performed at the ceremony. This is community worship. Also, one must chant the two-hour meditation. Then, one worships the spiritual master. The devotee states that one worships the master "as one would worship God, as if God were personally present there. Because he is receiving worship as God's representative." A senior devotee offers a class on the *Bhagavad-Gita*. Breakfast is served about 8:30 A.M. There are varieties of activities for the devotees to perform. One of the full-time jobs is cooking for the deity and offering *prasadam*. Cooking is done six times a day. Cleaning, dressing, feeding, and sewing for the deities take much time.

Maintenance of the temple compound and grounds is assigned to devotees. Some garden and farm. Some go into the city to sell society books and magazines. Some lecture and speak with college students on various campuses. Some start new businesses and operate established ones. The devotees who live outside the temple grounds are expected to give as high as 50 percent of their earnings to the temple. A devotee says, "One thing is, we don't need a lot of money because we lead such a simple life. We don't go to movies, we don't go to restaurants, we don't drink, we don't smoke, we don't need fancy cars and big houses; we wear simple clothes, and I have on about three dollars worth of clothes. We can maintain ourselves very simply."

Other services in the temple include a noon and a 5:00 P.M. worship ceremony around the deities. Asian peoples often come to the evening service, bringing their gifts of food to the deities and offering flowers as they parade before the colorful and exquisite images of Krishna, Rama, and others. All are invited to eat prasadam, especially after the evening worship. The vegetarian foods offered to Krishna are shared by the temple community with any who are present.

Devotees band together from various temple communities to celebrate important festivities within the Hindu tradition. The first annual Ratha-yatra chariot festival was held in Washington, D.C., in 1982, attracting over twenty thousand. It commemorated the ancient chariot rides of Puri, India, in which the image of Jagannatha, Lord of the Universe, was carried. Lord Chaitanya, in his time, participated in the festival, chanting the names of Krishna. The procession of thousands walked from the Washington Monument to the Capitol. Marion Barry, Jr., mayor of the District of Columbia, declared August 21 Ratha-yatra Day.

The Krishna commune in Moundsville, West Virginia, built the ornate Palace of Gold, costing millions of dollars. It has become a tourist attraction with its marble floors, precast-cement scrollwork, stained glass, teak carvings from India, and fourteen-karat gold leaf. Hotels and restaurants have become a part of this new Vrndavana in a town of twelve thousand native West Virginians. One Krishna member described the temple or Palace of Gold as a future "spiritual Disneyland."[25] A goal of each Hare Krishna is to make a pilgrimage to Vrndavana, India, the place of appearance of Krishna in the *Bhagavad-Gita* and the place where Chaitanya and Prabhupada resided for some time.

Since the death of Prabhupada in 1977, the Society has faced challenges and transitions. A leading Hare Krishna reports, "Although Prabhupada's departure was certainly a blow to his disciples, and although his physical absence initiated an era of institutional and spiritual adjustment, the movement has survived and, on the whole, is prospering—its institutional integrity intact."[26]

By 1970 Prabhupada had established the Governing Body Commission (GBC) to administer the institutional and spiritual affairs of ISKON. Each member of the GBC was assigned a geographical territory. By 1977 the GBC had begun to function as a semiautonomous, democratic body. At the swami's death the commission changed to a fully autonomous body. "As far as spiritual leadership is concerned, the movement has had to adjust to a plurality of gurus, initially eleven, who assumed their preceptorial rule in order to perpetuate a long-standing disciplic lineage within Caitanya-Vaisnave tradition. These gurus comprised nearly one-half of the total GBC body, which had grown, by 1977, to about twenty-three members."[27]

An issue which has faced the Hare Krishna is the relationship of the GBC and the several gurus who give spiritual guidance, train, and initiate new devotees into the movement. Another issue is the relationship of the several gurus to Prabhupada, to their devotees, and the devotee's relationships to the gurus and also to Prabhupada. Traditionally, the guru has had absolute and autonomous authority over his disciples.

According to Hare Krishna leaders the movement has shown steady and sometimes dramatic growth. Four indicators are used to measure their growth: physical property holdings (overall number of branches), the publication and distribution of books, the rate of recruitment, and the types of influence in the public arena. In Europe it is reported that the number of ISKON centers, full-time members, and books distributed have tripled since 1977.

> The movement has purchased historic estates, chateaus, and villas some of which are famous landmarks . . . has established a number of large farm communities. . . . approximately eight million books distributed annually in every major European language.[28]

Devotees spread the word through gourmet vegetarian restaurants like "Healthy, Wealthy, and Wise" in Oxford Street in central London;

> through devotee-owned and operated radio stations such as Radio Krishna Centrale in Florence and Radio Atma in Paris, as well as a popular weekly all-night call-in show in Stockholm on a commercial station.[29]

In Great Britain, the Mahabharata Association, a brand of ISKON, publishes the *Mahabharata Times* with wide readership in Europe's resident Indian communities.

In Australia the devotee population and literature distribution have tripled. In Latin America, the number of ISKON centers has doubled with twenty communes in Brazil and a solid presence in fifteen other countries. Over twenty million Spanish-language books have been distributed throughout Latin America and the Caribbean. In India, the Society in 1978 dedicated its largest center:

> an extensive complex in Bombay consisting of a massive, ornate temple, a modern theatre for the performing arts, a restaurant, and a twin-tower luxury hotel.[30]

ISKON has initiated the building of temples in Vrndavana and preaching movements throughout villages and publications in ten major Indian languages. Hare Krishna are growing in other Asian countries as well as in Africa.

ISKON leaders admit that since 1977, North America is the only region which has not demonstrated growth. The number of centers has increased by seventeen while the total number of devotees has remained constant, balancing new members with dropouts. Literature distribution has decreased. Leaders attribute the most significant factor of lack of substantial growth in North America to negative press.

> In spite of these problems, however, the movement in America continues to attract new members, organizes successful, well-attended religious festivals (such as the annual Festival of the Chariots in Los Angeles which attracts more than 100,000), has launched a major cultural center in Detroit funded by devotee Alfred Ford (great-grandson of Henry), and has attracted much positive press coverage of its lavish "Palace of Gold," a temple dedicated to Prabhupada at New Vrindaban, the Society's three thousand acre village in the hills of West Virginia.[31]

There has also been internal dissension. Suits have been filed against Hare Krishna leadership by ex-members. The guru of the New Vrindaban in West Virginia was brought to trial and imprisoned for a murder plot and its execution. In many temple locations, there has been much dependence on friends of India for financial and community support. In general, the leadership has been challenged with second generation accommodations to American culture including education for their children, relations to other religions and politics, and responses to followers who live beyond the commune and temple grounds.

A recent development in ISKON has seen the increase in "laity," those who live and work outside the communes or *ashrams*, and who are committed in various degrees to the movement.

> This less formal membership has derived, in part, from the wide dissemination of ISKON literature over the years, and a persistent interest, among young people, especially, in yoga, meditation, vegetarianism, and Eastern philosophical concepts. The size of ISKON's new laity far exceeds that of its core membership. In a 1978 Gallup poll reporting on the religious affiliations of American teenagers, one percent of the sample claimed involvement in the Krishna movement, a proportion which projects to roughly half million young people, a figure more than one hundred times the actual core membership of ISKON in the United States. Even if a mere tenth of those who claimed to be affiliated factually are, the figures still represent more than ten times the total core membership of the movement. . . .[32]

The Hare Krishna movement is a part of a spiritual tradition within the greater context of Hinduism with roots deeply in the *Bhagavad-Gita* and formal ties to Lord Chaitanya and A. C. Bhaktivadanta Prabhupada. It has served since 1965 as an alternate religious tradition to Americans. Since the guru's death in 1977, the movement has faced challenges and transitions. Nevertheless, it appears to have grown in centers and members worldwide and continues to serve as an alternate religion. Within the various expressions of Hinduism, the Hare Krishna stress the supremacy of the personal nature of God,

> following the Vedic theistic philosophy that the most complete understanding of the Absolute Truth is personal. . . . the individual spiritual self is an eternal servant of the supreme spiritual being.[33]

As Prabhupada stated, "oneness, the philosophy of monism or pantheism, is imperfect. When that oneness comes in understanding Krsna, that is perfection."[34]

Prabhupada once said,

The boys and girls who are my students have been very scornful of the materialistic way of life. Their fathers and guardians are not poor. There is no scarcity of food or material enjoyments. Why are they being frustrated? You may say that because India is poverty-stricken the people are frustrated, but why have American boys and girls been frustrated? That is the proof that the materialistic way of life cannot make you happy. You may go on for some time trying to become happy, but happiness will never come from materialistic life. That is a fact.[35]

The guru often speaks words of wisdom. He raises ultimate questions. He evidently has appealed to thousands. The Hare Krishna movement has been in America for over twenty-five years. Christian perspectives on its concepts and practices will be presented at the conclusion of the chapter.

Transcendental Meditation

Thousands of Americans have paid millions of dollars to attend classes where they learned a form of meditation focusing on a mantra assigned particularly to themselves. Transcendental Meditation (TM) centers sprang up by the hundreds, and a college offered degrees informed by the philosophy of the movement. Controversy centered upon TM's leader and upon whether the movement was a religion. What is Transcendental Meditation and who is Maharishi Mahesh Yogi, its founder?

Maharishi Mahesh Yogi was born in northern India about 1918. He graduated from Allahabad University with a degree in physics in 1949. He pursued an intense study of the Hindu Vedic scriptures, including the *Upanishads* and the *Bhagavad-Gita*. He sought out famous gurus for study in the Himalayan mountains, learning Hindu philosophy and meditation practices, or Yoga. His most noted teacher was Guru Dev who followed the philosophy of Shankara, a seventh-century A.D. interpreter of the Vedic scriptures. After the death of Guru Dev and further periods of retreats in the forests of the Himalayas, Maharishi Mahesh Yogi emerged to proclaim his wisdom and Hindu spiritual tradition to his own people. India had its abundance of gurus, and by the late 1950s he was ready to launch his philosophy and meditation in more fertile fields like Europe and America. His name was to be popularized widely in the Western media. *Maharishi* means "Great Sage." *Yogi* means one who practices Yoga or one who is united with god. *Mahesh* is his family name.

By way of England, he arrived in California in 1959 and established a nonprofit religious organization, the Spiritual Regeneration Foundation. It offered people "spiritual growth, peace and happiness through a system of deep meditation."[36] By 1965 he had founded Student's International Meditation Society (SIMS), and centers for meditation were placed near university campuses. Maharishi, with his long gray hair, white beard, and twinkling eyes, attracted many celebrities to take up meditation. The Beatles, Mia Farrow, the Rolling Stones, Shirley MacLaine, and Joe Namath tried TM and gave Maharishi mass media coverage. TM, however, faced decline, and Maharishi returned to India to rethink and to reorganize his movement. By the late 1960s and early 1970s he was back in the West offering his meditation in a new version. He publicized TM as a science, not a religion, more in psychological and mental language than in spiritual terms.

Publicity for TM classes claimed that it

> can be learned easily and enjoyed by everyone; provides deep rest as a basis for dynamic action; improves clarity of perception; develops creative intelligence; expands awareness; insures full development of the individual in a natural way.[37]

Maharishi had determined through his earlier American failure to change his language and methods of presenting meditation. He wanted to prevent conflict in the religion-state relationship and to appeal to a wider audience and support group, including the federal and state governments.

Consequently, he obtained endorsements from state legislatures for his classes and texts to be a part of school systems and also received grants from the federal government. To the general public, Maharishi appealed and appeared as a scientific genius and mental therapist. To his trained teachers and disciples, he was a Hindu *guru* offering some of the most ancient spiritual philosophy and yoga of India.

The basic and most elementary component of TM is the offering of several classes by a disciple of Maharishi which lead to one's initiation and reception of a mantra. Some four hundred TM centers, meeting in rented quarters or public places across America, offer classes for a fee. The climax of the basic TM experience is the initiation ceremony. The candidate brings three fruits, six flowers, and a white cloth. Shoes are removed, and one enters a candlelit and incense-filled room. A picture of Guru Dev is placed strategically, before which one bows. The teacher recites the words of the ceremony, the *puja*, which basically is a Vedic hymn of worship. Among the words recited with their Sanskrit origins are offerings to Guru Dev, Brahma, Vishnu, Shiva, Krishna, and other gurus and Hindu deities.

The initiant is given his personal *mantra,* whispered by the teacher. This mantra is to be kept secret by the initiant. After this ceremony one is prepared to meditate on one's mantra for twenty minutes each morning and evening. One is asked to return to the teacher for several "checking" sessions to make certain one's technique of meditation is correctly performed. Besides the basic course in TM, there are other advanced courses with appropriate fees, retreats, video lectures, and mailouts.

On his second foray into the American scene and the revival of his TM movement, Maharishi launched his "World Plan." That plan included establishing universities, academies of science, and consultation services with world governments. In full-page advertisements in *Time* magazine, "His Holiness Maharishi Maheshi Yogi" is described as:

Founder of the Science of Creative Intelligence and the Technology of the United Field (1971-1982); Founder of Maharishi European Research University, Switzerland (1975), and Germany (1982); Founder of Maharishi University of Natural Law, England (1982); Founder of Maharishi International University, United States (1971); Founder of Maharishi Academy of Vedic Science, India (1980); and Founder of the World Government of the Age of Enlightenment (1976).[38]

Maharishi bought the defunct Parsons College, a Presbyterian school founded in 1875, located in Fairfield, Iowa, for $2.5 million and opened it in 1974 as Maharishi International University (MIU). Its enrollment is about seven hundred, and many of its students are TM initiants before they arrive. The first year's curriculum focuses on courses under the umbrella of the Science of Creative Intelligence (SCI) which the Maharishi developed. They include: Astronomy, Cosmology, and SCI—the Galactic Symphony of the Pulsating Universe; Physics and SCI—Quantum Models of Pure Consciousness; Western Philosophy and SCI—From Plato's Republic to Maharishi's World Plan; and Vedic Philosophy and SCI—The Sources, Course, and Goal of Knowledge from the Vedas to the Maharishi. Students may major in various fields and graduate with a B.A. or B.S. degree.

The TM movement's impact on the town and nine thousand townspeople in Fairfield has been significant. Many TM meditators, not directly associated with the college, have moved to Fairfield. Some three thousand meditators have opened businesses which employ over a thousand people. These meditators have added two thousand to the town's population. In the summer of 1984, seven thousand meditators flocked to the town and to MIU to jointly meditate for peace and prosperity around the world. The town faces challenges, both economically and culturally, from the TM movement's presence.[39]

Perhaps the most ambitious part of TM's "World Plan" is the World Government of the Age of Enlightenment. Maharishi believes that meditators can have a global impact upon change and can facilitate change with effective mass meditation. Seven thousand meditators, who came for simultaneous meditation at MIU, represented a number which is the square root of 1 percent of the world's population. Maharishi asserts that a preliminary study in 240 American cities showed that when 1 percent of the people practice TM, there is a 17 percent drop in crime. He claims there is a cause and effect relationship. Through his World Government of the Age of Enlightenment, he invites governments to allow his movement to solve their problems, regardless of their magnitude or nature—political, economic, social, or religious, and irrespective of the system—capitalism, communism, socialism, democracy, or dictatorship.

> The World Government of the Age of Enlightenment, a non-political, non-religious, global organization with the participation of the peoples of more than one hundred countries, does not usurp any of the functions of existing governments, nor does it replace them in any way.

> The World Government of the Age of Enlightenment enjoys sovereignty in the domain of consciousness, authority in the invincible power of natural law, and activity in the eternally dynamic silence of the unified field of all the forces of nature from where the infinite diversity of the universe is perfectly governed without a problem.

The unified field of all the laws of nature has been glimpsed by the supergravity theory of quantum physics, and its complete knowledge is available in the ancient Vedic literature as recently brought to light by Maharishi. Application of this beautifully complete knowledge of the functioning of nature has given rise to Maharishi's integrated systems of education, health, administration, defense, and rehabilitation. New principles and programs to enrich and glorify all areas of life of the individual and nation have opened a new horizon of perfection for life everywhere.

This practical knowledge is the basis of the World Government's invitation to all governments to rise to a new level of governing without problems. The Maharishi Technology of the Unified Field, applied to daily living, will enliven the evolutionary power of natural law to uphold life in all positive values—the individual will enjoy freedom from problems and suffering; every nation will enjoy integrated national consciousness, cultural integrity, self-sufficiency, and invincibility; and the whole family of nations will enjoy permanent world peace.[40]

Transcendental Meditation has grown from a guru and a few noted celebrity initiants to a reorganized movement encompassing hundreds of thousands of meditators, universities, land and business ventures, and bank accounts of millions of dollars. Reports are that Maharishi's worldwide assets total over $400 million, and TM's world government with its ten ministries and representatives in 140 countries spends some $15 million yearly to maintain its organizations.[41] Maharishi has forecast some 3,500 teacher-training centers and some 3.5 million teachers to reach the world's population with TM.

In the United States, TM has found favor not only among individuals taking meditation courses but also among public schools, the armed services, the federal government, and educational journals. The state department of education in New Jersey, for example, provided a TM course for select high schools with a text funded by the state and written by Maharishi International University. The United States Army has used TM in programs on alcoholism and drugs. The National Institute of Mental Health has funded programs for TM teachers. TM has been taught on over three hundred college campuses, often at government expense. The University itself receives considerable tax support. Leading publications such as the *Harvard Law Record* and the *Yale Alumni Magazine* have included articles of endorsement.

To understand the TM movement is to understand its founder. Besides the history of his life in India and his training in India's spiritual traditions, Maharishi has also provided his philosophy in books. They include *The Science of Being and Art of Living* (1963), *On the Bhagavad-Gita* (1969), and *Love and God* (1965). Basic to the guru's thought is that "Expansion of happiness is the purpose of life, and evolution is the process through which it is fulfilled. . . . The purpose of individual life is also the purpose of the life of the entire cosmos. The purpose of creation is expansion of happiness which is fulfilled through the process of cosmic evolution."[42] He speaks of God as "Absolute Being" on one hand and as "Creative Intelligence" on the other hand. He also writes about God, "I am That, Thou art That, all this is That, That alone is, and there is nothing else but That."[43] Maharishi writes of karma, reincarnation, and transmigration of the soul.

With regard to religions he asserts,

> Because none of the scriptures of religion describe or teach TM, the effectiveness of religions in general has declined worldwide. The true spirit of religion is lacking when it counts only what is right and wrong and creates fear of punishment and hell, and the fear of God in the mind of men. The purpose of religion should be to take away all fear from man.[44]

He thus advocates the simple meditation practice twice a day of reciting one's secret mantra to achieve happiness, prosperity, and peace.

Maharishi Mahesh Yogi is forming a partnership with Doug Henning, the professional magician and TM advocate, to build a theme park in Central Florida near Disney World which will cost one billion dollars. The park will be named Vedaland, and its themes will be enlightenment, knowledge, and entertainment. The park is expected to cover 450 acres, will feature a five hundred room hotel and thirty-six attractions, including a time tunnel ride, a dive into the subatomic spaces of a DNA molecule, and a building that "levitates" fifteen feet above a pool of water.

Transcendental Meditation has impacted American culture as an alternative religious experience. It offers opportunities for individual practice rather than communities or communes of group worship. In recent times, however, the trend has developed for groups to worship simultaneously to bring change to the world. TM has brought controversy over whether it is a religion or a science, and legal action has been taken by groups who contend it is a religion under false guise. Maharishi has challenged Christianity with his negative statements on Jesus' suffering and on his interpretations of God, reality, and the world. Further consideration of Christian perspectives upon TM will be given at the conclusion of the chapter.

Bhagwan Shree Rajneesh

The small town of Antelope, Oregon, two hundred miles from Portland, was the center of attention of a guru from Poona, India. Antelope also was a seedbed of controversy between townspeople and Rajneesh's followers, who by the thousands descended upon the town and its environs. Who was Rajneesh? What kind of guru was he? What were his followers like?

Born Rajneesh Chandra Mohan in 1931 in central India, he died in 1990. He taught philosophy at Jabalpur University, and left that post about 1966 to pursue his own philosophical studies and meditation techniques. Sometime thereafter he changed his name to Bhagwan Shree Rajneesh. *Bhagwan* means god, and *Shree* is a title of respect to great teachers. He became, according to guru tradition, one of humankind's great enlightened ones. In 1969 he founded his ashram in Bombay and was active in Poona from 1974 to 1981.

Some attention has been given by scholars to tracing Rajneesh's connection with Western thought and Western groups which eventually led to his arrival in the United

States in 1981. "Human growth centers," demonstrating a blend of Western psychology and Eastern wisdom, grew up in the 1960s in California and attracted people like Alan Watts and Baba Ram Dass (formerly Dr. Richard Alpert, the former associate of Dr. Timothy Leary of LSD fame). In Europe "human growth centers" appeared in which the name of Rajneesh was mentioned. From these centers and also from those adherents of this kind of Western-Eastern blending of psychology, philosophy, and techniques of altering consciousness, people traveled to Bombay and then to Poona to sit at the feet of Rajneesh. During the 1970s his ashram became quite Westernized and thus less attractive to indigenous Indians.[45]

His ashram in Poona had begun to attract about fifty thousand Americans and Europeans yearly. He gave philosophical lectures. He taught his techniques of meditation. These techniques included *tantric yoga* (the use of sexual intercourse to achieve divine consciousness), Zen, dancing, and acupuncture. Rajneesh experienced mounting problems with local government officials, citizens, and tax matters. In June 1981, he was admitted into the United States on a temporary visa. Soon thereafter, he purchased a 63,229-acre ranch near Antelope, Oregon, for some $6 million; the ranch served as his world headquarters. His newly incorporated city, Rajneeshpuram, meaning "essence of Rajneesh," included some 2,100 acres and was home to about twelve-hundred permanent devotees.[46]

Gary Leazer reported in his article, "Bhagwan," that,

> A 1983 survey found disciples of Rajneeshpuram averaged 34 years of age; most were well-educated, one-third had advanced degrees. Most were from large cities and had been disciples for over three years. Three-fourths were married, but nearly one-fourth of those were not living with their spouses. Previous affiliations were about one-third Protestant, one-fourth Roman Catholic, one-fifth Jewish; the rest claimed no affiliation. One-half said their political background was lib-

eral; slightly more than half were women. Most were
white Americans.[47]

Plans were to have some 10,000 devotees living at
Rajneeshpuram. The devotees, called *sannyasi*, worked for
their lodging and food and the opportunity to practice meditation near the Bhagwan himself. Rajneesh claimed over
one-quarter million followers worldwide and some four thousand in the United States. He had buses bring the unem-
ployed and street people from California to give them food
and work and to provide the opportunity for them to see his
emerging city.

What were the basic foundations for Rajneesh's teaching
and practices?[48] His world view is monistic, and he teaches
that there is one energy called bioenergy. It may be
described as life, love, or light. In meditation, one experiences this bioenergy. The phases of the dance meditation
carry one through extreme physical exertion to ecstasy to
complete rest. As one contemplates one's inner life, one
may distance oneself from it. To become neutral, unin-
volved, or impartially observing is to become truly aware.
Rajneesh teaches that people have their energy perverted or
deformed by religious prejudices and social pressures. He
recommends tantric yoga to overcome inhibitions and allow
energy to flow. Spirituality and sexuality are two ends of the
same energy. Man and woman mutually surrender as in the
relation of master and pupil.

His role was not like that of a classical understanding of a
guru. His followers honored him in the Rajneesh centers on
his birthday, the day of his enlightenment, and the feast of
the full moon. His personal contact with his followers was
minimal. The master or enlightened one was the object of
that surrender which enabled one to overcome the ego. The
master's voice became one's inner voice. Trust was essential. His use of the sacred scriptures of religious traditions,
namely, the Taoist writings, the Buddhist *Vsutras* and Zen,
the Hindu *Upanishads* and tantric writings, and Sufi materials indicated his mysticism. He became the "I am the way"

and related to his followers as Buddha or Jesus related to their own.

Rajneesh taught that one's statements must be founded on experience alone. He rejected any demands for faith. He was the enlightened one, and others aspired to enlightenment through him. As one scholar has written,

> He has succeeded in satisfying equally such disparate needs as that for psychological relief and enrichment, that of the religious experience of being dissolved into oneness with the ground of all being, and that for the attainment of esoteric secret knowledge. He has succeeded in presenting himself in the role of the psychological healer, the religiously enlightened one, and the great initiate and adept. The boundaries between the different roles are fluid, and equally fluid are the distinctions among his followers.[49]

To have become a sannyasin, or initiated devotee to Rajneesh, one had to pass through a ceremony and vow certain principles and practices. One vowed loyalty to Bhagwan and carried his picture in a locket. A red or orange outer garment and a necklace of 108 beads was worn. A Hindu name was given, and one had to be a vegetarian and practice meditation daily. Two group activities were necessary. The *satsang* was a spiritual discourse usually held in the presence of Rajneesh. When Rajneesh took his vow of silence in 1981, however, the satsang was composed of readings from his many works. A second group activity was dynamic meditation which involved activities of jumping, screaming, and sometimes the removal of clothes.

The first annual world celebration was held at Rajneeshpuram in July of 1982.[50] Many of the twelve thousand devotees and friends of Rajneesh came from Europe on chartered flights to attend the five-day meet. A satsang was held each morning at eight o'clock. Rajneesh would arrive in one of his purported twenty-seven Rolls Royces surrounded by his admirers. He sat on a large reclining chair on the raised platform in the Buddha hall, in silence and with his eyes closed. He had taken a vow of silence in April of 1981. After someone read from his discourses, he would depart to the crowd's cheers. On the last morning, followers joined him on the platform, falling at his feet and kissing them. After each satsang an initiation ceremony was held by Rajneesh's assistants with two hundred to three hundred initiants each day taking the vows to wear the new clothes, the necklace of 108 beads, to assume the new name, and to perform daily meditation.

Five stages of dynamic meditation were held in the hall after each initiation ceremony. All participants were blindfolded or were requested to close their eyes. The first stage involved hyperventilating. The second was primal screaming, which consisted of shouting, beating the floor, and body contact. The third stage was jumping with hands above heads. The fourth stage was freezing, standing absolutely still when the music stopped. The fifth stage was celebration, a relaxation with the flow of music. Most meditations cost $100 in addition to the admission fee of $400 for the five-day meet.

There were some two thousand tents which served as sleeping quarters, with four persons to a tent. "Continual announcements over the loudspeaker reminded the sannyasins that tents were the only place where free and open sex could take place."[51] One tent housed a boutique which sold Rajneesh's 360 books, 150 videotapes, 1,500 cassette tapes, posters, coffee mugs, paperweights, yo-yos, and frisbees with Rajneesh's picture. In the evenings devotees danced before Rajneesh in the hall and then had an enormous banquet of fruits and vegetables. The entire meeting was organized and managed well, from sanitation to food to impeccably manicured grounds.

Rajneesh broke his three-year silence in October of 1984. Reports are that his personal secretary, Ma Anand Sheela, approached him on behalf of the press when he was on his daily drive around Rajneeshpuram. The press wanted to know why he called his movement a religion. Rajneesh responded, "Tell those guys this is the only religion. Christianity has failed. I say to you this is the first religion and perhaps the last religion."[52] The devotees of Rajneesh controlled the Antelope city council and the school district. Plans were underway to continue purchasing available land. Controversy continued between the townspeople and the newcomers. Legal suits were impending. Ma Prem Isabel, a spokesperson for the guru, vowed that Rajneesh and his devotees would fight for their rights and for justice.

By 1985 Rajneesh had been interviewed on television and quoted in newspapers that his top leaders had been involved in poisoning restaurant food, in setting fire to government offices, in tapping phones, and in attempting to murder the guru's doctor and dentist. Among those alleged leaders was Ma Anand Sheela, his outspoken personal secretary, who supposedly left Rajneeshpuram for Europe. Rajneesh had accused the leaders of leaving his movement $55 million in debt. Law enforcement officials began to pursue the allegations.[53]

Rajneesh was caught attempting to flee the United States, and he was imprisoned amidst the scandal of the Antelope, Oregon, affair. The organization's leaders had embezzled large sums of money and had plotted the murders of uncooperative members and even Rajneesh himself. Rajneesh was deported to India, where he revamped his movement. His movement in America was in disarray.

Golden Lotus Temple and Gandhi Memorial Center

In Washington, D.C., on Western Avenue is the Golden Lotus Temple, known as the Self-Revelation Church of Absolute Monism. Adjacent to it are its church-school building and the Gandhi Memorial Center. Also on its grounds are residential quarters and a printing press. Each Sunday morning at eleven o'clock there is a worship service of prayers, hymns, offering, and discourse led by its minister and swami. The children have church school, studying the founders and the spiritual traditions of the world's religions.

Who began the temple and the center? What are their purposes? How do they represent the Hindu tradition?

In 1928 Swami Premananda came to the United States from India. His guru had been Swami Yogananda Paramhansa, who had represented India at the Congress of Religions in Boston in 1920. Swami Premananda began his classes of philosophy and meditation in the Washington, D.C., area.

> The Golden Lotus Temple of the Self-Revelation Church of Washington, D.C. was designed and built by Swami Premananda. The cornerstone of this most distinctive edifice was laid by the Grand Master of Masons in the District of Columbia, assisted by the officers of the Grand Lodge, on May 17, 1952. This was the first time in the history of Masonry and religion that a Grand Master laid the cornerstone of a house of worship of which a Swami is the minister. Upon the completion of the Golden Lotus Temple the first service was held on November 23, 1952.[54]

In 1959 Swami Premananda founded the Mahatma Gandhi Memorial Foundation, and in 1976 the Gandhi Memorial Center was dedicated. After the dedication the Swami retired to a farm sixty miles from Washington. He not only founded the temple-church and the center, but he also authored over thirty books on Advaita Vedanta, including translations of the *Bhagavad-Gita*, *Dhammapada* (from the Pali language), and eleven of the thirteen principal *Upanishads*. "He is the only Swami in the world coronated a 33rd Degree Scottish Rite Mason."[55] To continue his disciplic succession, he founded the "Swami Order of Absolute Monism."

> In order to assure the continuity of the philosophy of Advaita Vedanta, Swami Premananda has established the Swami Order of Absolute Monism in the United States of America. Open to both men and women, married and unmarried, its purpose is to inspire the life of spiritual ministry. Membership in the Swami Order is

identification with and life guided by the idealism of the Swami Order as founded by Swami Sankarachariya of India in the 8th century A.D.[56]

His successor is Srimati Kamala. She was initiated by Swami Premananda and ordained a minister of the Swami Order by him in 1973. Since 1975 she has served as minister of the temple-church and as director of the Gandhi Memorial Center. She was consecrated as a swami by Swami Premananda in 1978. Kamala, nee Sally Slack, was born in Madison, Wisconsin. Her father was vice-president of Phillips Petroleum Company. She graduated in 1968 from Saint Lawrence University, majoring in philosophy, language, and literature. She studied in Paris at Cite Universitaire and at the University of Rouen where she received the National First- and Second-Degree Certificates.

Raised in an affluent family with a Unitarian background, she had been interested in philosophy and religion. Visiting the temple-church, she met Swami Premananda and decided to study with him.

> I was always groping. Even as a child, I bought my own Bible and would set up an altar and have my own prayers under a tree. It just gave me great joy and was something special and sacred to me.[57]

The swami sent her to earn her master's degree in special education from the University of Maryland. She taught in the fashionable schools of suburban Washington and in a ghetto school of the inner city. After years of living on the grounds of the temple and of study with the swami, she was ordained a minister and consecrated as a swami. After Premananda's retirement, she became the administrative president of the Mahatma Gandhi Memorial Foundation and the director of the Gandhi Memorial Center. In addition, she is the full-time minister of the Self-Revelation Church of Absolute Monism.

Kamala has visited India and the institutions inspired and established by Mahatma Gandhi. She has received numerous awards for her efforts in fostering the cultural and spiritual heritage of India in North America. She is a founding member of the new council for Indo-U.S. Relations formed to evaluate the interaction between India and the U.S.

The administration of the Gandhi Memorial Center is separate and distinct from that of the temple-church. The church centers its activities around Sunday morning worship, the church of the children, special lectures, and community life. A Sunday worship bulletin states that the church promotes a nonsectarian philosophic religious service and Sunday School. The church's ideal is:

> Every man is essentially divine. Man is the divine self. The ideal of human existence is the recognition of man's spiritual self. Religion is the realization of man's divine nature, otherwise called self-realization. When man realizes his true self, spirituality guides his daily life and conduct. Life guided by spiritual vision insures inner contentment and world peace.[58]

In 1944 the church founded an India Mission located on 120 acres in West Bengal. The services of the Mission include free school, vocational school and teachers' training college, medical clinic, emergency relief, and other charitable services to the community. In each Sunday worship service the church states in unison its belief with the following words from the bulletin, "I am an Absolute Monist. I believe:"

> Truth is one; men call it by various names.

> God, Brahman, is Consciousness-Existence-Bliss Absolute. Everything is the manifestation of God, the Divine Reality. The soul of man is of identical nature with the God of the universe. Realize thyself. By the realization of one's own self, the absolute Self is realized.

> God is the light of the heavens and the earth.

> He who realizes God becomes one with God.

> I am that I Am.

I and my Father are one.

I am Brahman, the absolute Self.[59]

A Kriya Meditation Series may be offered in the church for seven consecutive Wednesday evenings. The topics addressed by Kamala are as follows:

The Metaphysics of Meditation

Karma: The Law of self-manifestation and self-unfoldment

Atma-Jnan (Self-Knowledge)

The way and the ideal of life

Mind: The Key to realization

The Heart of the Mystic

Cycles of Infinite Perfection

The Breath of Life (Hong Swa)

Aum: The Symbol of the Absolute

The mystic word and ritual

Light on Kriya

Sound and Light at the Seven Mystic Centers.[60]

As director of the Gandhi Memorial Center, Kamala organizes and directs a group of some fifty workers, including about twenty residents who maintain its activities and services. The Center has a library of three thousand volumes, representing the life and ideals of Mahatma Gandhi and the cultural and spiritual heritage of India. There is a hall where meetings for films, lectures, and programs presenting Gandhi's life and India's cultural heritage are held. There is a graphics studio where composition work for publication is produced. A printing press and a book bindery are located in a nearby building. Classes in Indian classical dance and music are offered as a benevolent project for a scholarship for a deserving student in India. All programs at the Center are open to the public free of charge, and all work at the

Gandhi Center is rendered by workers who serve year-round with no remuneration (honoring Gandhi's own avowed solicitation of neither funds nor co-workers).

The Center offers a correspondence course on the life and message of Mahatma Gandhi in conjunction with Gujarat Vidyapith, the university founded in India by Gandhi in 1920. The Center has prepared a large photographic display of over sixty (two-by-four-feet) panels on Gandhi which it loans to schools and civic groups. Recently it began the New Age Montessori School located on the grounds. The school is a state-certified private institution for children two-and-a-half to six years.

Swami Kamala presides over a tradition and a community with roots in a guru's lineage back to the seventh century A.D. and an American root back to 1928. Membership and donations are not required. Seventy percent of the worshipers are Americans, racially and culturally mixed. One is a retired head of the FBI, another a retired English professor, and another an engineer who has his own corporation. There is a trust lawyer and a vice-president of a large bank as well as a man who has his own trash collecting company. Twenty percent of the congregation is Indian. Kamala leads her community in singing "Abide With Me," in praying the Lord's Prayer, in recitations from the Bible, the *Upanishads, Bhagavad-Gita,* and in lectures and discussions on yoga. She serves as a Gandhian gadfly to the American public. She and her community offer their expressions of Hinduism in America.

A Christian Perspective on Hindu Peoples

This study has offered Hinduism in the United States as a complexity, as a diversity, and as a variety of religious experiences. While one Hindu may appear atheistic and another agnostic, others may seek truth, God, or the deities through offerings, meditations, and various devotional statements and practices. One will want to be sensitive to the particular Hindu or follower of his/her spiritual tradition, and to learn of that person's religious experience. One does not encounter Hinduism but persons who claim components of Indian spirituality. There are obvious differences among the Hare Krishna, Transcendental Meditation adherents, Rajneesh and his devotees, and the Golden Lotus Temple and Gandhi Memorial Center.

Nevertheless, one should be aware of general orientations in the great body of Hindu thought and ritual. Hinduism stresses the universal and speaks of the Absolute, Brahman, and the world soul. It moves from monistic to theistic philosophies about the ultimate, being, and essence. It speaks of the world as illusion. It points to the great dilemma of humankind as ignorance and offers ways of salvation or liberation through temple ceremonies, knowledge, meditation, and devotion. History also becomes illusory, absorbed into the idea of timelessness. Individual souls are reborn in cycles until such a liberating process has occurred and the individual soul is absorbed into the great soul. Often this is the negative evaluation of the world and the desire to escape it. There tends to be the assumption of the identity of divine and human or the nonseparation of the two. A primary goal, therefore, is not necessarily the worship of God and personal communication with God, but it is self-realization or the understanding and affirmation that finally there is no difference between the individual self and God.

A Christian view understands God to be supremely personal as well as absolute. God has created humankind for dialogue and communion with Him. Humankind is made in God's image. Humankind, however, does not become God. We are granted participation in God's life which is given and communion with Him. Creation is by and from God, and humankind, as expressions of that creation, is distinct from God. The human dilemma does not rest alone in ignorance and enlightenment; but it rests in humankind's willful rebellion against God and the sin against God's will, love, and creation. Creation and the world are real, not illusory, nor is the consuming goal of life to escape the world. History is the arena in which life is lived under God and in relation to the welfare of humankind. The Christian clue to understanding the nature of God, creation, and salvation and reconciliation is found in Jesus Christ. The nature, love, will, and salvation of God are revealed uniquely in creation and in history in the incarnation, life, teachings, death, and resurrection of Jesus Christ. For the Christian, Jesus Christ as revealed in the Bible, as experienced personally, and as witnessed in the Christian church and throughout history, is the Way for life and salvation, as well as the Giver of salvation.

Hinduism tends to be inclusive and tolerant of varying religious concepts and practices. The Bible may be used to express and conform to the ancient Vedic scriptures of truth and reality. Jesus Christ and His sayings may be seen in the same lineage of the appearance of other great souls in Hindu scriptures. Christian symbols such as the cross may be assimilated in temple ceremonies. Hindu spiritual traditions, however, remain authoritative in establishing the hermeneutics of Christian symbols and teachings and rely on the gurus and swamis as authoritative voices. A Christian view is inclusive as it affirms the truths of God in creation and in human history. That view is exclusive as it is based on belief and faith in the revelation of God in nature and history with criteria and norms from the biblical tradition, Jesus Christ, and the teachings and practices of the church.

A Christian may appreciate orientations within the Hindu tradition on a spiritual search, on the meaningfulness of the inner life and the disciplines for its maturity and growth, and a critical examination of the world. One may also examine and value the teachings of Mahatma Gandhi and their effect upon bringing change to the social classes of India, namely the caste, and to India at large. Hindus who have accepted Jesus Christ as Lord and Savior have added a dimension of Jesus' social teachings to their backgrounds as well as an understanding of Jesus Christ as the selfless one who brought God to persons and thus introduced persons to God.

A Christian may be concerned with the four Hindu spiritual traditions presented in this chapter and with the persons associated with them in America as well as in India. The Hare Krishna tend to offer a critique of the materialistic and antispiritual (Kali-yuga) age. Their temples traditionally have been simplistic and austere. They have attempted to remain faithful to indigenous Indian cultural values and forms. One may ask about the opulence and the entrepreneurship associated with the "Palace of Gold" temple in West Virginia. How does this example fit with the Hare Krishna's previous call for self-sacrifice? Does Krishna demand this expression in West Virginia as devotion? One may appreciate the Hare Krishna emphasis upon nature, natural foods, and the simplistic life-style while raising questions of their idea of Krishna being everywhere and in everything, a part and parcel of all. Although Prabhupada says otherwise, is this a form of pantheism? One may also wonder, even with the Hare Krishna, of the question of disciplic succession after the death of their founder of the American movement, Prabhupada. Will there be one guru to whom all others give loyalty, or will there be several? The Hare Krishna worship Krishna as Lord, and also make worship to their spiritual guru. They find their source of scriptural inspiration and authority in the *Bhagavad-Gita*. American Hare Krishna who have had Christian backgrounds often bring their Christian beliefs and practices and fit them into the Krishna world view and ceremonies.

The Transcendental Meditation movement, under Maharishi Mahesh Yogi, offers varying Hindu traditions of guru worship, secret mantras, levitation, and meditation. Rajneesh also provides guru worship, ecstasy in song and dance, sex in meditation practices, and communal living. Both of these movement's teachings and practices, often offering pop psychology and instant therapy, blend ancient Hindu texts and traditions of yoga with popularized techniques appealing to American culture. Some Americans are ripe for hope, are involved in spiritual search, are feeling alienated, and are prepared to contribute to the guru's coffers.

The Golden Lotus Temple presents a philosophical tradition of the Vedanta adapted to Western concepts and practices, especially those of American society. Its view of absolute monism qualifies its approach of nondualism as advocated by the Shankara school of thought. The Christian view, as stated above, would encounter this Hindu philosophy and mysticism. The Gandhi Memorial Center preserves and presents the impact of the life and teachings of Mahatma Gandhi. The Temple and the Center state their philosophies and traditions clearly, precisely, and noncommercially. The dedication of the residents who live on the grounds and work in their vocations full time and who nevertheless give their time and energies freely to the work of the Gandhi Center can be appreciated.

There is a profundity about Hinduism. Yet there is a simplicity, too. A Hindu is on a spiritual search. Someone asked, "How do you communicate your Christian faith and experience to a Hindu?" Perhaps a Christian may respond, "I communicate out of my knowledge and experience and community of faith to another person who may be a pilgrim in spiritual search." The apostle Paul, in the midst of various religious philosophies and traditions, because he felt commissioned by God to be in the midst, told persons that he saw them as very religious. He then shared his faith.

7

BUDDHISM IN AMERICA

■ ▬▬▬▬▬▬▬▬▬▬▬▬▬▬▬▬▬▬ ■

Introduction

India is the birthplace of Buddhism, and Siddhartha Gautama, popularly known as the Buddha, its founder. Born about 560 B.C., the Buddha was a contemporary of Confucius in China, Zoroaster in Persia, and Ezekiel in Palestine. In the India of Buddha's birth, Hinduism had already been the major spiritual tradition for centuries. The *Vedic* and *Upanishad* scriptural traditions were available. Hindu teachings on the gods, the soul, *karma*, rebirth, transmigration, and the *dharma* were evident. The classic stages of the life of student, householder, forest dweller, and holy person *(sannyasin* or *arhat)* were known, and the caste system was a reality of the social order. Buddha faced the issues within Hinduism and became a reformer of it and a founder of his own movement; Buddha became the enlightened one. That is the meaning of his name.

Gautama was born into an affluent family. Tradition holds that his father desired him to be a king. He gave his son all the amenities of life and attempted to shield him from unpleasantries and evils. Guatama had a wife and a child; however, he was restless. He began his search for deeper meanings of life. It is reported that four sights caused him

241

concern and questioning. He saw (1) an old man, (2) a sick man, (3) a corpse, and (4) a holy man. Aging, sickness, and death distressed him; and the sannyasin intrigued him.

> Consequently, he left his family to begin a life of spiritual pilgrimage in the forests. He became a student of Hindu gurus. He meditated upon Hindu philosophy. He followed the strict discipline of an ascetic life, often in self-flagellation. There was no satisfaction in his quest for the Hindu holy life.[1]

Gautama had become an agnostic with reference to the existence of the gods. He did not accept the Hindu teachings on the souls (Brahman-Atman), and he rejected the concept and the practice of the caste system. He had left home, family, the good life, and a promising future. He had intensely explored the concepts and practices and life-style of Hinduism and found them wanting. There was no guru, no community, and no meaning. Gautama accepted the Hindu ideas of karma (one's good and bad actions) and transmigration. He taught that the individual is composed of skandas, described as predispositions or psychological forces. The skandas are like atoms, but they are not eternal. They serve as the means by which karma is transferred from one rebirth to another. The skandas are body, sensation, perception, volition, and consciousness. There is no permanence in the self or the skandas.

Gautama came to his enlightenment while seated in meditation beneath the Bodhi Tree (tree of wisdom). He became known as Buddha, the enlightened or awakened one. His enlightenment included his teachings on the Four Noble Truths and the Eightfold Path. The Truths served as the core of the Buddha's world view, and the Path indicated the way to live ethically and to attain enlightenment.

The first truth posits the universal human experience of suffering (dukkha). There is physical, emotional, and mental suffering which results from past karma. All life is suffering. The second truth is that the cause of suffering is desire or craving *(tanha)*. The third truth is that suffering can be overcome by ceasing to desire. The fourth truth teaches that the Eightfold Path provides the solution for suffering.

> Birth is suffering. Decay is suffering. Illness is suffering. Death is suffering. The presence of objects we hate is suffering. The separation from objects we love is suffering. Not to obtain what we desire is suffering. Everything from A to Z is suffering. The Buddha issued a judgment upon all of life and rejected the current ways of answering the dilemmas of life.[2]

The Eightfold Path is the answer to suffering. The individual, through knowledge, correct living, and meditation, may become enlightened, may obtain the Buddha-Mind, and may become Buddha. Of course, one must understand the causes of suffering *(dukkha)*. One must know of everything's impermanence *(anicca)* and that there is constant change in phenomena and existence. And one must be aware there is no soul or ego *(anatta)* and that this world has no substantial reality. There is ignorance *(avidya)*, and the goal of life is to become enlightened and attain *Nirvana*. Deities do not help. There are no prayers to deities. The individual through self-reliance attains enlightenment. A path is there for one to follow.

The Buddha taught The Eightfold Path, which includes three divisions or patterns of living—right beliefs or resolves, moral life, and the mystical or meditative life. Right beliefs have their foundation in understanding the Four Noble Truths. One takes an oath to resolve the wheel of becoming (birth and rebirth) and eliminate sensuality, craving, and malice. Both the understanding and the will are affected by correct belief and resolve. The next stage in the Path is the moral life. Morality is involved with right speech, right conduct, and right occupation. A proper Buddhist refrains from rumors, stealing, and violence toward all creatures. The ideal is celibacy. The third component of the Path is concerned with the life of meditation and right-mindfulness and composure. One roots out attachment to physical objects and distractions of the world and focuses on good qualities. Meditation includes postures, exercises, and trances (dhya-nas) and lifts one into serenity of body and mind and above both joy and suffering. In this final stage of meditation, one has achieved enlightenment and is ready for nirvana.

The Buddha advocated the principles and practices of the truths or laws (dharma) he experienced in the context of a middle way. He counseled neither the hedonistic nor the ascetic life. One was to eat moderately and to refrain from frivolous activities. He did ask his disciples to take a vow to Buddha (enlightenment), to Dharma (truth), and to Sangha (monastery).

To become a monk was to choose the ideal life, but also there was room for the laity who supported the monks and the monastery. Whereas the laity could achieve a portion of the Eightfold Path, only the monk could have the time and the disposition to complete the Path. A discrepancy developed between the monks and the laity. The idea developed that the laity supported the monks, and in return through their meritorious service, the monks were able to bless them. The monk gains good karma by renouncing the world, and the laity merit good karma by assisting the monks. The goal of life is Nirvana, which means extinction or the cessation of birth and rebirth. The Buddha was not concerned to define or describe Nirvana. He refused to speculate about life after death.

India with its temples to deities and caste system did not readily accept Buddha and his followers. Buddhism built its monasteries, emphasized the life of the monk, the teachings of Buddha, and the laity's meritorious support. This form of Buddhism became known as Theravada, the way of the elders. It sometimes has been referred to as Hinayana, meaning "the little wheel." Its major scriptural tradition is the Tripitaka. The Theravada tradition claims to be the correct teaching of the Buddha, and it has been the primary Buddhist expression in India, Burma, and Thailand.

As Buddhism migrated to China, Korea, and Japan, it encountered other religious traditions, and adaptations occurred. A new and major Buddhist tradition developed known as Mahayana. The Mahayana:

> were willing to move beyond considering the monk as the only religious elite and beyond the monastery. They appealed to more people and became missionaries to other lands. They looked upon themselves as a universal religion. And the Mahayana interpreted and transformed the Buddha into a divine being of personal nature and transcendence. The Buddha became like a god. Others could become like him. These transcendent divine beings offered more than a way of enlightenment. They offered grace to those who would have faith in them and give them devotion.[3]

The idea of Bodhisattva emerged and meant one who had attained enlightenment but who remained in the world to help others. The Mahayana scriptures, called *satras*, included diverse writings like the *Lotus of the True Law*, the *Discourses on the Perfection of Wisdom*, and the famous *Heart Sutra* and *Diamond Cutter Sutra*. These texts stress the infinite and universal nature of Buddha.

Buddhism developed into two major traditions. The *Theravada tradition* emphasized the Buddha as a great teacher and a saint. The monk sought enlightenment through study and meditation of the Buddha's teachings. Laity depended on the monks for supplementing their progress toward enlightenment. The key virtue was wisdom, and meditation by individual effort was the highest means toward Nirvana. On the other hand, the *Mahayana tradition* perceived the Buddha as transcendent and divine. He became more than teacher or saint. He became savior. Other special individuals could partake of his nature and become Buddhas or *Bodhisattvas*. A key virtue became compassion, and Buddhists became more dependent on special Buddhas for salvation than upon their own efforts.

Outside of India, Buddhism became a migratory and missionary religion as it grew in China, Korea, and Japan. South and Southeast Asia welcomed its teachings and practices. It adapted to and incorporated some of the aspects of ancestral traditions, Confucianism, and Taoism in China; some of the native religious traditions of Korea; and some of the ancestral traditions and Shintoism of Japan. Ch'an Buddhism in China became Zen in Japan. Soka Gakkai in Japan became Nichiren Shoshu in America.

Through Chinese immigrations to the West Coast in the 1840s, Buddhism had initial entry into the United States. Temples were constructed in San Francisco. Earlier, Buddhism had migrated to Hawaii which became an American possession in 1898 and in 1959 a state with great Buddhist influence. When the World Parliament of Religions met in Chicago in 1893, several Zen Buddhists were among noted spokespersons of the major world religion communities. Zen Buddhist masters returned in the early 1920s to inaugurate Zen Centers. Perhaps the most noted Zen Buddhist in America has been D. T. Suzuki of Japan. Through his writings, lectures, and students, Zen became widely known across America after the 1950s. His teachings and his presence in America attracted followers like Christmas Humphreys, Edward Conze, and Alan Watts.

Zen Buddhism became the most noted form of Buddhism in America. Zen meditation centers were established early in San Francisco and Los Angeles, and other centers spread across the country. Philip Kapleau traveled to Japan to study under Zen masters, returned to establish the Zen center in Rochester, New York, and to publish *Three Pillars of Zen*. Kapleau was the pioneer in Americanizing Zen. "Beat Zen" promoted by Jack Kerouac and Allen Ginsberg in the 1950s merged the beat culture with Zen teachings and techniques into a pop culture expression. Alan Watts, through his writings, introduced Zen to Americans as an intellectual and meditative possibility.

Other forms and sectarian expressions of Buddhism appeared in America during World War II and especially after the Korean War and the Vietnam experience. Inter-marriages, immigrations, and curiosity and interest about the Orient brought Buddhists and Buddhism more into the cultural stream. The Buddhist Churches of America (BCA) were formed in 1942. These churches are a part of the Jodo Shinshu movement and claim over 100,000 members. The Soka Gakkai came from Japan in the 1960s with appeal to Japanese Americans. They promised health, happiness, and success to those who chanted the magical formula to the Lotus Sutra. Soon, Soka Gakkai directed their Buddhist faith and practice to Americans, and they changed their name to Nichiren Shoshu of America (NSA). NSA has over two hundred centers and over 200,000 members in the United States.

Zen, the BCA, and the NSA came from Japan from the Mahayana form of Buddhism. Theravada Buddhism also migrated to America. In the 1960s Theravada monks came from Sri Lanka and Malaysia to establish the Buddhist Vihara Society in Washington, D.C. Other Theravada organizations are located in the United States. Tibetan Buddhism arrived in the late 1960s to establish meditation centers in California and Vermont. Several Chinese Buddhist groups have formed across the United States, including the Sino-American Buddhist Association with its Gold Mountain Monastery in San Francisco and the Buddhist Association of the United States located in New York City.[4]

Buddhism in America is represented by various sectarian movements arising out of the Theravada and Mahayana traditions. Mahayana groups, by far, have the most organizations and members. Japan has been the central migratory source of Buddhists to America, especially seen in the prominence of Zen, BCA, and NSA. Buddhist missionaries came with the rise in immigration from Buddhist countries and with the rise of intermarriage between Americans and Orientals after the war periods. Buddhist study programs in universities have highlighted American interest. Zen Buddhism, in particular, appealed to Americans in the counterculture movements. Zen offered a viewpoint, a psychology, a life-style, and art forms which influenced Americans and American culture beyond the Zen Meditation Center. Zen influences were established in the tea ceremony, painting, dance, writings, flower arrangements, and the martial arts. Modern psychiatry and psychotherapy have been influenced by Buddhist meditation and its emphasis upon mental discipline and control of the unconscious mind.[5]

American culture has also influenced Buddhism and has demonstrated the adaptability of some forms of Buddhism to other cultures. Zen has been able to move across cultures from China to Japan to America and influence cultural values and forms, if not gain great numbers of persons into institutional membership. The Buddhist Church of America (BCA) adopted in its name the word *church*, a term amenable to America. The BCA has worship services on Sundays using organ and piano. Children sing "Buddha loves me, this I know" in their Sunday School. They distribute a book, *The Teaching of Buddha*, on the inside cover of which is noted, "This Buddhist Bible is Donated by Buddhist Promoting Foundation, Japan."[6] The Nichiren Shoshu sponsor "We Love America" rallies where thousands of their members march in the streets carrying an American flag. One such rally drew over ten thousand marchers in Washington, D.C., as they marched from the Capitol to the White House.

Buddhism in America offers meditation and retreat centers for those who seek contemplation and quietude in a meditative life-style. It has temples, churches, and Sunday Schools. It provides for community life, social activities and concerns, and fosters a variety of institutions of membership. Monks may preside in their saffron robes as they criss-cross the country to lecture and to lead meditation. The laity, composed of a cross-ethnic and nationalistic blend, may chant to Buddha, Nichiren, or Amida in worship centers with focus on the Buddha statue or on some sacred object of worship.

Americans may readily pick up copies of Watts' *The Way of Zen*, Kopp's *If You Meet the Buddha on The Road, Kill Him*, and Pirsig's *Zen and The Art of Motorcycle Maintenance*. America has many varieties of alternate religious traditions in addition to Protestant, Roman Catholic, and Jewish churches and synagogues. Buddhism is one of these alternatives. A representative sample of Buddhist communities will be presented, including Zen Buddhism, the Soka Gakkai or Nichiren Shoshu of America, and the Buddhist Vihara Society. These samples will provide the diverse flavor of the variety of Buddhism in the United States.

Zen Buddhism

Zen Buddhism arrived in America in the twentieth century via China and Japan. Reports indicate that Zen originated with the Buddha. Once when the Buddha was seated, an individual brought him a flower and asked him to speak the dharma. The Buddha took the flower, held it up, and looked at it in silence. After some time, the Buddha smiled. Thus, Zen began. Is it a philosophy, a psychology, a religion, an indescribable experience? It has been described variously as each of the above, which presents the paradox of Zen.

Origins of Zen

Zen is said to have been handed down by twenty-eight consecutive patriarchs until it arrived from India to China about A.D. 520. In China it became known as Ch'an. During the twelfth century it migrated to Japan where it became known as Zen. Two major traditions developed in Zen under the leadership of masters or *roshis*. The older tradition is *Rinzai*, and the younger but more prominent tradition in America is *Soto*. The two differ particularly on the practices toward attaining enlightenment or *satori*. The Rinzai may stress the attempt to solve intellectual puzzles called *koans*, while the Soto may emphasize "just sitting." Although Zen was introduced into America at the turn of the century, Zen centers became prominent only after the 1950s. Two of the more noted centers in America are the San Francisco Zen Center and the Zen Meditation Center in Rochester, New York.

The San Francisco Zen Center opened in 1961 under the leadership of Shunryu Suzuki Roshi. Soon, a group of Americans were practicing *zazen* or the sitting meditation with their roshi. Growth occurred. More land and buildings were purchased. By 1969 the center in San Francisco had moved to a fifty-room building with seventy students in residence, with the Buddha hall, and the administrative and dining facilities. The center bought a former hot springs resort and named it Zen Mountain Retreat. In 1972 the seventy-acre Green Gulch Farm was purchased. The farm, with its buildings, served as a source of food for the Zen community. The Zen Meditation Center of Rochester was begun in 1966 by Philip Kapleau. Kapleau had been influenced by the teachings of D. T. Suzuki who lectured at Columbia University. After returning from study under roshis in Japan, he founded the New York Center. Kapleau introduced Zen in the American context by emphasizing the wearing of "regular" American clothing during zazen and by chanting the meditation in English. There are several dozen Zen centers across America.[7]

Zen and Buddhism

Although Zen has been historically viewed as a form of Mahayana Buddhism, some have raised the question if it is Buddhism at all. Others have stated that Zen is the apotheosis of Buddhism. Zen comes from the *Sanskrit* word which means meditation. One meditates in order to experience satori. Satori is enlightenment of dhyana. As satori lies beyond the intellect, it cannot be described. Perhaps the best way to describe it is through silence. The purpose of Zen, then, is to experience a reality or be in a condition beyond the intellect. Zen becomes tired of learning about something and desires actually to know. The aim is to integrate the one who perceives or experiences with that which is perceived or experienced. The knower becomes the known.[8]

The Practice of Zen

Zen may utilize objects, rituals, and scriptures to attain satori; but Zen may not depend upon them and certainly must move beyond them. In the ultimate sense, it relies on no concept of God or soul or ritual or vow. A Zen center may have a Buddha statue in the meditation hall. The statue may be used for devotional aid. If the meditator becomes too cold to meditate, however, the wooden statue may be made into kindling wood for warmth. Scriptures from ancient Buddhism, like the *Heart Sutra*, may be read for meditation. One must not be attached to them, just like one must not become attached to the Buddha or to his teachings. A Zen saying is, "He climbs best who carries the lightest load."

There are five key words which describe Zen. They are *zendo, zazen, satori, mondo,* and *koan.* The *zendo* is the place where the meditators gather. *Zazen* is the practice of meditation, and there are varieties of *zazen. Satori* is the enlightenment itself. Zen has developed several techniques by which to break into the closed doors of the mind and to transcend rational thought. One is the *mondo*, a form of question and answer between the Zen Master and the pupil. "Why do you meditate all day long?" said the Master to the pupil. "I want to become a Buddha," said the pupil. The master picked up a brick and began to rub it. He said he wished to make a mirror. The pupil said, "But no amount of polishing a brick will make a mirror." The master replied, "If so, then no amount of sitting cross-legged will make you a Buddha."

The *koan* is a phrase or word insoluble by the intellect. It is like a riddle or a puzzle. But it has no rational answer. There are several thousand *koans* which have been handed down by Zen Masters. A *koan* is like a pebble in the mouth of a man who walks in the desert. It does not quench his present thirst, but it stimulates the means of quenching it.

Two hands when clapped make a sound. What is the sound of one hand clapping?

A man hangs over a precipice by his teeth, which are clenched into the branch of a tree. His hands are full, and his feet are dangling. A friend leans over and asks him, "What is Zen?" What answer would you give?

Two monks were returning home. They came to a stream where a pretty girl waited, fearful to cross and wet her clothes. One monk picked her up in his arms, crossed the stream, and having put her down, walked on. The other monk was horrified at his fellow monk touching the girl, and he upbraided him, mile upon mile. The first monk suddenly became aware of his fellow monk's scolding. He said, "That girl! I put her down at the stream. Are you still carrying her?"

Through these sayings we pick up a part of the spirit of Zen. Someone has said that Zen is a joke within a joke. The koans often are puzzles of nonsense. Another has said, "When you desire Zen as much as a man whose head is held under water wants fresh air, you are truly seeking." And the answer to achieve it lies within oneself.

Zen Monasticism

Although Zen has become popularized in both Eastern and Western cultures through the arts and other cultural forms, it has a deep tradition of the role of the monk and the monastery. The monastery has served the needs of full-time monks as well as the needs of laypersons for briefer periods of time. The zendo life may be characterized as a life of humility, labor, service, gratitude, and meditation. A Zen monk learns humility through begging. With his bowl or bag he canvases the streets and homes for money and food. This teaches self-denial. A life of labor is essential for "a day of no work is a day of no eating." Labor is performed by all in a democratic spirit. The life of service is exemplified in shared responsibilities in the zendo. Gratitude is cultivated and shown in calling out the names of Buddha and the Bodhisattvas, and in reciting the *Sutras*.

The life of meditation is observed individually and collectively in the privacy of one's own quarters and as group meditation in the meditation hall. One may practice Zen as a resident full-time monk, or one may reside at the zendo temporarily. Zen is not limited to place or time, and may be practiced at home and at one's employment. The zendo has stringent rules for all who live within it. There may be men and women and married couples in American zendos.

The day begins early at the zendo. By 4 A.M. all must be in place for meditation. Sitting meditation may be interrupted by occasional periods of exercise until breakfast sometime after 8 A.M. Then, there are tea times, clean up periods, work responsibilities, attendance at lectures, and a closing zazen in the evening. Zen meditators are vegetarians, and meals are usually simple. By 9:30 P.M. it is bedtime; but sleep is not sought after, with some having only several hours of sleep each night. Study and meditation fill much of the time, and there is little waste of time, energy, food, and wakefulness. The roshi or abbot of the zendo is respected, and his wisdom as well as his counsel are sought. More formal lectures are offered to the public at times. At certain meditation periods there are the clapping of bells, the smell of incense, the bowing before the Buddha statue, chanting, and the recognition of others' presence. As one Zen Center counsels, "In practicing Zazen, let each person put forth great, persistent effort so that we and the world together may attain maturity in Buddha's wisdom."[9]

The Appeal of Zen

Zen Buddhism's influence goes beyond life at the zendo and the zazen of the individual. Literature, poetry, painting, garden arrangements, tea ceremonies, and martial arts are among the objects and events which the Zen "spirit" may influence. Arrangements, designs, word suggestion, gestures, posture, and movement may all suggest the Buddha-nature. Zen tea ceremony in its simplicity and graceful movements points to profundity in the ordinary. Zen martial arts, through their appearance and posture, tame an adversary without physical contact. A Zen garden with its rocks and stones and shrubbery and trees is arranged to demonstrate natural beauty. Zen painting may suggest emptiness in design with strokes and spaces appropriately inviting the idea and feeling of empty space and few details. Zen poetry is more concerned with intuition and feelings rather than words and obvious statements.[10]

Zen's appeal to America has been diverse. D. T. Suzuki, one of the leading Zen writers who has greatly influenced Americans, has written that Zen has no God for worship, no rituals, no doctrine of eternal life, no concept of soul or immortality, and no real concern to look after someone's soul or life. Some have seen Zen as a religionless religion with no transcendent authority, no binding scripture, and no legislation of morality. This has been a part of its attraction. Others have gravitated to Zen for its various therapies upon the mind, the emotions, and the body. The meditation postures have provided, for some, the health of the whole body. Others have chosen to associate either full time or occasionally with a Zen center and its roshi to experience the varieties of Zen under the supervision of a master. Some have chosen to apply Zen's emphasis upon silence, discipline, order, and meditation techniques to their own spiritual awareness and development, and to practice Zen in this way along with their involvement and commitment to other religious communities. These would make a distinction between certain Zen techniques and Zen Buddhism.

Zen centers, in terms of their numbers and members, have declined since their proliferation in the 1970s. Nevertheless, Zen remains an alternate movement in new consciousness search. Even though it originated out of the Mahayana Buddhist development, it is highly individualistic in its concepts and techniques. Within the zendos there is a tradition of master and pupil, authority and obedience, and monk and laity. Although Zen tends to be extremely iconoclastic, it does use Buddha statues, and it does place authority in a succession of masters or roshis who have been consecrated in a disciplic order. There are different sects, different disciplines, different techniques, and different orders in Zen. One in America who chooses to taste of Zen or participate more fully in the zendo would not expect to find discussion of and commitment to the Christian understanding of God as presented in the life and teachings of Jesus Christ, in the biblical tradition, and in the Christian Church.

Nichiren Shoshu (Soka Gakkai)

More than ten thousand American flag bearers march down Constitution Avenue in Washington, D.C. in a "We Love America Rally." In a worship center in Washington, several hundred followers chant in rhythm a strange sounding phrase to an outsider's ears. Outside the worship center a young woman grabs your attention and gives you her testimony of how this chanting has brought her health, happiness, and success in her personal life, her family life, and her work. Adjacent to the center thirty young men dress rehearse for their international convention to be held in Honolulu beginning July 4. Who are these energetic, youthful, aggressive, and missionary people? What do *Nichiren Shoshu* and *Soka Gakkai* mean? What are the beliefs and practices of this religious community in America?

Soka Gakkai in Japan

The Nichiren Shoshu form of Mahayana Buddhism was founded in America in 1960. Coming from Japan, it took the name of Nichiren Shoshu of America (NSA). The followers of NSA believe that Guatama Buddha predicted that a special teacher would appear in the thirteenth century A.D. to present the correct form of Buddhism for the new age. "Nichiren Daishonin, born in Japan in 1222, fulfilled all the conditions of the prophecy."[11] Japan was in the midst of social upheaval and faced outside invaders. On April 28, 1253, Nichiren founded Nichiren Shoshu Buddhism by establishing the chant *Nam-myoto-renge-Kyo* and the worship object the *Gohonzon*. Nichiren proposed a simpler approach to Buddhism with chant and worship object. He became the Buddha of the new age for his followers. He died in 1282, but not before he had become what some consider the Amos of Japan. He attacked the government for not keeping the Buddhist dharma. After all, his name meant "the great holy one," and he claimed that his movement was the true and orthodox expression of Buddhism.

The NSA assert that a succession has been handed down from their founder to a present abbot. Several sects had split off of Nichiren's founding community. From the thirteenth century until 1928, the movement continued with relative growth. In 1928 two Japanese, Makiguchi and Toda, were converted to Nichiren Shoshu. Makiguchi, an elementary schoolteacher, founded the Soka Gakkai (Society for the Creation of Value), basing Soka Gakkai on Nichiren's idea of chanting. Both he and Toda were imprisoned by authorities. After Makiguchi's death in 1944, Toda became the organizational genius behind the movement. He used the founder's book, *Kachiron*, as the ideology, and he gave the movement its shape. Toda, also a schoolteacher, revived the movement in 1951 and vowed, "You must not give Toda a funeral if 750,000 family units have not been won. Throw my bones into the ocean off the coast of Shinagawa."[12] Todo made Soka Gakkai a lay movement, aggressive, missionary, and quite evangelistic. At the death of Toda in 1958, the movement claimed that 750,000 family units had been won to Soka Gakkai. In 1960 Daisaku Ikeda was named the third president. During the initial days of his reign, Soka Gakkai was founded in America. By the early 1960s the Soka Gakkai had become such a powerful religious movement that it was the third most powerful force in the Upper House of the Japanese National Diet.

Soka Gakkai Comes to America

President Ikeda visited the United States in 1960. His close disciple, Masayasa Sadanaga, founded the Los Angeles headquarters in 1963. The first convention was held in Chicago in 1963 with fifteen hundred in attendance. By 1968 national headquarters were opened in Santa Monica, California, and an annual convention was begun in Hawaii. As the Soka Gakkai reached more Americans, Sadanaga changed his name to George Williams and changed the names of the Soka Gakkai meeting halls, called *Kaikans*, to community centers. The name of the movement became NSA. NSA spread over the United States and to other countries. When the new temple was dedicated at Mt. Fuji in 1972, about eighteen thousand Americans made the pilgrimage to Japan. There are approximately three hundred thousand members of NSA in the United States with over two hundred fifty chapters. Worldwide, there may be over ten million followers in more than ninety countries. NSA is composed of the laity. There are also temples administered by the priesthood in America in Los Angeles, Washington, D.C., Chicago, New York, and Honolulu.

NSA has roots in a fanatical and aggressive missionary movement in Japan. Nichiren, himself, was seen as a fanatic, opposing all religious traditions of his day. Soka Gakkai, in modern Japan, has been one of the most aggressive religious groups. Members have smashed the Buddha images of other Japanese, claiming that the images represented false religion. Their conversion techniques have often been based on intimidation, coersion, and rumor, in order to divide family members from one another and gain converts by threat. Religion and politics were viewed as a unity where the law of the Emperor and the Buddhist dharma should be one. Government should be the organization to bring happiness and success to all. It has been suggested that the name change to Nichiren Shoshu of America was to downplay the Soka Gakkai image known in Japan. In America, NSA has become adaptable to American society and has basically appealed to tens of thousands of Americans.[13]

NSA Teachings and Practices

The philosophy of NSA is utilitarian. Truth has to do with concepts and speculation. Value has to do with beauty, benefit, and personal and public gain. Humans can create values, and this is humankind's greatness. The goal of life is to achieve happiness, or to attain Buddhahood. The path to happiness or Buddhahood is the Nichiren Shoshu faith. Faith, then, is placed in the truth taught by Nichiren, which is that Buddhahood or happiness can be realized in the present, and that the simple prayer and the chanting of it, *Nam-myoho-renge-Kyo*, is the means to attain happiness.

> The first steps in beginning to practice Nichiren Daishonin's Buddhism are based on the expectation that it will lead to desired results. Confidence, or stronger faith, comes from seeing actual proof, i.e., from prayers being answered.
>
> The practice for oneself consists of chanting Nam-myoho-renge-Kyo to the Gohonzon, supported by gongyo, the morning and evening recitation of two chapters of the Lotus Sutra. To practice for others means to share with other people one's experiences. Practice in Buddhism is what makes faith real.
>
> The purpose of study . . . is to strengthen one's faith, to enable one to work more effectively for world peace, and to establish happiness in one's life. NSA members study Nichiren Daishonin's teachings through such books as the *Major Writings of Nichiren Daishonin,* the organization's newspaper, *The World Tribune,* and its study magazine, the *Seikyo Times.*[14]

The chanting of *Nam-myoho-renge-Kyo* before the Gohonzon is one of the primary rituals and worship experiences for the members both at the NSA center in group worship and at home privately. Gohonzon is a scroll containing the names of the Buddhas found in the *Lotus Sutra*. The scroll is contained in a cabinet, often decorative, before which the worshipers chant. Large Gohonzons are found in the central place of the worship center, and small Gohonzons are used in the homes. Nichiren taught that the *Lotus Sutra* is the primary text of Buddhism. He advocated that a simple devotion of chanting to the *Lotus Sutra* scroll is more meaningful than deep study and practice of philosophy and meditation over the *Lotus Sutra*. To chant the Daimoku, "Glory to the sacred teaching of the *Lotus Sutra*," would bring one's Buddha nature to realization and give one happiness and material prosperity.

- What does the sacred phrase, *Nam-myoho-renge-Kyo*, the Daimoku, mean?
- Nam means dedication, specifically to fuse one's life with the fundamental life-force of the universe.
- Myoho literally means the mystic law, the essential principle of the universe.
- Renge means lotus flower, the symbol of simultaneous cause and effect. Causality, as taught in Buddhism, is a strict law which penetrates the past, present, and future. Furthermore, it is not something imposed by others, some "god" for example. Though this implies personal accountability for one's fate, the practice is always oriented toward the present and future. Nichiren Daishonin's Buddhism enables one to face and overcome trouble and obstacles and live with confidence. The lotus flower which grows from a muddy swamp symbolizes the emergence of Buddhahood in the life of an ordinary person.
- Finally, Kyo means Sutra, the teaching of a Buddha.[15]

There are two major practices of NSA: gongyo and daimoku. Gongyo involves reciting part of the second and all of the sixteenth chapter of the *Lotus Sutra* five times in the morning and three times in the evening. It is chanted in Japanese before the Gohonzon at one's private altar in the home. After the chanting of gongyo, one chants the daimoku. This chanting brings one in harmony with the universe and one's own Buddha-nature as well as brings one material benefits and success in this life. In home meetings, as well as at the NSA centers, members give their testimonies of the benefits of chanting. They often testify that chanting has aided them in securing a job, a promotion, a wish, a house, a cure, and other tangible and material benefits. In the center a leader sits in front of the group to lead the chants. Often, there is singing of songs in a pep rally fashion.[16]

Members of NSA are missionary. They are fervent in their chanting, faithful in center activities, and aggressive in promoting NSA ideals and practices. *Shakubuku* is the word used for their conversion strategy; it literally means "to destroy and conquer." It implies intolerant propaganda and coercion to attain a conversion. In Japan, intimidation, harassment, and frenzied and fanatical activity were associated with Soka Gakkai efforts to convert others to their movement. President Ikeda described the reasons behind shakubuku. One may achieve Buddhahood and happiness. One may break the chain of karma. One reaps more merit. Thus, to convert another means to reap happiness, overcome evil, and earn more merit. Competition among NSA members exists to see who can win the most converts and gain the most merits and testify to the greatest results of chanting. Shakubuku within the American Nichiren Shoshu centers is not of the Soka Gakkai brand in Japan. NSA members, however, present their belief and faith in an energetic and aggressive manner. One member, from a NSA in Philadelphia, described the ups and downs of his life and points to skakubuku as a part of the solution to his struggle:

> From that point onward, I began to do Shakubuku again and practice honestly. I really applied myself to my district and attempted to make every cause I could. Within three months, I landed what is probably the most influential job in Philadelphia in the field of video production. . . . During this time, my district has become a chapter and the chapter has doubled in size.

. . . I know that with the guidance of my leaders and through sincere practice to the Gohonzon, I can accomplish anything.[17]

Behind their devotional practices is a simple and pragmatic view of life. They believe if you are serious in practice, physical illness will be healed. A doctor may be consulted also, but worship of the "true worship object" will facilitate and speed up healing. The day of death may be postponed through practice. One may have more time to gain more merit before death comes. Karma, the belief that one's present life has been affected by deeds of a former existence and will affect a future life, can be improved through practice so one may attain Buddhahood. Suffering is viewed as a result of false beliefs, and it may be overcome through devotion to the Gohonzon. Life is to be happy, successful, and abundant. Any person can become Buddha in this life. Success is measured by a cheerful home, a good business, a healthy and happy spirit, and peace. President Ikeda stated,

A passage from the Gosho, Nichiren Daishonin's writings, reads, "Is there any sin not to be forgiven or happiness not to come if one only chants Nam-myoho-renge-kyo?"

This maxim promises anyone a happy life filled with good fortune and blessed with the ability to erase all bad causes provided that that person sincerely embraces the Gohonzon. Where else can we find anyone who promises us true happiness with such confidence?[18]

The NSA Organization

Nichiren Shoshu of America has a nationwide network of leaders and centers. George Williams, now an American citizen, is general director. He presides over the national headquarters in Santa Monica, California. Beneath him are executive directors, regional directors, and administrators of territories, areas, districts, and groups. In the NSA centers there are peer groups for men, women, young men, and young women. New members are placed by age in their groups. George Williams, born in Korea, grew up under Soka Gakkai parents in Japan. He immigrated to America in 1957, studying at George Washington University and the University of Maryland. He was named by President Ikeda to his position in NSA. In 1975 the organization of all laypersons in Nichiren Shoshu Buddhism was founded as Soka Gakkai International (SGI) with Ikeda as president. Williams also serves as vice-president of SGI.

Some several hundred thousand Americans have been attracted to NSA. Increasingly, non-Oriental Americans have become members. About 60 percent are between the ages of twenty-one and forty. NSA appears to attract more blacks and Latin Americans than other Buddhist groups. Nearly one-third come from Roman Catholic backgrounds, and nearly a third come from Protestantism. Some 40 percent of Protestants are from Baptist backgrounds.[19]

About forty NSA community centers are located across the United States from Seattle, Los Angeles, and San Francisco to Washington, Louisville, Dallas, Fayetteville (North Carolina), Philadelphia, and cities in between. Centers tend to be beehives of activity with chanting periods, clean-up and work responsibilities, sewing rooms for making costumes and flags for parades, and testimonials to one another and to new converts. The publications offered are the *World Tribune,* a weekly newspaper of NSA events, of statements by Ikeda and Williams, and testimonies of members; the *NSA Quarterly,* a journal presenting the philosophy of the movement; and the monthly *Seikyo Times* with a magazine format.

The Nichiren Shoshu of America has been one of the fastest-growing Buddhist groups. Its emphasis upon the power of positive meditation and chanting has been attractive. Testimonies by members of receiving material benefits for right religious practice have appealed to tens of thousands. Zealous missionary activities have influenced friends and neighbors to join. The movement claims celebrities like television's Patrick Duffy and singer Tina Turner. Their talents are displayed on videos in the centers. NSA is intolerant of other religions, since it focuses completely on a highly exclusive saint (Nichiren), an authoritative scripture *(Lotus Sutra)*, and a sacred phrase and worship object *(Nam-myoho-renge-Kyo* and *Gohonzon)*. It claims itself as the way and the truth and the happy life. The Christian concept and understanding of God, Jesus Christ, salvation by grace through faith, and the life and fellowship of the Christian Church are not a part of NSA's doctrine or practice.

Buddhist Vihara Society

The Buddhist Vihara Society, located at 5017 16th Street N.W. in Washington, D.C., is the only one of its kind in the United States. It is the first Theravada Buddhist center in the United States. Three or four monks usually live at the Vihara. They wear the traditional yellow robes with shaven heads. Several have come from Sri Lanka, and there may be an American monk at times. Since 1980 its president has been Venerable Gunaratana, a monk from Sri Lanka.

Origins

A pamphlet from the Vihara describes its beginnings:

> The Washington Buddhist Vihara is the first Theravada Buddhist Vihara center in the United States. It was set up under the guidance of eminent members of the Sangha in Sri Lanka, who saw the need for a center in this country offering the Theravada perspective and way. On the initiative of the Most Venerable Madihe Pannaseeha Maha Nayaka Thera, the Buddhist Vihara Society was founded in 1965 with Ven. Bope Vinita Thera as first president. In 1967 the Ven. Dickwela Piyananda, a senior scholar-monk of wide repute, became the Society's president, joined the next year by the Ven. Henepola Gunaratana. In 1968 the Society acquired the present building as a Sangha residence, which thus became the Washington Buddhist Vihara.[20]

Vinita had enlisted the aid of the ambassador of Ceylon (now Sri Lanka) and his staff to found the Vihara Society. Later, with the assistance of the governments of Ceylon and Thailand, a building previously owned by Thailand on 16th Street was purchased. The house is modest with a basement, two stories, and a small back yard.

Venerable Gunaratana, the present senior monk and president, was born in Sri Lanka in 1927. He entered the sangha at age thirteen, receiving his Buddhist training in traditional monastic schools. For some fifteen years he did dhamma (missionary) work in India and Malaysia. In 1968 he came to the Vihara from the Buddhist temple in Kuala Lampur, Malaysia. In 1980 he received his Ph.D. in philosophy from American University. Venerable Gunaratana presides over the administration and daily activities of the Vihara.

Other monks who have resided recently at the Vihara include Venerable Bhikkhu Bodhi and Venerable Bhikkhu Ajita. Bhikkhu Bodhi (*bhikkhu* means monk), an American, was born in New York in 1944. He received a Ph.D. in philosophy at Claremont Graduate School in 1972. After studying Buddhism in Asia and becoming ordained in the Sangha in Sri Lanka, he returned to be a resident at the Vihara in 1979. He served as general secretary, edited the newsletter, and gave lectures and classes. In May of 1982, Bhikkhu Bodhi left for Sri Lanka to continue his study and practice of the dhamma. Venerable Bhikkhu Ajita arrived at the Vihara in 1980. Born in Sri Lanka in 1951, he studied Buddhism at the Maharagama Bhikkhu Training Center and was ordained a monk in 1965. He taught Buddhism in several centers before coming to the Vihara. He has served as secretary and has offered lectures and classes. Other monks have temporarily resided at the Vihara.

Vihara and Buddhism

The Buddhist Vihara Society adheres to the Theravada school of Buddhism, generally recognized as the oldest and as the "School of the Elders." It is distinguished by its close adherance to the original teachings laid down by the historical Buddha.

> The Theravada lineage began with the Buddha's closest immediate disciples, who settled his doctrine in unison at a council held only three months after his passing. From its original Indian homeland the Theravada teaching reached Sri Lanka around 300 B.C., brought there by the monk Mahinda and the Nun Sanghamitta, son and daughter of Emperor Asoka, the great Buddhist ruler of India. Thereafter Sri Lanka became the glorious "island of the Dhamma," preserving the Buddha's authentic teachings intact for over 2,200 years. From Sri Lanka Theravada Buddhism further spread to mainland Southeast Asia, where it shaped the traditional cultures of Burma, Cambodia, Laos, and Thailand.

> Theravada Buddhism is grounded upon the "triple gem"—the Buddha, Dhamma, and the Sangha. The Buddha was a perfectly enlightened man who found the way to deliverance from suffering and taught this way to others openly and freely. The Dhamma, the teaching, is a body of doctrine and practice aimed at helping us uncover the deepest most urgent truths about our existence. The Dhamma does not so much give us ready answers as a path to enable us to make our own discovery of truth. For guidance in treading the path the disciple looks to the Sangha, the order of bhikkhus (monks), which has maintained the Dhamma in unbroken continuity from the Buddha's time to the present. The shaven-headed, safron-robed monks, like the Buddha himself, lead a life of homelessness dedicated to spiritual development and service to others.[21]

Theravada Buddhism stresses the Four Noble Truths and the Eightfold Path as taught by the Buddha. Focus is on the sacred written tradition of the Tripitaka in the Pali and Sanskrit languages. Its view is that the basic experience or reality is suffering, and the cause of suffering is desire. Suffering has a solution; however, it can be overcome by following the

Eightfold Path. The path consists of stages of correct knowledge and commitment, of correct behavior or conduct, and of correct meditation. The goal of the path is the attainment of enlightenment or nirvana which liberates one from suffering (dukkha) and from impermanence (anicca). The Theravada School stresses the difference between the monk and the layperson. Monks rely on the support and generosity of laypersons. Laypersons expect to gain merit through their support of the monks in order to overcome bad karma of past lives and to achieve sound karma. They also hope to attain nirvana. The Vihara (Sangha) is most important in the Theravada school.

Vihara Practices

The major activities of the Vihara occur in the building itself. The main floor contains the shrine room, kitchen facilities, and the book store. The shrine room is the primary focus of the building and the activities. A gilded Buddha image, about five feet tall depicted in a meditation posture, rests on a slightly elevated stage at one end of the shrine room. Flowers decorate the stage area, and there are secondary altars with small images and with elephant horns prominently displayed. A deep red carpet covers the room, which may seat over a hundred. One of the monks may sit near the Buddha statue and may use a microphone to lecture or to lead in meditation. The book store contains a variety of books and audio visuals on Buddhism. The second floor includes the library with a complete set of the *Pali Tripitaka*, an office, and living quarters for the monks. The basement is used primarily as a meditation hall. The small backyard has an eight-foot-tall bronze figure of Ananda the close disciple of the Buddha.

Programs at the Vihara are held daily; and they are publicized as follows:

> The practice of Buddhism involves a harmonious fusion of study, meditation, and devotion. Study provides the eye to guide progress along the path; meditation, the

actual work of practice; and devotion, the breath of inspirational warmth that encourages renewed effort. The Vihara's programs aim at a balance of these three elements. Dhamma classes, held generally on Wednesday evenings, explore the teachings of Buddhism. A service every Sunday at 2 P.M. involves devotion, Pali chanting, and a Dhamma talk; at the same time a class for children is often in progress. Following a tea break, from 4 to 5 there is a group meditation, sometimes followed by a talk about meditation practice. Ven. Gunaratana leads meditation at 7:30 P.M. Monday through Friday and at 2:00 P.M. on Saturday. Beginners are welcome at any of the group sittings, but are advised to receive individual instruction beforehand. From time to time meditation retreats are held, sometimes in the county or at colleges. Besides these programs, annual celebrations commemorate events of special significance, the most important being Vesak, in May, Great Disciples Day in February, Kathina Day in October, and Sanghamitta Day in December.[22]

Vesak Day celebration simultaneously observes the birth, enlightenment, and death of Gautama Buddha. The December Festival celebrates the founding of the Vihara. There are one-day retreats. The one-day retreat includes devotion (puja), walking and sitting meditations, meditation and discussion, chanting, and the recitation of vows.

Monks are engaged in special lectures on yoga in the Vihara. Venerable Gunaratana travels extensively across the United States and Canada visiting other Buddhist centers and also presenting lectures in various colleges. Monks make hospital visits and hold blessing services for newly-wed couples.[23] Monks operate the Vihara Book Service, preparing a book list each year, and conducting a mail-order service. A newsletter, "The Washington Buddhist," is published quarterly. Membership in the Vihara requires interest in Buddhism rather than personal involvement in its activities. A life membership is $150, an annual membership is $15, and a student membership is $5. Recently, the Vihara has purchased a tract of land in West Virginia and has begun the first building on a retreat center. A pamphlet, "Washington Buddhist Vihara, A New Center," urges the membership to improve and expand the Vihara:

> There is a consensus that the present activities of the Vihara and any future expansions are constrained by the limited space available in the present premises. The limitations are particularly felt in the meeting hall for services, accommodation for resident and visiting monks, Vihara Book Service, library, kitchen and dana rooms, and parking facilities.
>
> To achieve the noble goal of providing a larger Vihara, the Buddhist Vihara Society has launched a fund raising campaign. The existing assets of the Society should cover a significant part of the cost of the project. Our target is to raise $200,000 to supplement these assets. The initial phase of fund raising has a target of $100,000 to be met by Vesak, 1986.
>
> We appeal to you to make a generous contribution to make the new Vihara project a success.[24]

The pamphlet has an artist's impression of the proposal for the New Center and a pledge cutout.

The Buddhist Vihara Society of Washington, for nearly twenty years, has maintained a tradition of monks and lay-persons in the study and practice of Theravada Buddhism. Monks wear their traditional robes and adhere strictly to their tradition's rituals. The Vihara welcomes interest at any level, and anticipates a building program to meet present and future needs.

Christianity and Buddhism

A Christian view of Buddhism sees varieties of beliefs and practices among Buddhists.[25] Theravada Buddhism, of which the Buddhist Vihara Society of Washington is a part, follows the classical teachings of the historic Gautama Buddha. Those teachings include the Four Noble Truths and the

Eightfold Path. The problem of life is suffering. Suffering may be overcome through one's own individual efforts following the Truths and the Path. Impermanence is everywhere, and there is no soul. One is to escape this world, but there is little concern for what lies beyond. A Christian view is based on a good God whose good creation including humankind is tainted through humankind's sin and rebellion. Suffering is affirmed by a Christian as a human dilemma, like the affirmation of a Buddhist. The origin, meaning, and solution to suffering for a Christian, however, resides in human sin, the presence of evil in the world, and the crucifixion and resurrection of Jesus Christ. A Buddhist concern about the impermanence and anxiety-producing experiences of the world can be appreciated. A Christian affirms, however, the world as it may be changed by God's activity through humankind. A Buddhist excludes God from both discussion and experience; reliance is upon one's knowledge and own efforts to liberate oneself from the world.

Buddhism's stress upon goodwill, compassion, honesty, integrity, and peacefulness can be deeply appreciated by a Christian. Emphasis upon respect for nature and the preservation of its many ecological balances can be affirmed. Christian ethics and moral values are rooted, not in oneself, but in the knowledge, grace, and power of God as revealed through the Bible, through the revelation of Jesus Christ, and through the obedience and faith of humans as they respond to God. The commitment and dedication of the monk in the Theravada tradition can be admired. A Christian may raise with the monk the idea of merit-making. If Buddhists are to be self-reliant, why does a layperson have to rely on the monk for merits as the layperson gives gifts to him? Also, what does the tradition offer for social and political and economic orders in the world besides the monk and monastery tradition?

Mahayana Buddhism builds upon the foundations of the Theravada teachings, but there are different interpretations and practices. A main teaching of the Mahayana tradition holds to the doctrine of the Bodhisattva, one who has attained enlightenment but remains in the world to help others attain it. Also, there are many Buddhas and Bodhisattvas for different ages who function as savior types for others. The individual through faith relies on the grace and efforts of others for liberation or salvation. It appears that just as the monk may serve a saving function for the laity, the Buddha or Bodhisattva serves as savior for those who believe and place trust in the savior. The Nichiren Shoshu of America regard Nichiren as a Bodhisattva who revealed a way to get help through chanting to all the Bodhisattvas and Buddhas of the *Lotus Sutra*. The Pureland School claims that Amida Buddha resides in a heaven, and one only has to chant Amida's name, trusting in his name, to attain heaven. There emerges in the Mahayana tradition a religious experience which focuses on a god, on grace and faith, on humankind's dependence on another, and on an afterlife.

A Christian view notes the wide divergences between the two traditions. What has happened to the concept of self? If there is no self in the classical Buddhist understanding, why does the Mahayana tradition attach such importance to preserving it, for example, in some heaven? What has happened to disinterested goodwill? Is there a movement within Buddhism from a system of teachings on philosophy and psychology to one of religious beliefs and practices and devotion?

Zen Buddhism offers a complex psychology and a simplistic life-style. Nichiren Shoshu of America presents a Bodhisattva tradition. The Buddhist Vihara Society is classical Buddhism at its best with monk and layperson.

A Christian view toward Buddhists denotes tensions and possible contradictions within their teachings and life-styles. But this may be true in all religions. Buddhist psychology is complex and is often difficult to translate into other cultural thought forms and terminologies. One can be appreciative of the serious empirical and pragmatic quest of Buddhists as they delineate the problems inherent in the human situation and as they attempt to validate their answers from personal experience. They continue to have concerns about God and transcendent reality, human nature, evil, salvation and liberation, and a savior. A Christian perspective would invite Buddhists to consider the full meaning of the gospel as it is presented in Jesus Christ and His teachings.[26]

8

ISLAM AND THE
BAHA'I IN AMERICA
■   ■

Islam

During the 1970s Islam made an indelible impact upon
the American consciousness. The oil embargo and the rapid
rise in oil prices, led by Saudi Arabia and other Islamic
nations, initiated presentations in the American mass media
on Islam, its history, its beliefs and practices. The fall of the
Shah of Iran and the rise of Ayatollah Khomaini during
1978-1979 brought to the American public the Shi'ite form
of Islam.[1] During 1979-81, with the holding of American
hostages and the taking of the United States embassy in
Tehran, Iran, America again was impacted with Islamic
terms and meanings. The Gulf War of 1991 also brought to
American consciousness the Islamic world of Iraq, Saudi
Arabia, and Kuwait. The Iranian Revolution also brought
reports of the persecution and execution of persons of the
Baha'i religion which had its origins in Iran. The Baha'i, too,
have become known in a new way to Americans through
these events.

Islam has had a presence in America since the beginnings
of the twentieth century with migrations of Muslim nationals

from Middle Eastern countries. Estimates indicate there may be over three million Muslims in America including citizens, international students, and temporary visa persons. The Baha'i also came to America in the early 1900s, and it is estimated that there are some 100,000 living in the United States. Although Islam and the Baha'i have been present in America for decades, attention and relationships with them have been highlighted only recently.

Islam may be described as a religion based on unity, uniformity, and universality. There are little differences in dogma and rituals wherever Muslims are found, and the religion has a missionary vision of global impact. Some one billion Muslims reside on the earth, and it has been characterized as one of the fastest-growing religious communities in the world—second only to Christianity in numbers of adherents. The heartland of Islamic peoples is in the area of its birth, the Middle East; but Africa, Asia, Europe, and North America have become centers of Muslim presence and religious activity. Indonesia has been the most populous Muslim nation with some 90 million of its 140 million people professing Islam. Recent reports out of China indicate there may be from forty to eighty million Muslims within its boundaries. Muslims travel the globe to study in universities, to transact business, and to visit relatives and friends.

The Language of Islam

Islam means submission to God (*Allah*), and *Muslim* means one who submits.[2] The roots and expansion of Islam began with the city of Mecca in Saudi Arabia, from which its prophet came, and extend to the moon, whose crescent symbol Muslims place on their flags. Clues to the history and development of Islam may be found in eight words beginning with M: *Mecca, Muhummad, Medina, mosque, minaret, mambar, mihrab,* and *moon.*

Mecca in Saudia Arabia is the birthplace of the Prophet Muhammad (A.D. 572-632) and the holiest city in Islam, which contains the Ka'ba, the central shrine to which Muslims are to make a holy pilgrimage before death. Muhammad was born of a tribe in Mecca and was a resident when he received revelations to preach to the people of the city the law of the one God, Allah. Because his preaching upset the people who worshiped various idols, he had to flee the city in 622. He was welcomed by the people in *Medina,* some two hundred miles to the north. Muhammad became the religious and political leader of Medina and raised an army. He took Mecca, established the holy shrine, and from the two key cities of Mecca and Medina after his death in 632, followers took Islam across the Middle East through North Africa, into Europe, and eastward through Persia, India, and China in about one hundred years. Muslim merchants, inspired by missionary zeal, carried Islam to East and West Africa and to other parts of Asia by the sixteenth century.

The mosque (*masjid*) with its minaret, mambar, and mihrab, became the worship center in Medina and in Mecca. *Mosque* means "place of prostration." Prophet Muhammad made the mosque a place for varied religious activities. The *minaret,* with its spirals skyward, served as the elevated column attached to the mosque proper from whose top one could call the people to prayer. *Mihrab* was the niche in the mosque wall which signaled the direction to the Ka'ba in Mecca toward which the people bowed in prayer. *Mambar* was the raised seat attached to the mosque wall from which Muhammad preached. Muslims came to the mosque for legal counsel and judgments by Muhammad on all matters of life, both civil and domestic. People came to pray, hear the sermon, visit in the courtyards, plan marriages for their children, and socialize. The mosque became the focal point in Muslim consciousness for all matters pertaining to God and man. The mosque has continued many of its traditional functions, including Islamic education and missionary propaganda.

Islam adopted the lunar calendar to measure time, and the crescent symbol of the moon became a symbol for Muslim identity. The flags of Islamic nations may carry the crescent. Cities, shrines, sermons and prayers are most important to traditional Islam. Besides Mecca and Medina, Jerusalem is important to Muslims. Prophet Muhammad chose Jerusalem as the focal direction for prayer, which he later changed to Mecca. There is an Islamic tradition that Muhammad visited Jerusalem and was uplifted to heaven from the spot now known as the Dome of the Rock.

There is both unity and uniformity in what Muslims believe and practice. Ideally, one would not be able to differentiate between what an African Muslim believes and practices from an Asian Muslim. Islam holds that there are no sectarian or denominational divisions within its community. There appear to be some differences among the Sunni, Shi'ite, and Sufi Muslims, however. Muhammad taught that there was one God to be obeyed, one revealed Scripture to be followed, one law to be known, and one last prophet to be trusted, regardless of geographical boundaries or social positions.

Islamic Beliefs

Allah, which means "the God," is the one and only God. Allah does not share his divinity with anyone or anything. Islam is a monotheistic religion, a prophetic religion, and a revealed religion. Allah has revealed his truth and law through the prophet, Muhammad. Muhammad was the human channel to receive the infallible and perfect revelation and law of Allah which became codified in the *Qur'an,* the sacred scripture of Islam. Muslims believe that the *Qur'an* is literally in heaven and that Muhammad only recited what the angel Gabriel brought from Allah.

There have been other prophets and other scriptures. The Qur'an names at least twenty-eight prophets beginning with Adam and moving through Abraham, Moses, and Jesus to Muhammad, who is considered the "seal of the prophets." Other scriptures have been the *Torah,* revealed to the Jews, and the *Injil* (Gospel), revealed to the Christians. Jews and

Christians, however, distorted the Scriptures revealed by the prophets, and the true and correct revelation of both Torah and Injil is found in the Qur'an. Muslims refer to Jews, Christians, and themselves as "People of the Book," with the understanding that they have the correct book in the Qur'an.

Muslims believe that God has revealed his law in the Qur'an and that it is a perfect and complete roadmap for life. Life is lived under the judgment and in the will of God. History has a beginning and an end, and at its conclusion is a heaven and a hell. Muslims are often heard saying, "If God wills." They tend to view their destiny under the strong will of God. Angels are messengers from God, and Gabriel brought the Qur'an from God to Muhammad who later codified it. The beliefs of Islam, then, include monotheism, prophets, holy scripture, a strong ethical life, and a judgment day with eternal consequences for one's soul.

Islamic Practices

Regular religious practice is mandated in the Qur'an for the one who faithfully obeys God. Five major practices or "pillars of faith" exist in Islam.

(1) Confession—"There is no deity but Allah, and Muhammad is the messenger of Allah." Some say the mere confession of God and Muhammad in this context is enough to make one a Muslim. Others would hold fervently that one must make the confession as well as perform and complete the four other practices.

(2) Prayer—The practice of prayer is a stated ritual some five times each day. It may be stated in the home, the mosque, or at one's work; however, it is time consuming. Before each time of prayer, one must wash hands, arms, and feet ceremoniously for purification. Specific words are used, especially in Arabic, and postures and genuflections are coordinated with the words to symbolize one's relationship to God. Prayer in the mosque is said in Arabic because Muslims believe that Arabic is the language of God, since the Qur'an came down from heaven in that

language. Muslims may also pray more personal prayers in their vernacular languages.

(3) Fasting—This is observed for twenty-eight consecutive days in the special lunar month. During the month from sunrise to sunset, there is no consumption of food or liquid, and there is no sexual intercourse. The fast may be broken at sunset each day. Muslims view fasting as a healthy measure as well as a season to meditate upon God and to give to the needy. Fasting is an especially difficult time in countries where the stated month falls in the hottest season.

(4) Giving—Muslims are required to give certain percentages of their income and their possessions to the causes of Islam. This fourth practice is explicitly stated in the Qur'an. Almsgiving supports the work of the mosques and the livelihood of the clergy.

(5) The pilgrimage of hajj—The Qur'an states that each Muslim must make the pilgrimage to Mecca once in a lifetime if health and economic means are sufficient. The pilgrimage may take up to one month. Shrines are visited in Mecca and Medina. Rituals and prayers are performed around the shrines, and the pilgrims return to their neighbors and friends back home with a special status of *hajji* (male) or *hajjieh* (female).

Some add a sixth pillar to the practices of Islam. It is the *jihad*. Jihad means "holy efforts" or "holy conquest" in the name of Allah. Each Muslim is obligated to be on jihad for Allah. That means to be a missionary for the Islamic faith. Jihad is sometimes used when a Muslim nation goes to war against the infidels. Islam has spread to every continent because of its emphasis upon personal and community jihad.

Islam is perhaps one of the most monolithic religions of all. Its major beliefs and practices are stated explicitly in the Qur'an, and conformity and unity are quite obvious across cultures. The Muslim life-style is most conspicuous in the activities of the mosque. The leader of the mosque is the *imam*.[3] He serves as the model for the people in their rituals. Muslims line up behind the imam for prayer; they recite the words he announces as they bow behind him in unity. They sit and listen to the imam expound from the truths of the Qur'an. They give the imam their alms for distribution to meet the needs of the mosque and the needy.

The lunar calendar characterizes the life-style of all Muslims as well as the set times of each day for prayer. Muslims pray together in the mosque at stated times each day. They fast the same month, they take the pilgrimage the same month, and they hear the stated sermon at high noon on Friday around the world. Although Muslims may perform their religious obligations individually, the primary duty is to be together in their practices. It is to be the umma, the brotherhood of Islam.

Branches of Islam

Islamic history demonstrates much unity in doctrinal statements and ritualistic practices. Since its origins there have been sectarian divisions. A major disagreement occurred soon after the death of Muhammad from which several branches of Islamic communities emerged. The most noted branches are the *Sunni* and the *Shi'ite*. The question of leadership arose after the prophet died. The Sunni branch claimed that the prophet left no heirs and no individual preferences, thus, they favored an election of a leader from the community. The Sunni established the calliphate with the *caliph* ruling in religious and political matters.

The Shi'ite branch claimed that the prophet named his successor. It was Ali, the cousin and son-in-law of the prophet, married to his daughter Fatimeh.[4] The leaders of the Islamic community were to remain in the prophet's family. The Shi'ite established the imamate and named Ali as the first imam. His two sons, Hasan and Husain, became the second and third imams. Twelve imams ruled until the end of the ninth century when the twelfth imam disappeared. Many believe that the twelfth imam went into occultation. He is the hidden imam and will return one day. Until that time, it is the duty of a *mujtahed* or an *ayatollah* to preside over the community as an agent of the hidden imam. In modern times Ayatollah Khomaini was the classic example of the Shi'ite tradition.

The Sunni claim to be the true bearers of the Islamic tradition. Sunni means orthodox or traditional. Sunni are the great majority of Muslims represented in all parts of the world with their strong ties to the heartland of the Middle East. Saudi Arabia is the strong Sunni nation and is guardian over the sacred precincts of Mecca and Medina. Shi'ite means partisan and came to mean partisan to Ali and his family. Shi'ites are represented heavily in Iran, Iraq, and Lebanon. Their major shrines are in Iraq and Iran where many of the imams are buried. The shrine of Husain in Kerbala, Iraq, is especially sacred.

Differences between the Sunni and the Shi'ite over succession do not prevent them from worship and prayer together. Major beliefs and practices, as described above, are the same for both. Both may attend the same mosque, stand beside one another in prayer, and make the pilgrimage to Mecca at the same time.

Other prominent groups of Muslims include the *Ahmadiyyas,* the *Sufi,* the Nation of Islam and the American Muslim Mission. The Ahmadiyyas represent a distinct sect of Islam in which their founder claimed to have superseded the prophet Muhammad. The *Sufi* are the mystical wing of Islam, led by their sheiks and formed by their brotherhoods, who view God in personal terms and stress more the love of God than the law. The Nation of Islam, led by Elijah Muhammad and referred to as Black Muslims, was a segregationist movement appealing to American blacks. Major branches of Islam around the world did not accept the Nation of Islam; it has continued under the leadership of Louis Farrakhan. The American Muslim Mission emerged after the death of Elijah Muhammad under the leadership of his son, Wallace Muhammad. The American Muslim Mission attempted to align itself with orthodox Islam in order to find more acceptance among worldwide Muslims.

There has been great unity as well as some fragmentation among Muslims since their early beginnings. Conflicts have emerged in the twentieth century between Islamic nations and other nations and among Islamic nations themselves. The emergence of the state of Israel and the Palestinian problems have both united and also divided Muslims. Egypt, a Muslim nation, made accommodations with Israel at the displeasure of surrounding Muslim countries. India was partitioned to include nations of Muslims. Iran and Iraq, both claiming Shi'ite majorities, have waged war over boundary disputes and demonstrated endless battles between various factions, including Muslims fighting Muslims.

Conflict among Islamic nations and among Muslim peoples suggests the strength and importance, at times, of national, tribal, ethnic, and sectarian priorities over the unity and brotherhood espoused by Islam. Disputes and fragmentation often involve a background of religion and politics. Although the ideal of Islam is unity, the reality is often diversity and conflict. However, Islam has strong symbols and practices of unity, especially as they unite around prayer and pilgrimage.

Muslims in the United States

No land or people are beyond the missionary heart of Islam. The United States has attracted Muslims during the twentieth century. Reports are that some Muslims entered the new world with Spanish explorers and with slave trades. Significant numbers of Muslims, however, began entering the states before World War I. They came from the heartland of the Middle East, namely, Palestine, Lebanon, Syria, and Jordan. They settled in the Northeast and the Midwest. Others came from the Balkans. After World War II, immigration rules changed, and many Muslims entered from the Middle East, Asia, and Africa. For the most part, they were professional people. Some came for political asylum. Many came to study. Some married Americans and became citizens. Accurate figures are not available, but there are estimates of over three million Muslims living in the United States, and some sixty nations are represented by Muslims.

Muslims often form communities based on ethnicity and nationality. These may be called immigrant communities.[5] The Toledo, Ohio, and the Detroit, Michigan, areas have large numbers of Arabs. A Turkish community is evident in Patterson, New Jersey. Lebanese began an Islamic center in Quincy, Massachusetts. Tens of thousands of Arabs are in southern California and many more Iranians across California. Over thirty thousand Yemenis are in Dearborn, Michigan. Albanians form a strong Muslim association in Waterbury, Connecticut. Fifteen Sunni mosques are in New York City, and a mosque was built for eight thousand Albanian Muslims in New York City. Active Muslim centers exist in Atlanta, Jacksonville, Raleigh, and Trenton. Yugoslav Muslims have built an Islamic center in suburban Chicago. Thus, immigrant communities in large cities and small towns form associations and build Islamic centers to meet their religious needs.

With the oil wealth expanding the budgets of some Muslim countries, students flocked by the tens of thousands to American colleges and universities. Support was given by individual families. Governments sent many students on scholarships, anticipating their return to aid their nations in becoming modern societies. It is estimated that before the Iranian Revolution, Iranian students numbered over fifty thousand. Saudi Arabia and the Arab Gulf States are placing thousands of students in American universities.

Since 1963 the Muslim Students' Association of the United States and Canada (MSA), with headquarters in Plainfield, Indiana, has involved thousands of students on college and university campuses. MSA has over 150 chapters across the nation, publishing newspapers, magazines, and holding conferences to promote Islamic understanding. The association is at the forefront of fostering social justice and making political statements about the concerns and welfare of Muslims across the world.

Alongside the immigrant and student populations, there are Muslims married to Americans, and there are Native American Muslims among the black population. World Islam has entered a renaissance period, it seems, if not a revival, and the presence of Islam in America has widened. Renewed interest in Islamic history, literature, art, and religion is present. Muslims indeed have come West. There are more Muslims in England than Methodists, and Islam is the second largest religion in France. Islam is growing in America too.

On February 6, 1992, Iman Wallace Dean Muhammad, the former director of the American Muslim Mission, delivered the opening prayer for the United States Senate. He was the first Muslim cleric to give this prayer. Muslim leaders have suggested that banks, post offices, and other businesses should honor Islamic holidays as they do Christian and Jewish ones. A group of Muslims have initiated a plan to build the "Islamic Way Community" near Talbotton, Georgia. The community will include a shopping mall, one hundred residential homes, schools, and an Islamic university.

Islamic Centers

There are over three hundred Islamic centers across the United States. They range in size from a small rented room to an exquisite mosque with Middle Eastern decor and minarets. The Islamic Center of Washington, D.C., located on Massachusetts Avenue, is striking in its Middle Eastern architecture; its minarets point skyward. Inside, plush Persian carpets, intricate tile mosaics, and fine-crafted mambar make it a special Islamic place in America. The Center is a quiet place for Muslims to read the Qur'an and to recite their prayers. A room with water for purification is available. A library, conference room, and a courtyard are included for study and rest. The board of directors is composed of ambassadors from Islamic nations, and a recent director has been a Palestinian with an American Ph.D.

At Shaw University in Raleigh, North Carolina, Muslims worship in the Mosque of King Kahlid Ben Saud.[6] The late king of Saudi Arabia financed its building. This mosque and Islamic center serves the Raleigh-area Muslim community of several thousand members. Muslims have also built a two-story mosque adjacent to the campus of North Carolina State University. The imam-director is from Syria.

Perhaps one of the largest and most recent centers is the Islamic Center of Greater Toledo. The first immigrants to Toledo from Syria and Lebanon established the Syrian American Muslim Society in the late 1930s. In 1954 the first Islamic Center was built in Toledo. With the increase of Muslims to greater Toledo, the center could not meet the religious and social needs of its members. In 1978, forty-eight acres were purchased at the junction of I-475 and I-75, a prime location. The center was designed by the noted Turkish architect, the late Talat Itil of Toledo. It incorporates the traditional Islamic architecture. Construction began in 1982 and was completed within a year.

> Built with white brick, reinforced steel and poured con-
> crete, the center occupies 1/3 of an acre and has
> 26,000 square feet covered area. Flanked by two 135
> feet tall minarets, the sixty foot dome sits on a carpeted
> octagonal prayer area with accommodation for 1,000
> people. The upper floor contains a 500 seat sermon
> hall, suite of offices, council chambers, a library and
> medical clinic. The basement contains 10 full size class-
> rooms, a large kitchen and a dining area for accommo-
> dation for 300 people.
>
> Made of faceted glass, seventy-two windows adorn the
> building. There are 32 small windows in the dome with
> attributes of God written in Arabic calligraphy. The
> large windows in the prayer area and on the front carry
> verses from Qur'an, the holy book, written in different
> styles of Arabic calligraphy. The rest of the windows in
> the building are also inscribed with Qur'anic inscrip-

tions. The windows were designed by Roy Calligan of the Calligan Enterprises International of Pennsylvania.

The new building of the Islamic Center of Greater Toledo is one of a kind in North America because of its size and its classic Islamic architecture.[7]

The paved parking area around the mosque is neatly lined for one thousand vehicles. The kitchen contains ultramodern appliances. Long-range plans include a retirement home and a school. Officers of the Center for 1984-85 included a president, a vice-president, and a secretary-general counsel who held the Ph.D., the M.D., and the J.D. respectively. The imam holds a B.S.W. from Egypt, an M.A. from the prestigious Al Azhar University of Cairo, and an M.A. from Alberta. The Islamic Center of Greater Toledo can be seen from great distances as the two heavily traveled interstate highways converge at its door. It draws Muslims from as far away as Canada.

Islamic centers across the United States appear to be healthy and growing. Centers such as those in Toledo, Los Angeles, and Washington depict deep roots in American culture and appeal to internationals as well as American citizens. Some centers have received funds from Muslim nations affluent in oil and zealous in mission. Others have been built by the immigrant population who want facilities for worship and community service. Recently the Islamic Center of Virginia opened in Richmond in an affluent suburb, alongside various churches. Muslims in America are committed, visionary, and able to gather and build their centers.

The American Muslim Mission

The Nation of Islam and the American Muslim Mission are indigenous expressions of Islam in the United States. They have attempted to preserve and portray an Islamic perspective, and their appeal has been primarily to the American black community. Since the early 1930s Islam has made inroads among blacks, introduced by leaders capitalizing on the racism in American society and mixing Islamic religion with the cultural values and politics of the day. Until recently, Islamic leaders outside the United States had little to do with "Black Muslims." They considered them distortioners and heretics of true Islam. With the death of the founder of the Nation of Islam and its name change to American Muslim Mission, its leaders changed their teachings and programs toward orthodox Islam, and their movement found more favor in the international Muslim community.

The American Muslim Mission had its origins in the appearance of Fard Muhammad, sometimes called Mr. W. D. Fard, in Detroit in 1930.[8] He sold silk to the black community. His identity continues to be shrouded in mystery. Various reports describe him as half black and half white as well as half black and half Syrian. He claimed to have been born in Mecca. He preached black supremacy, that God is black. Fard claimed that he had come to bring the "lost-found nation of Islam." His charismatic personality attracted followers; and he organized the University of Islam (elementary and secondary school) and the Fruit of Islam (organization to teach defense and security). His movement became known as the Nation of Islam.

His successor was Elijah Muhammad, formerly known as Elijah Poole, born to a black Baptist preacher in Georgia. Elijah Muhammad had been named Minister of Islam by Fard and had helped found the Islamic worship centers in Detroit and Chicago. In 1934 Elijah assumed leadership of the Nation of Islam after it was purported that Fard had disappeared. Elijah preached the doctrines of Fard, and he also spoke of Fard as being divine. "Elijah Muhammad was almost single-handedly responsible for the deification of Fard and for the perpetuation of his teachings in the early years after Fard disappeared."[9] Elijah became for his followers the Messenger or Prophet of Allah, appearing to usurp the place of Prophet Muhammad of the seventh century.

Elijah Muhammad told the story of "Yacub's History," which depicted Fard Muhammad as God who came to destroy the white race and restore the black race to its superior place in the world. During the late 1950s and 1960s, the Nation of Islam grew, caught up in the momentum of the civil rights movement. Elijah claimed that he had a half million followers by 1962, but others suggested some ten to fifteen thousand. The movement's expansion was due in large measure to Malcolm X, formerly known as Malcolm Little. Elijah appointed Malcolm to be minister of Harlem Temple No. 7 in New York City. He was a charismatic preacher, a good organizer, and the ideologue of the movement as he edited the weekly newspaper, *Muhammad Speaks.*

American black Muslims heard Malcolm, with Elijah's blessing, tell them to segregate from whites, seek their own territory, refuse to fight for the nation, and refuse to pay taxes. Personal hygiene was emphasized; prohibition of extramarital sex, alcohol, tobacco, gambling, movies, and dancing was announced. Black education and black businesses were encouraged. "Be black, think black, and buy black" became the emphasis. The Universities of Islam became parochial schools with certified teachers. The curriculum included the Arabic language and Islamic history and culture.

In the midst of prosperity as a movement, dissension emerged between Elijah and Malcolm. Malcolm was extremely popular. He had helped to found many temples across the nation. He learned from several women of their impending paternity suits against Elijah. Malcolm made a statement at the time of President Kennedy's assassination that it was "the chickens coming home to roost." Elijah prohibited Malcolm from publicly speaking. About this time Malcolm made the hajj to Mecca.[10] This experience profoundly influenced him to see Islam at its roots, the meaning of the brotherhood of Islam, and the distortions brought to Islam by Elijah and his teachings. He consequently resigned the Nation of Islam in 1964 and formed his own black nationalist group known as the Muslim Mosque Inc. In 1965 Malcolm was assassinated while speaking to a group in Harlem.

After Malcolm X's death, Elijah named Louis Farrakhan the National Minister for the Nation of Islam and minister of the Harlem temple, succeeding Malcolm in both positions. Farrakhan had been a close friend of Malcolm, but he had loyalty to Elijah. Farrakhan had been a nightclub calypso singer. During the 1970s the Nation grew, and properties were bought in places like Michigan, Alabama, and Georgia. The Nation claimed by the mid-1970s to have temples in over 150 cities, forty-six universities, and a multitude of business enterprises including banks, restaurants, supermarkets, canneries, and apartment units. There were reports of impending financial crisis, loan defaults, and little cash flow; and it was obvious that the organization faced a catastrophic financial crisis.

By 1975 the Nation of Islam had achieved wide recognition throughout black communities as an alternate religious choice for blacks. It had appealed to the idealism of young blacks for new status and dignity; and sports figures, including the heavyweight champion Muhammad Ali, formerly Cassius Clay from Kentucky, brought Islam wider publicity. There was considerable tension within the Nation and between the Nation and the other Muslim groups. There were estimates in 1973 of some seventy Muslim groups in America, many of which were small groups of blacks with various social and religious agendas. A Hanafi Muslim family death in Washington, D.C., in 1973 was attributed to tensions between the Hanafi group and the Nation. Within the Nation there was discontent over the use of funds and the life-styles of the leaders. There was a growing voice for the Nation to heed some of the changes which Malcolm X heralded.

Elijah Muhammad died on February 25, 1975, and his son, Wallace Muhammad, assumed leadership the next day. Wallace was born in 1933. He had been active in the youth and adult activities of the Nation of Islam, and he had served as the minister of the Philadelphia temple. He had been imprisoned as a conscientious objector, was married several times, was suspended from the Nation by his father for immoral behavior. Wallace had been friends with Malcolm X and had become aware of some of the shortcomings of his father.

Wallace Muhammad began to make changes in both the beliefs and practices of the Nation of Islam.[11] He talked more of God being mind than black. He talked more of the white devil being in the mind of whites than the white race being the devil. He downplayed his father's teaching on the divinity of Fard Muhammad. He forecast a new mission for his people. They began to call themselves Bilalian Muslims and changed their newspaper to *Bilalian News*. Bilal was an African slave who became the first prayer leader for Prophet Muhammad. This change by Wallace appeared to place his movement more in the mainline Islamic tradition. In 1976 the Nation of Islam became the World Community of Islam in the West (WCIW). The name change indicated the emerging strategy of Wallace to align his movement with orthodox Islamic teachings and practices and to open up membership to nonblacks.

Wallace had inherited a financial crisis institution, with business enterprises running at $2 million yearly deficit and outstanding loans of some $10 million. He turned his attention to financial matters and to the administration of the business affairs. He also brought changes to the organization and dismissed those disloyal to him. He transferred Louis Farrakhan from New York to the Chicago mosque. Farrakhan had become a popular leader and possibly a challenge to Wallace. Farrakhan resigned in 1978 to begin his own Muslim movement based on the teachings of the Nation of Islam as led by Elijah Muhammad.

As the 1980s began, Wallace continued changes in his movement toward greater appreciation of America and toward orthodox Islam.[12] He had established a Council of Imams, numbering six, with administrative responsibilities for six territories across the United States. He took the title of Chief Imam and appointed the council, which was responsible directly to him. He had the symbol of the American flag printed on the newspaper, and had the children in the schools give allegiance to the flag. In 1980 the WCIW's name was changed to the American Muslim Mission. The *Bilalian News* was changed to *World Muslim News* in 1981, and in 1982, it became the *A.M. Journal.*

The Islamization of Wallace's organization continued with name changes and the initiation of orthodox practices. Wallace took on the name of Warith Deen Muhammad. Temples became mosques (*masajid*). Ministers became imams. Chairs were removed from the temples, and worshipers sat on carpeted floors. Imams were trained in Arabic studies to understand Islam and to lead the people in prayer in the Arabic language of the Qur'an. Muslims were given classes in the study of the Qur'an and in Arabic. The fasting season of *Ramadan* was observed according to the Muslim lunar calendar.

Warith encouraged his people to prepare for and to make the pilgrimage (*hajj*) to Mecca, and imams organized tour groups for the hajj. Warith warned his followers away from their cultic worship of his father, Elijah Muhammad, by teaching them the Islamic confession of faith to mean belief in the Prophet Muhammad as the seal of the prophets, not his father. The Fruit of Islam security force of males was disbanded, and men were engaged in other mosque activities. The Universities of Islam became the Sister Clara Muhammad Elementary and Secondary Schools (Clara was Elijah Muhammad's wife).

A special committee was formed by Warith, the Committee to Remove All Images of the Divine (C.R.A.I.D.). Its purpose was through writings and meetings to sensitize churches to remove statues and pictures of Jesus. Warith claimed that blacks in churches were being led to look at a white Jesus and thus compound their inferiority and continue emphasis upon race. In the formation of the American

Muslim Mission with a new direction, he had opened up membership to all peoples.

The American Muslim Mission Committee to Purchase 100,000 Commodities was launched in 1982 to foster collective buying power by members of the organization. The American Muslim Teachers College was inaugurated in 1980 with certification in Chicago and with the intention of having a campus and training school in Sedalia, North Carolina. Down payments on property were made, and administrators arrived in North Carolina, but due to financial crises and poor administration, the Teachers College never blossomed. Wallace authored several books in the new period of his movement, As the Light Shineth from the East, Religion on the Line, and Prayer and Al-Islam.

Beginning in 1982, it became obvious through speeches made by Warith and through publications, that there was a crisis in the American Muslim Mission. Warith made statements that inferred that the Council of Imams could no longer be trusted with responsibilities. He stated that he was severing his ties with the council. It was rumored that the imams of key mosques were competing among themselves for power and prestige, and that even some of them were in communication with Louis Farrakhan.

Not only was there dissension within the household of imams, there was also the court case involving the family members of Elijah Muhammad who claimed Elijah's holdings belonged to them, and not to the Muslim organization. The family, which consisted of the illegitimate children of Elijah, was awarded millions of dollars by the court. Warith appealed the decision. The courts ruled that the American Muslim Mission turn over its funds to settle the court case. Some speculated that this action would cause Warith to have to declare bankruptcy.

At a convention of some twelve thousand held in Georgia in 1982, Warith was snubbed by some of the imams. By 1984 Warith had declared that he had severed all relationships with the existing imams and that he was only responsible for being imam of the Chicago mosque. He also established the Muslim American Community Assistance Fund. Warith indicated that only those imams who would personally pledge their support to him would be part of his movement. A financial crisis existed. Imams had been fired; others had expressed dissension with the direction of the movement. Warith Deen Muhammad had disassociated himself from the imams and called for a new beginning.

One of the imams, who publicly declared his support of Warith and his withdrawal from relationship with other imams until they proved their loyalty to Warith, was Warith's nephew, Sultan Muhammad, imam of the Washington, D.C., mosque and member of the old Council of Imams. The Washington Masjid, located at 1519 4th Street, N.W., Washington, D.C., was one of the oldest buildings of the American Muslim Mission. From a pamphlet published in the early 1980s, it was described as follows:

> With the Name Allah, the Gracious, the compassionate, As-Salaam-Alaikum/Peace Be Unto You

> The Washington Masjid (Mosque) is one of 150 places of worship (masajid) and centers of the American Muslim Mission (AMM). The AMM is the largest Muslim community in America and has places of worship in every major U.S. city and the Caribbean Islands. This community follows the principles and practices of the religion Al-Islam and is guided by Allah's (God's) instruction in the Holy Qur'an (revealed Scripture) and the Sunnah (work, action, word) of Prophet Muhammad, Peace Be Upon Him.

> The physical building was constructed in 1960. It was the first Temple built by Elijah Muhammad and his followers in the Nation of Islam (N.O.I.). The N.O.I. began in 1930-34 with the teachings of W.D. Fard. These symbolic teachings were designed to attract African-Americans through emphasis on mystical theology and the separation of the races. The Honorable Elijah Muhammad assumed leadership of the community in

1934 and stressed the establishment of respect and dignity with all members of society through economic development and moral excellence.

The community experienced a phenomenal transition from the N.O.I. to the World Community of Al-Islam in the West March 1975 and again to the American Muslim Mission May 1980. This development is viewed by many as the work of the Almighty Creator. The major element of the transition has been the full acceptance of and adherence to the Holy Qur'an as the guidance of God as well as respect from the entire Muslim world.

Imam Warith Deen Muhammad, son of Elijah Muhammad, was thrust into leadership of the N.O.I. by the sudden death of his father on February 25, 1975. This Imam (leader by example) brought the N.O.I. through its transformation and into great prominence as a social reformation movement. Through sensitive leadership, piercing scriptural interpretation, and profound commentary on major social issues, Imam Muhammad has received numerous awards and is becoming established as a global leader. Mr. Muhammad has taken bold steps to encourage and improve communications between all major faiths in America and is viewed by many as the leader to survive true religion for the whole human race.[13]

The Washington Masjid held its *jumah* congregational prayer service each Friday at noon. On Sundays at 1 P.M., Tal'alim instruction classes were held. The Community Night Service was held on Tuesday evenings. Other classes held throughout the week included Islamic studies, orientation classes, prayer classes, Qur'anic reading classes, and Holy Qur'anic Arabic classes. A Sister Clara Muhammad Elementary School and Muslim Sunday School were also operated. It had committees for prison services, youth, and missions. A resident imam and an assistant imam administered the mosque.

The American Muslim Mission with the Washington Masjid and its five hundred families demonstrated a vigorous religious community. Efforts by Warith Deen Muhammad led to adaptations to American society as well as to alliance to orthodox Islam.

The vitality of the Washington mosque was not enough to keep the American Muslim Mission a viable organization. There had been too much internal dissension. There were too many legal battles for monies and properties. The American Muslim Mission lost its status, and its leaders and followers scattered to other Muslim communities or dropped out. Wallace continued to be a symbolic leader of a small band of followers.

Meanwhile, Louis Farrakhan, the former loyal minister to Elijah Muhammad, continued the themes of the Nation of Islam. While Wallace Muhammad attempted change, Louis Farrakhan became the leader of a "revitalized" Nation of Islam. He has stirred controversy by referring to Judaism as a "dirty" religion and to Hitler as the "wickedly great" architect of Nazi Germany. In an issue of his newspaper, *The Final Call,* Farrakhan said that Jewish involvement in the slave trade justified his anti-Jewish rhetoric. Farrakhan has his base in Chicago, and mosques belonging to his Nation of Islam are scattered across the United States.

The Baha'i

Origins

The Baha'i religion made its way to America at the turn of the twentieth century. It was founded in Iran, formerly known as Persia, by Mirza Husayn Ali (1817-1892). He became known as *Baha'ullah,* which means Glory of God. The word *Baha'i* comes from *Baha* which means glory or splendor, and it is used to refer to a follower of *Baha'ullah.* In mid-nineteenth century Persia, Shi'ite Islam was strong. One of the major beliefs of the Shi'ite faith was expectation of the return of the twelfth imam who would renew religion and be the true guide to the faithful. The twelfth imam was the successor to Prophet Muhammad. Many believed that the imam had gone into occultation and at a propitious time would return.

On May 22, 1844, in Shiraz, Persia, Siyyid Ali Muhammad pronounced that he was the expected twelfth imam. He said this to a prominent member of the Shaykhi sect of Islam who especially awaited the return of the imam. He gained disciples and assumed the title of the *Bab,* which means gate. He preached across Persia the coming of "Him Whom God Shall Make Manifest." The government and the Shi'ite clergy were alarmed at his preaching. After some years of imprisonment, the Bab was executed in Tabriz, Persia in 1850. Tradition holds that the first shots fired left him unharmed, and a second attempt was necessary.[14]

A disciple of the Bab, Mirza Husayn Ali, was imprisoned in Tehran when two of the Bab's followers attempted to assassinate the Shah. While in prison, Mirza began to understand his impending role as a messenger of God, as Baha'ullah. He was exiled to Baghdad in 1853. In April of 1863, he declared to some of his followers that he was the messenger of God as prophesied by the Bab. He was transferred by Ottoman authorities to Constantinople and then to Adrianople. He issued a series of letters, known as tablets, to the leaders of Persia, Turkey, Russia, Prussia, Austria, Britain, and the pope and certain Christian and Muslim leaders informing them of his mission of unity and peace. Again, he was exiled from Turkey to Akko (Acre), Palestine. He died in 1892, but not before he had named his elder son, Abdul Baha (1844-1921), which means "servant of the Glory," as leader of the Baha'i community.

Abdul Baha was both administrator and interpreter of the movement as it moved out of Persia and the Ottoman Empire. He traveled in Africa, Europe, and America during 1910-1913, and before his death Baha'i groups had been formed in North Africa, the Far East, Australia, and the United States. Baha appointed his oldest grandson, Shoghi

Effendi (1896-1957) as Guardian of the Cause. Shoghi Effendi served as the official leader of the Baha'i until his death. He named no individual successor, but established the Universal House of Justice located in Haifa, Israel, to serve as the governing body for Baha'i work around the globe.

Baha'i in America

The Baha'i faith was publicly introduced to Americans at the World Parliament of Religions in Chicago in 1893.[15] A talk on the Baha'i faith, prepared by Reverend Henry H. Jessup, was delivered in his absence by another speaker. Groups of the Baha'i were formed in several cities. In 1898, the first group of American pilgrims visited Haifa to meet Abdul Baha and returned to spread their faith. Professor E. G. Browne, a Cambridge University orientalist, wrote of both Baha'ullah and Abdul Baha in his *A Traveller's Narrative.* An American writer, Ethel Stevens, visited Palestine and stayed with Abdul Baha and his family. In 1911 her account was printed in *Everybody's Magazine,* in which she described his worldwide significance. Americans had written access to the Baha'i founders.

The visit of Abdul Baha to the United States from April 11 to December 5, 1912, was what gave great impetus to Baha'i presence and growth. He described his visit as his "purpose to set forth in America the fundamental principles of the revelation and teachings of the Baha'ullah. It will then become the duty of the Bahais . . . to give these principles unfoldment and application in the minds, hearts, and lives of the people."[16] He traveled for 230 days visiting major cities. In Chicago he laid the foundation stone for the first Baha'i House of Worship in the western hemisphere. The House became the headquarters for the National Spiritual Assembly located in Wilmette, Illinois, a suburb of Chicago.

The Baha'i in America, as well as worldwide, have grown quietly and surely. There are 100,000 adherents in the nation, and an estimate of 3.5 million in the world. Baha'i have achieved worldwide attention with their persecution and execution in Iran under the Shi'ite revolution and its continuation.[17] They have been discriminated against by the majority Muslim population since their beginnings in Iran. Some consider them a false religion. Others have classified them as an heretical sect of Islam. The Shah of Iran provided an umbrella of protection for all religious minorities in Iran, including the Baha'i, who were the largest minority with some three thousand followers. With the Iranian revolution and Ayatollah Khomaini's regime, systematic persecution against them ensued with executions. Reports state that since 1979 over 150 have been executed, 550 have been imprisoned, and thousands have lost their homes and possessions. Their cemeteries and assembly halls have been desecrated, and their holiest shrine, the House of the Bab in Shiraz, has been torn down. Their leadership has been virtually wiped out.

Baha'ullah, the prophet/founder, left a plan by which all the people of the world could be united. That plan is described as follows:

> Free from any form of ecclesiasticism, having neither priesthood nor man-made ritual, and forbidding asceticism, monasticism, and mendicancy, the Baha'i Faith relies on a pattern of local, national, and international administration, created by Baha'ullah, elaborated by Abdul Baha, and implemented by Shoghi Effendi. Each locality, for instance, of nine or more adult Baha'is, elects each year a council—a Local Spiritual Assembly. At present, there are over 25,500 assemblies throughout the world.

> National Spiritual Assemblies are also elected annually by previously elected delegates who come together in a national convention. There are over 130 National Spiritual Assemblies. Once every five years, at an international convention, these assemblies gather to elect the Universal House of Justice, the supreme institution of the Baha'i Faith. All Baha'i elections take place by secret ballot, with no nominations or electioneering.

Appointive institutions also exist in the Baha'i International Community. Among them are the Hands of the Cause of God and the Continental Board of Counsellors, who are assisted in their work by Auxiliary Boards. Their functions are educative and center on teaching the Baha'i Faith and protecting the community.[18]

Organization

There are three levels of administration. When there are at least nine Baha'i in a community, they may form a Local Spiritual Assembly, with nine individuals serving on its council. At the national level there is a National Spiritual Assembly composed of nine Baha'i who administer the affairs. In America, this Assembly is located in Wilmette, Illinois, and was initiated by the visit of Abdul Baha in 1912. In Wilmette there is also the House of Worship, a beautiful facility which overlooks Lake Michigan. Other houses of worship are located in Frankfurt-am-Main, West Germany; Kampala, Uganda; Sydney, Australia; and Panama City, Panama.

There are plans for a House of Worship in every locality of sufficient numbers of Baha'i. The Local Spiritual Assembly serves as the base for worship and educational programs, and the National Spiritual Assembly serves for the national convention and administrative affairs of the country. Worship consists of readings from the Scriptures of many of the world's religions and a cappella music. Local meetings are often held in homes. The Baha'i Center of Washington, D.C., operates out of a house it owns on Sixteenth Street Northwest.

The third level of administration is the Universal House of Justice composed of nine individuals. The Universal House of Justice is located at the Baha'i world center in Haifa, Israel, on Mount Carmel overlooking the Mediterranean Sea. It functions as the supreme governing body, applying the laws taught by Baha'ullah and ruling on matters not included in the sacred texts. It is located in the immediate vicinity of the shrines of the Bab and of Abdul Baha. The shrine of Baha'ullah is located just outside of Akko at Bahji, the beautiful gardens.

Teachings

The sacred literature of the Baha'i includes the writings of Baha'ullah and the interpretations and clarifications of those writings by Abdul Baha and Shoghi Effendi. The Baha'i believe that these writings are inspired and are the revelation of God for this age. The *Kitab-i-Aqdas* (The Most Holy Book) and the *Kitab-i-Iqan* (The Book of Certitude) are Baha'ullah's teachings on the laws of and nature of God and religion. His *Hidden Words* is composed of brief statements on the nurturing and edification of the soul. There are many meditations, prayers, and letters. Baha'ullah has more than one hundred writings in print. There are also Abdul Baha's *Some Answered Questions* and Shoghi Effendi's *The World Order of Baha'ullah*.[19]

The teachings of the Baha'i focus on the oneness of God, the oneness of religion, and the oneness of humankind. Baha'ullah taught:

> that Divine Revelation is a religious truth is not absolute but relative continuous and progressive process
>
> that all the great religions of the world are divine in origin and
>
> that their missions represent successive stages in the spiritual evolution of human society.[20]

Baha'is believe that God reveals Himself through messengers or manifestations for each age, about every thousand years. These messengers have included Abraham, Moses, Zoroaster, Buddha, Jesus, Muhammad, the Bab, and for this age Baha'ullah. Each has brought the light of divine knowledge for each new age.

The essence of all religions is one, while each religion has specific features needed for a given time and place and level of a civilization. Therefore, a new manifestation like Baha'ullah comes for this age, while another may appear a thousand years after him. The purpose of humanity is to know and worship God and to lead forward an ever progressing civilization. Humans have immortal souls that enter a new form of existence after death. Heaven and hell are symbolic. Good deeds bring one near to God, while distance from God brings evil and suffering. To know God and worship Him fully, one must not only accept the manifestation of the age but also obey and fulfill the teachings.

> Since the Baha'i Faith teaches that the purpose of religion is the promotion of concord and unity, and that religion is the foremost agency for the achievement of peace and orderly progress in society, the Baha'i writings provide the outline of institutions necessary for the establishment of peace and world order—such as a world federation or commonwealth, with its executive, legislative, and judiciary arms, an international auxiliary language, a world economy, a mechanism of world intercommunication, and a universal system of currency, weights, and measures.[21]

Characteristics of the community, based on laws and obligations and teachings, include the reciting of specific prayers, a fasting season, a new calendar for religious obligations, and work with the United Nations. Fostering of good character through the development of spiritual qualities such as honesty, trustworthiness, compassion, and justice is essential. Stress is upon the elimination of all prejudices of race, creed, class, nationality, and sex. Each Baha'i through independent investigation sees the harmony of science and religion as two facets of truth. Males and females equally participate in all elective, administrative, and decision-making matters. Universal education is fostered.

> Daily Prayer—Baha'ullah tells us to pray daily. There are many Baha'i prayers, but Baha'ullah has given us three special prayers. We must say one of these each day.

Fast—Each year from March 2 to March 21 is a time of fasting; Baha'is have nothing to eat or drink from sunrise to sunset.

Nineteen Day Feast—Baha'is have a new calendar. The year is divided into 19 months. Each month has 19 days. On the first day of each Baha'i month the local Baha'i community comes together for prayer and readings from the Baha'i Holy Books community consultation from recent and future activities fellowship.

Drinking of alcohol (beer, wine, etc.) is strictly forbidden.

The use of drugs (including marijuana, peyote, heroin, L.S.D.) is strictly forbidden.

Baha'is must have their parents' consent before they marry and a Baha'i marriage ceremony is necessary.

Baha'is must obey the laws of the country in which they live.

Baha'is must not join political parties or become involved in politics.

Each Baha'i has the privilege and obligation to give regularly to the Baha'i Fund. Contributions are voluntary.

Every Baha'i should study the Baha'i teachings every day.

It is the duty of every Baha'i to teach the Baha'i Faith to others.

Every Baha'i should be honest and truthful and courteous to his fellow man.[22]

Membership in the Local Spiritual Assembly is open to those who place faith in Baha'ullah and who accept his teachings. There are no clergy and no sacraments. The calendar's year is divided into nineteen months of nineteen days each. There are four intercalary days with five days in leap year. New year begins on March 21. Other holy days when Baha'is do not work are the days in commemoration of Baha'ullah's announcement of his mission (April 21, 29, and May 2), the declaration of the mission of the Bab (May 23), the birth of Baha'ullah (November 12), the birth of the Bab (October 20), the passing (ascension) of Baha'ullah (May 29), and the martyrdom of the Bab (July 9). Marriage is monogamous and requires the consent of the parents. Divorce is discouraged, and there is an obligation by Baha'i law of a year of trial separation before a divorce may be finalized.

The Baha'i International Community has had a relationship with the United Nations since 1948. It has consultative status with the United Nations Economic and Social Council (ECOSOC), the United Nations Children's Fund (UNICEF), the Environment Program (UNEP), and the United Nations Department of Public Information. Baha'i has representatives with the United Nations in New York, Geneva, Vienna, and Nairobi. It participates in United Nations committees and agencies on human rights, the status of women, science and technology, population, narcotics and drugs, the family, and disarmament.

The 100,000 Baha'i in America are a part of 3.5 million followers living in more than 111,000 localities in 363 countries and territories (including 173 independent nations). They come from 1,600 ethnic tribes and groups, and their literature can be read in over 700 languages and dialects. Their appeal is across all nationalities, races, and classes. In America in particular, leaders in their administrative orders represent both black and white and male and female. An article about Baha'is in North Carolina indicated there were 1,100 Baha'is in the state with some 100 located around Raleigh, the capital. Most are Americans, and many convert to the Baha'i religion from Judaism and Christianity. The majority are white, but almost one-third come from the black communities. Several are Iranians.[23]

The religion of the Bab, Baha'ullah, Abdul Baha, and Shoghi Effendi is represented by the laity from local assemblies to the world headquarters at Haifa on Mount Carmel.

American Baha'is, for the most part, assemble in homes or rented quarters for their local meeting, and they have their beautiful and well-placed national assembly and House of Worship in Wilmette. The Baha'i Publishing Trust provides their literature, and their faith commits them to be missionary. Their concern has been with the plight of their fellow believers in Iran, and they have sensitized the president of the United States, the United States Congress, and other bodies to speak out against the persecution and execution of the Baha'is in Iran, where over 150 have been put to death. Baha'is, then, are an independent world religion with sacred writings, prophets, and a religious life-style located within the context of American religious pluralism.

A Christian Perspective Toward Muslims and the Baha'i

Christianity has had a particular relationship to both Islam and the Baha'i. Islam was birthed in a time and place where Christianity had centuries of the development of churches, theology, and Church Councils which had debated certain doctrines and practices of the church. Islam had its roots in dealing with the theological and presuppositions as well as the practices of Christian churches in and contingent to the Arabian peninsula. Likewise, the Baha'i religion had origins in Persia where both Christianity and Islam had presence for over one thousand years. Both Islam and the Baha'i, like Christianity, stand upon monotheism, prophets, revealed scriptures, and the significance of history. There are significant differences between the three religions, and a Christian perspective includes both appreciation for Muslims and Baha'i as people aware of God and awareness of the obviously different beliefs and practices of Christians from those of the others.

Christians and Muslims have been interacting with one another to some degree for 1,300 years.[24] A part of that interaction has included the crusade period of the medieval ages of hostilities and death between them. The crusading history and spirit has remained to influence both religions in contemporary relationships. Prophet Muhammad certainly was aware of Christian teachings. He made strong statements of belief in one God, of angels as messengers from God, of prophets of God, of a revealed scripture, of strict ethical conduct in the significance of human history, of a judgment day, and of rewards and punishments toward a heaven and a hell.

A Christian perspective may appreciate the emphasis that Muslims place on God, God's righteousness, mercy, and justice, and on the importance which they place on prayer and on the family. There are, however, crucial differences which Christians have with Muslims over key beliefs and practices. Muslims view Jesus Christ as one of the prophets, and Muhammad as the last of the prophets. They do not accept Jesus as the incarnate Son of God, though they accept the virgin birth of Jesus. They do not believe that Jesus was crucified on the cross and that He was resurrected from the dead. It appears they believe He was rescued from the cross, lived a long life, and was taken to heaven by God. The Christian view holds that Jesus Christ was fully God and fully man who died on the cross for humankind's sin and was resurrected from the grave, demonstrating God's power over sin, death, and Satan, and God's will that salvation be for all.

Muslims hold that both the Jews and the Christians corrupted the true revelation offered by God through His prophets and that the Bible is contaminated. The infallible word of God is contained in their Qur'an as delivered from heaven word for word by the angel Gabriel to Muhammad. Materials in the Qur'an referring to the Old Testament and the New Testament are true. A Christian view, however, states that the revelation of God sufficient for salvation is found in the Bible and particularly in the life, teachings, death and resurrection of Jesus Christ. Christians believe that God may communicate to individuals through the Holy Spirit; but beyond the nature and function of Jesus Christ as God's unique revelation and humankind's Savior, there is no need for other prophets, and there is no need for Muhammad to be the seal of the prophets. The Bible is the necessary guide for the knowledge and understanding of God, for the ways of salvation, and for the directions of ethical living in the world.

The commitment and discipline which faithful Muslims display in their religious life may be appreciated by Christians. Prayer, fasting, and the giving of much of their time, energies, and financial means to religious duties are emphasized. They consider the mosque a place of prayer and devotion to God, and reading their scriptures is most important. A Christian view points to a personal relationship with God based on freedom and the liberty of the individual, not on ritualism or a rigid pattern of uniformity. This does not mean that Muslims are coerced or do not have freedom. Muslims are caught in patterns of rigidity in both confession and practice that often remove them from considerations of a personal God. To be a good Muslim, one must pray the basic same words so many times a day; one must fast for so many days; one must face Mecca; one must go on pilgrimage. These activities or works are required in the Qur'an and make one a correct Muslim. A Christian view claims that the essential relationship with God rests on God's free grace received by the individual through faith. Then, worship of God and service to one's neighbors ensues through community in the church.

Christians and Muslims have much in common in terms of their intertwining history, the similar terms used both in theological beliefs and religious practices, and their common views of the challenges in the world and the ways to overcome them. Perhaps the crucial areas where Christians sharply differ with Muslims are in the understanding of revelation, authority, and the nature and function of Jesus Christ. These crucial issues affect any discussions on salvation, church, and life-style.

The Baha'i arose out of both Christian and Islamic soil in Iran, most directly, however, from Shi'ite Islam with its emphasis on eschatology and the return of an imam to bring new light for the establishment of a better age. A Christian view also may deeply appreciate the stress which the Baha'i place on belief in one God, a God of justice and unity, as well as the Baha'i focus on prayer. Baha'i efforts at world peace and their constructive ideas and plans for education and for strengthening the morals of civilization are admirable.

The Christian view does not affirm the Baha'i belief in the manifestations of God for succeeding new ages. They treat Jesus like they treat Buddha or Muhammad. He was good for his age as Baha'ullah is good for this age. The Baha'i claim revelation as progressive. Each prophet or manifestation of God offers people what they are best able to receive for their particular condition and time and place. The Baha'i indicate that their teachings are progressive for this time and age. Their assumptions are that humankind can evolve or progress in ethics, morals, unity of purpose, in benevolent and peaceful communities, and in world order with the enlightened teachings and plans announced by Baha'ullah.

A Christian view sees Jesus as more than a spokesman for God or one of the manifestations of God. A Christian view sees the problem of humankind not as a collective problem primarily, but as an individual problem of sin. The individual has rebelled against the will of God; the problem is sin, not knowledge or enlightenment or ignorance. The problem has to be dealt with by God, not with an enlightened message or manifestation, but with judgment, mercy, and grace, as shown uniquely and emphatically in the life, death, and resurrection of Jesus Christ. No further prophets are needed, and no new manifestations of God in singular persons are necessary. Jesus Christ is the Son and Savior of God who takes away the sins of the world through the cross and the resurrection. God's action in and through Jesus Christ and operative in individuals who avail themselves of God's grace and power is sufficient to bring the Kingdom of God to fruition. Baha'is have little to say of sin and salvation and more to say of enlightenment and progress.

Muslims and the Baha'i are increasingly visible in the United States. They have their worship centers, distribute literature, serve as missionaries, and grow in the context of religious pluralism. Christians need to be aware of them, and to be prepared to communicate with them. Their roots are Middle Eastern and their religions are similar to Christianity in terms of doctrines and practices and the use of the same and often similar words. There needs to be a sensitivity to their family, friends, and neighbors in other parts of the world who suffer in war, in persecution, and in death. A Christian may be ready not only to reach out to a Muslim and a Baha'i in understanding, but also with a word out of one's own experience of grace and fulfillment in the knowledge and love of God through Jesus Christ.

9

THE NEW AGE
VOICES, VISIONS,
MOVEMENTS

■   ■

Introduction

During the 1970s the term "New Age" became a part of
the scholarly literature on religious and spiritual developments in America and other parts of the world. What does
this term mean? What are its origins? Is it a movement or
movements? Is it highly centralized in organization, or is it
loosely structured? What are its characteristics in terms of
religion, philosophy, and social organization?

What is new in the New Age? Ecclesiastes 1:9-10 states,
"What has been will be again, what has been done will be
done again; there is nothing new under the sun. Is there anything of which one can say, 'Look! This is something new'?
It was here already, long ago; it was here before our time."[1]

The New Age presents many themes and practices that
remind us of the past, often of the ancient past. They
include God and self as one, the unity of all things, beings
from the spirit world, and mediums to contact those beings
and serve as their voices to the present generation, power in
crystals and pyramids, and reincarnation. The New Age

often presents ideas and practices of the past in the vocabulary and culture of the present.

Marilyn Ferguson is a leading spokesperson of the New Age. Her book, *The Aquarian Conspiracy,* has been called by *USA Today* the handbook of the New Age. Ferguson writes, "A leaderless but powerful network is working to bring about radical change in the United States. Its members have broken with certain key elements of Western thought, and they may even have broken continuity with history."[2] She labels the network the Aquarian Conspiracy and indicates that it is without a political doctrine or a manifesto. It is a network "with conspirators who seek power only to disperse it, and whose strategies are pragmatic, even scientific, but whose perspective sounds so mystical that they hesitate to discuss it. Activists asking different kinds of questions, challenging the establishment from within."[3]

Ferguson calls the conspiracy benign with a human agenda. It is a paradigm shift. "It promotes the autonomous individual in a decentralized society. . . . Human nature is neither good or bad but open to continuous transformation and transcendence. . . . The New perspective respects the ecology of everything: birth, death, learning, health, family, work, science, spirituality, the arts, the community, relationships, politics."[4]

Russell Chandler, in his book *Understanding the New Age,* writes that the term "New Age" is an umbrella term and to give it a more precise term would be a chimera. It is "a hybrid mix of spiritual, social, and political forces and encompasses sociology, theology, physical science, medicine, anthropology, history, the human potential movements, sports, and science fiction."[5] Chandler echoes Ferguson's description of New Age as a paradigm shift, although he labels it a radical shift in which the old order will give way "to a new Order of peace, prosperity, and perfection."[6] He prefers the label New Age Movements since he views the movements as elusive and open.

In *Unmasking the New Age,* Douglas R. Groothuis describes the New Age as "a kind of ecumenical movement of Eastern occult and new consciousness groups network."[7] He writes that the groups are eclectic and diverse, emphasizing and exalting change and evolution.

Lowell D. Streiker, in *New Age Comes to Main Street,* writes that there are two kinds of New Age. One is the left hand or ecstatic kind of New Age filled with gurus, channelers, psychics, crystal healers, witches, and other visionaries. The other kind is the right hand or social transformationists who are concerned with ecology, social conscience, and feminism.[8]

In *The Hidden Dangers of the Rainbow,* Constance Cumbey describes the New Age Movement as "a movement which includes many thousands of organizations networking throughout every corner of our globe with the intent of bringing about a New World Order—an order that writes God out of the picture and deifies Lucifer."[9] Cumbey further writes that the Movement "includes organizations teaching mind control, holistic health, esoteric philosophy, scientific workers, political workers, and organizations dedicated to peace and goodwill. It also includes many consumer, environmental and nutritional organizations as well as religious cults of every shade and description."[10]

Diverse scholars and writers about the New Age describe it as religion, philosophy, education, politics, health, and ideology. Cumbey views the New Age as a more coherent movement both organizationally and ideologically, while Ferguson writes more of its diversity and loose networking. Whatever the New Age is, writers are attempting to analyze it, to describe any themes and patterns of it, and to place it in the context of social and cultural views and organizations.

New Age Themes
According to Non-New Age Writers

Literature about New Age thinkers, practitioners, and writings is growing. Some of it attempts to be objective, and some of it is unashamedly critical. New Age themes are being announced by writers who are not proponents of New Age. These themes will be explored by writers such as Chandler, Groothuis, Streiker, David Clark, Norman Geisler, and Cumbey.

The premises of the New Age, according to Chandler, are based on its views of ultimate reality, humanity, God and religion, humanity's problem, solution to humanity's crisis, and an agenda in society. A foundational premise is a common vision, a shared world view concerning the nature of existence, and the purpose of life within it. Ultimate reality in much of New Age thought centers on the word *unity*. The cosmos and all within it are one interconnected process.

All is One

Chandler denotes this reality as "pure, undifferentiated universal energy . . . a consciousness of 'life force.'" He describes this premise as monism, "where distinctions of apparent opposites disappear, as does the line between material creation and the force of energy that creates it. Consciousness is not confined to human beings, but applies to all reality. It is best described in impersonal terms such as Principle, Mind, Power, Unity, and especially, Energy."[11]

From the idea of "All is One" flows the premise that "humanity is All One." Chandler asserts that humanity is only "congealed energy," the "solidification of thought." Humanity is "an extension of the Oneness, which is all the divinity there is." According to Chandler the unity of all things is usually named pantheism, in which "there are not many selves, but one Self, the One."[12]

In the premise based on God and Religion, New Age thinking progresses from "All is One. We are all One. All is God. And we are God." Chandler says that the New Age God is expressed in terms of the "Higher Self" or "Infinite Intelligence."[13] He refers to Marilyn Ferguson's view that reality is "a larger Self," to Shirley MacLaine's statement that "I am God," and to Jack Underhill's writing, "You are

God, honest. . . . I know your driver's license says differently, but what does the DMV know?"[14]

New Age views religions as many spiritual paths to the same goal of cosmic unity. The founders of religions and their teachings are basically the same: "how to become one with the One." The final goal in the quest to become one with the One may be reached through a series of life cycles based on the theories of karma and reincarnation. "The final goal is to merge with the cosmos, or God, and end the repetitious and painful birth-death-rebirth process."[15]

What is the dilemma in which humanity finds itself? Why is the self not the Higher Self? Why does one not attain the higher consciousness, godhood, or merge with the Unity of the cosmic order? Chandler writes that the problem is "Metaphysical amnesia." Humanity has forgotten its true identity, its true Self, its oneness with God. Much of the problem lies with humanity's ignorance, its misplaced world view, and the corruptions of western culture in both its beliefs and practices.

The solution to the crisis of humanity involves a "paradigm shift." An awakening is needed, a new perception is called for, knowledge is to replace ignorance, and personal transformation is to occur. The paradigm shift will result in the premises: "All is One; God is All, and All is God." Chandler asserts that New Age premises rest on the shift in thinking and living that "Humanity is deified, death is denied, and ignorance—not evil—is the enemy. . . . Each individual may 'actualize' his or her divine nature and achieve union with the Ultimate Unifying Principle by applying a plethora of consciousness-changing techniques, or 'psychotechnologies' to body, mind, and spirit."[16]

The agenda of the New Age is based on personal awareness, planetary transformation, mass enlightenment, and social evolution. Chandler writes that the agenda is broad and includes "ecology (nature and God are merged); androgyny (because all are One, male-female distinctions are irrelevant); world peace and nuclear disarmament (including rapprochement and possible political unification between the United States and the Soviet Union); and natural foods and healing processes . . . organize global politics, an emerging global civilization and one world government . . . an "eclectic" world religion."[17]

While Chandler delineates his selection of premises of the New Age, Groothuis sets forth six basic distinctives of the New Age Movement. He notes that the movement is eclectic and diverse. Since it emphasizes change and evolution, there are often shifts in perspectives among its adherents and writers which make them difficult to pin down. Groothuis' six distinctives are All is One, All is God, Humanity is God, A Change in Consciousness, All Religions Are One, and Cosmic Evolutionary Optimism.

The All is One concept is foundational to the New Age. According to Groothuis "it permeates the movement in all its various manifestations—from holistic health to the new physics, from politics to transpersonal psychology, from Eastern religions to the occult. Another name for the idea is monism. Monism, then, is the belief that all that is, is one. All is interrelated, interdependent and interpenetrating. Ultimately there is no difference between God, a person, a carrot, or a rock."[18] Groothuis cites the New Age physicist and philosopher, Fritjof Capra in his book *The Turning Point,* that the ultimate state of consciousness is one "in which all boundaries and dualisms have been transcended and all individuality dissolves into universal, undifferentiated oneness."[19]

All is God

Groothuis concludes that if All is One, then it follows that All is God, and this is pantheism. All things are a part of one divine essence, of a cosmic unity, of the One. The One is beyond personality. Groothuis asserts that "the idea of a personal God is abandoned in favor of an impersonal energy, force or consciousness. Ultimate reality is god, who is in all and through all; in fact, god is all."[20]

Humanity is God

Groothuis claims that this is one of the most seductive premises of New Age. Humanity is god in disguise. New Age writer Theodore Roszak is quoted that the goal is "to awaken to the god who sleeps at the root of the human being." Stewart Brand, in *The Next Whole Earth Catalogue,* is quoted, "We are as gods and might as well get good at it."[21] According to Groothuis, "Whether it comes from Eastern religions such as Hinduism—'Atman is Brahman' (the individual self is really the universal Self)—or from the new self-actualizing psychologies—all knowledge, power, and truth are within and waiting to be unlocked—the New Age raises the placard of pantheism high: you are god!"[22]

A Change in Consciousness

If All is One, and All is God, and Humanity is God, then what is the problem with humanity? The answer is ignorance and humanity's contentment with its limitations and finitude which are basically an illusion in humanity's thinking process. There is a need for enlightenment, a new perception, a change in consciousness, and transformation.

Groothuis writes that "there are many names for this transforming experience: cosmic consciousness, God-realization, self-realization, enlightenment, illumination, Nirvana (Buddhist), satori (Zen), at-one-ment or *satchitananada* (Hindu)."[23] Shirley MacLaine portrays the change of consciousness: "We already know everything. The knowingness of our divinity is the highest intelligence. And to be what we already know is the free will. Free will is simply the enactment of the realization that you are God, a realization that you are divine: free will is making everything accessible to you."[24] A realization of oneness leads to spiritual power and well-being, a release of human potential or the divine from within.

All Religions Are One

Differences among the religions are external and superficial, and although there may be many paths and methods to Oneness, or god, or higher consciousness, the essential of each religion is the same: the vital experience of the god within. New Age thought is syncretistic in the sense that the stated exclusivity and uniqueness of religions is dissolved into the cosmic oneness and unity.[25]

A last distinctive is Cosmic Evolutionary Optimism. Groothuis refers to the thinking of Julian Huxley that, "Man is that part of reality in which, and through which, the cosmic process has become conscious and has begun to comprehend itself." And Groothuis notes that Teilhard de Chardin "prophesied a progressive evolutionary harmonization and unification of world consciousness eventually reaching the 'Omega Point' where all consciousness is fused and all become one with the One."[26] New Age futurists expect a massive transformation in which there may be a suprahuman species.

In *The New Age Comes to Main Street,* Lowell Streiker posits two kinds of "New Age phenomena" of persons, expressions, and life-styles. "Left hand" or "ecstatic" New Age, is represented by a variety of gurus, psychics, channelers, and visionaries. "Right hand" or "social transformationist" New Age includes the areas of ecology, social conscience, and feminism.

Streiker acknowledges the diversity within New Age and describes it in several ways. Rather than theistic, integrating creator and creation and emphasizing self-realization rather than moral law, it is pantheistic. New Age is spiritually ecological, with mutual dependence between nature and humanity. It is more transformative than reformative, with the key theme of the transformation of consciousness. It utilizes reflection and meditation for self-understanding.[27]

New Age is androgynous in placing importance upon the feminine aspects of reality. Streiker observes that female dominance does not replace male dominance. New Age is characterized as xenophilic, with comfort toward the strange and the alien. "For better or for worse, the imagination of New Age is riveted to the far away, to the spatially and temporally alien, to other civilizations and worlds, to past lives and parallel dimensions, to higher planes and superhuman beings."[28]

New Age is ecstatic in that it "thrives on novelty, is open to the exploration of the limits of human consciousness, and celebrates the transpersonal and psychic dimensions of human experience. New Age is committed to pursuing sources of knowledge that transcend both sensory data and logic."[29] Streiker continues, "New Age is life-affirming and death-denying. It is expressive rather than repressive. It is afraid of neither imagination nor inspiration. It maintains that death, disease, poverty, and suffering do not speak the final word about the destiny of the individual or humankind. It is more interested in human possibilities than in limitations."[30]

Toleration and inclusiveness are seen as traits of the New Age. "It is open, accepting, and nonjudgmental, even uncritical. . . . There is a powerful New Age impulse to absorb corruption without itself being polluted. For New Age, the origin of evil is error rather than rebellion. The primal force of error is egocentricity, the belief in the ultimate significance of the separate self."[31]

In describing New Age, Streiker has attempted to focus on attributes which are accessible to ordinary folk on "Main Street." He writes that even if the label "New Age" becomes worn and discarded, the substance of New Age will continue.

In *Apologetics in the New Age,* Clark and Geisler discuss common New Age themes. They indicate that New Age is not new and that its philosophical roots reach back centuries, based on a pantheistic world view. That view is based on the oneness of reality, that all is within the being of God. In reality, there is no duality in that God rises above the personal into the impersonal. God is impersonal. Creation arises out of God and is the same substance. Humans are the extension of God and consequently are divine; they partake of the same substance of God.[32]

Clark and Geisler write of the knowledge of mystical consciousness. They write that there are two levels of knowledge, the higher and the lower. The most important knowledge comes through the direct apprehension of reality based on the "self certifying nature of mystical intuition." Logic and language have their inadequacies, and New Age stands on the ineffability of mystical objects and intuition. With regard to the problem of good and evil, the individual bears responsibility, with an illusory nature to both good and evil, pain and sorrow. Ethics is the means to salvation.

The religious dimensions of pantheistic mysticism on which New Age thought stands includes the themes of knowledge as salvation and ignorance as evil. Salvation occurs through human effort and results in mystical ascent. A pluralism of beliefs among New Age exists.[33]

A noted critic of New Age is Constance Cumbey, author of the widely read *The Hidden Dangers of the Rainbow*. She writes, "Make no mistake about it! The New Age Movement is a religion complete with its own Bibles, prayers and mantras, Vatican City/Jerusalem equivalents, priests and gurus, born-again experiences (they call it 'rebirthing'), spiritual laws and commandments, psychics and 'prophets' and nearly every other indicia of a religion."[34]

Cumbey views the New Age Movement as a monolithic entity whose organizations and networks are singularly related together in purposes and goals. She portrays the movement as a comprehensive body of doctrine. There is belief in a "God Transcendent" known as "The Source" and a "God Immanent" meaning "god within" or the divinity of man. There are beliefs in reincarnation, the perfectability of man, the interconnectedness of all things expressed through "holistic thinking," and the existence of "masters" and an occult hierarchy.[35] Cumbey draws her assumptions concerning those tenets particularly from the writings of Alice Bailey and David Spangler.

Diverse themes of the New Age have been presented by various authors. In conclusion, the New Age was described by an article in *Time* magazine as follows: "All in all, the New Age does express a cloudy sort of religion, claiming vague connections with both Christianity and the major faiths of the East . . . plus an occasional dab of pantheism and sorcery. . . . The underlying faith is a lack of faith in the orthodoxies of rationalism, high technology, spiritual law and order. Somehow, the New Agers believe, there must be some secret and mysterious shortcut or alternative path to happiness and health. And nobody ever really dies."[36]

Ancient Roots of New Age Thinking and Practice

Whether New Age is considered in religious, philosophical, or cultural terms, it is influenced by the ancient and near past. Literature associated with New Age draws from several world view traditions, the teachings of the founders of religions, and philosophers. Indian spiritual and philosophical paths of the subcontinent of India, known as Hinduism and Buddhism, are its roots. Taoism of China; spiritism and shamanism of Africa, Asia, and Latin America; and Zen Buddhism out of China and Japan lend their influences.

The mother goddesses of the ancient Mediterranean and the astrology of Egypt and Babylonia make their impacts. Early Gnosticism of Greece, Rome, and Palestine contribute to New Age. The mysticism of Judaism and Christianity, as well as master teachers and "messiah types," have been influential in the seminal thought of New Age.

New Age draws much from traditional Hinduism, which includes a variety of views of ultimate reality and paths to reach it. New Age particularly likes the concept of Brahman and Atman—a world soul, higher self, higher consciousness, force (energy), or "God" which is generally known as Brahman. Various schools of thought in Hinduism define Brahman differently, according to the above terms.

Atman is the individual expression of soul, self, consciousness, force, or "god." Hinduism teaches the concept of Maya which means illusion or being in a state of ignorance. Illusion or ignorance is not knowing or realizing that Atman is really a part of Brahman. Proper knowledge will help one to self-realization, to know that one is already or can be united and become one with Brahman.

As Hindu philosophical views may include monism, pantheism, and even a proximate monotheism, New Age may find diversity in these roots and express diversity. From the school of Advaita Vedanta, which represents impersonal monism, to Krishna Consciousness, representing unity in the one Krishna God, New Age may express secular humanistic views as well as spiritual, religious concepts. One may study New Age terminology including unity, holistic, higher consciousness, God in you, self realization, Brahman, and Atman in light of Hindu views.

Other Hindu views incorporated in New Age thought include karma, reincarnation, transmigration or soul travel, and paths to Moksha or liberation or freedom or to God. Karma is a view that one reaps what one sows, or effect naturally follows cause. A good cause gives good karma, and a bad cause gives bad karma. Bad karma results in samsara, or cycles in and out of existence, or transmigration of the soul, or reincarnation. Good karma makes possible the end of reincarnation and unity with Brahman or God.[37]

There are stated paths or ways to good karma, and therefore, to Brahman. These paths include Yoga or meditation, Jnana or knowledge, and Bhakti or devotion. There are many schools of meditation in Hinduism. New Age focuses on meditation in terms of mind and body exercises, trances, channeling, and special or sacred words or phrases known as mantras. One may through meditation remove illusion or ignorance known as Maya and become united or yoked with Brahman. This path is also one of mind over matter.

Another path is pure knowledge. If ignorance is bad karma, then knowledge is good karma, and it yields unity with the higher consciousness or God. Early gnosticism taught a mystical or hidden way to achieve ultimate reality or God. It was "pure mind." A body of literature is important for containing the correct knowledge, and a teacher is needed to show the secrets of its truth. New Age places much importance on correct knowledge, or a paradigm shift of world view, and on certain bodies of literature which give not only the correct content but the proper assessment of the meaning and function of knowledge in the emerging New Age.

Bhakti is the path of devotion. In Hinduism, devotion may be given to images, to worship in temples, to gurus, to avatars (reincarnated saints or master teachers or pure consciousness individuals), or to a pantheon of deities both male and female. Devotion may also be focused on oneself as the locus of Brahman or divinity.

New Age presents lectures and literature on realizing one's potential, getting in contact and communion with oneself through self-realization, and through being all one can be. Gurus, or avatars, are available and are portrayed as mediators or mediums for one to give devotion to in order to use their teachings or methods, or to become united with their souls or consciousness on the way to the higher consciousness. New Age trance-channeling combines many attributes of classical Hindu paths.

Just as Hinduism provides a world view and ethos from which New Age is nurtured, so are the roots of Buddhism, which sprang up in the milieu of Hinduism in India. Guatama Buddha was a reformist of Hindu traditions, being an agnostic toward deity and an iconoclast toward images and temple ritual. Indian tradition has considered him an avatar, along with the Hindu deities of Brahma, Vishnu, Shiva, Krishna, and others.

The Buddha had an experience of enlightenment. *Buddha* means the enlightened one. His experience led him to teach the four noble truths and the eightfold path—(1) all in the world is suffering; (2) the cause of suffering is desire; (3)

there is a way to overcome suffering and desire; and (4) the way is the eight-fold path. The path basically includes right knowledge, right action, and right meditation. The Buddha gathered disciples and required that they take a three-fold vow to the Dharma (law of the universe), to Buddha (to become enlightened to one's own nature and thus become a Buddha), and to the Sangha (the community of monks or saints).

Through proper knowledge, correct action, and right meditation, one could break the cycle of karma and the transmigration of one's entity and attain Nirvana, the cessation of suffering. Buddhism developed into two basic movements, the Hinayana and the Mahayana. The Hinayana emphasized the strict teachings of the Buddha and the role of the monk as teacher and guide. The Mahayana accommodated other traditions of teachings to include a pantheon of deities, Bodhisattvas (savior types or mediators to help ordinary folk to break the cycle of karma and to enjoy the fruits of a Buddha heaven or Buddhahood), and a dependence on someone and something beyond the self for liberation and freedom. Zen Buddhism developed out of China and Japan and emphasized the pursuit of enlightenment or the true Buddha nature.[38]

New Age has gone to school on the enlightenment of Buddhism. To turn inward, to examine one's nature, to have proper knowledge of the universe and all entities within it, to know the power of the mind and be mindful of it are nourishing elements of Buddhism. The monk and Bodhisattva as teacher and mediator, or as exemplary Buddha-nature, to which all should ascribe are models for New Age teachers and gurus. Zen meditation practices enable one to be mindful of all ecological relationships within one's world of experience and to appreciate the laws of the universe.[39]

The emphases of New Age of holistic health, mind over body or the unity of mind and body, ecology of beings and entities, universal or higher consciousness, and the teacher/

lecturer/exemplar of intuitive truth find their bearings in Buddhist literature and teachings.

The world view and ethos of Hinduism and Buddhism have not only been sought by New Age thinkers who traveled to India and Japan to study them, but these traditions have migrated from their homelands to other lands including the United States to influence New Age. Ralph Waldo Emerson and Henry David Thoreau laced their writings in nineteenth-century America with Eastern thought, as well as the school of Theosophy, Christian Science, and other American philosophical and sectarian movements.

Roots of New Age also extend to the traditional Chinese religion of Taoism. Lao Tzu, its founder, emphasized philosophy and mysticism. The word, *Tao,* referred to a way of life in balance with the nature of the universe as well as the power of it. When one follows the Tao, it brings harmony and unity. *Yang* and *Yin* are concepts important to Taoism. Yang is the power in the universe representative of masculinity. Yin is the power of femininity. For one to attain harmony in life, both Yang and Yin are to be brought into balance. Perhaps because Yin was stressed in Lao Lzu's time, it was thought that the feminine needed to balance the assertive masculine Yang. Emphasis was placed on communion with nature and unity and kinship with the underlying natural forces.[40]

New Age not only draws on Taoism's teachings on unity and balance with universal principles and energies, but it stresses the balance of the role and function of femininity and masculinity. The view of introspection into self and of proper relationship to nature are fundamental to New Age and Taoism.

Pre-Christian nature religions of the Mediterranean basin of the Great Goddess type and Neo-Pagan expressions of witchcraft have been influential on New Age. The goddess in many forms, including Isis and Diana, has represented themes of fertility, prominence of femininity, a return to nature, and the harmony with the Whole or the One. New

Age has been the theme of the goddess as a corrective to the dominance of masculinity and to the separation from nature. Witchcraft, known as Wicca, is seen as a return to ecological wholeness similar to the themes of the goddess.

Shamanistic traditions of various cultures have impacted New Age. The shaman has been described as "the first voyager into the realms of the superconscious." "The shaman is "a technician of ecstasy," whose purpose is to reconnect people with the sacred, as mystic, mediator, guide, and healer."[41] From trance-channelers to wholistic health, New Age draws upon the shamanistic teachings and practices.

Ancient religions, philosophies, and traditions from across the cultures of the world have influenced New Age thought, writings, and practices. In this sense the newness of New Age is clothed in the ancient and adapted to the modern. Much of the past has been replicated in the present with the anticipation that it will be the wave of the future. New Age is the umbrella covering the variety and the diversity of thousands of years of humanity's search within itself and beyond itself.

Modern Foundations of New Age

Reports say that Alice Bailey coined the phrase, "New Age," in the first half of the twentieth century, and Marilyn Ferguson popularized it with her book *The Aquarian Conspiracy* in the 1970s. In noting recent historical influences upon New Age, the latter half of the nineteenth century and the first half of the twentieth century in America are particularly significant.

Transcendentalism

The transcendentalism of Ralph Waldo Emerson, Henry David Thoreau, and others of the mid-nineteenth century drew on a variety of sources, including Quaker and Puritan traditions, Greek and German philosophers, and Eastern religions. Transcendentalism was schooled in the Hindu sacred writings of the *Vedas* and the *Bhagavad Gita* that had been translated into English. Emerson wrote of the "Over Soul," a mystical force within all nature and human personalities. God was sought in nature. Thoreau wrote about Brahma and the Ganges. Emphasis was upon self-realization and the development of human potentiality.

J. Gordon Melton has characterized transcendentalism as "a uniquely American form of mysticism . . . the first substantial religious movement in North America with a prominent Asian component."[42] It was a backdrop for the later developments of Spiritualism, Theosophy, New Thought, Christian Science, Unity School of Christianity, and others.

Spiritualism

Spiritualism is a religious phenomenon which stresses mental healing of the Franz Mesmer movement in Europe in the 1800s, as well as the mid-nineteenth century American Fox sisters who claimed to have heard voices from the dead. Basically, it focuses on communication with the spirits of the dead. From spiritualism has sprung seances and mediums to facilitate conversations with spirits as well as clairvoyance, slate writing, and mysterious appearances from departed spirits. Trance-channeling of the present, with J. Z. Knight channeling the voice of a millennia age Ramtha, finds its roots in spiritualism.

In 1875, Madame Helena Blavatsky founded the Theosophical Society of New York. Born in Russia, she traveled extensively, including India, and studied various religions. She became a channeler for a spirit-guide who was called King John. She stated the major purpose of Theosophy in her book, *The Secret Doctrine,*

> (1) An Omnipresent Eternal boundless and Immutable PRINCIPLE, on which all speculation is impossible, since it transcends the power of human conception. . . . (2) The Eternity of the Universe in toto as a boundless plane. . . . The absolute universality of that law of periodicity, of flux and reflux, ebb and flow, which physical science has observed and recorded in all departments of

nature. (3) The fundamental identity of all Souls with the Universal Over-soul, the latter being itself an aspect of the Unknown Root; and the obligatory pilgrimage for every soul . . . The pivotal doctrine of the Esoteric Philosophy admits no privileges or special gifts in man, save those won by his own Ego through personal effort and merit throughout a long series of metempsychoses and reincarnations.[43]

Blavatsky has been called the "godmother" of the New Age movement, and her biographer wrote that she "paved the way for contemporary Transcendental Meditation, Zen, Hare Krishnas; yoga and vegetarianism; karma and reincarnation; swamis, yogis and gurus."[44] After her death in 1891, her successors, Annie Besant and Alice Bailey, continued her teachings which included "Theosophy's messianic vision of a coming new world religious teacher, inspired by channeled prophecies from a hierarchy of 'ascended masters.'"[45]

Annie Besant attempted to portray her adopted son, Krishnamurti, who was educated at the Sorbonne, as the new messiah or the reincarnated World Teacher. The attempt was not successful. Alice Bailey helped found the Arcane School, the New Group of World Servers, Triangles, and World Goodwill while writing some two dozen books. Lucifer Publishing Company was begun in 1922 to disseminate her writings. The name was changed to Lucis Publishing Company. In the lineage of Theosophy, Lord Maitreya has been a term used for the reincarnation of ascended masters, including Jesus.

Other Movements

Along with the development of the Theosophical Society came the establishment of New Thought groups. In 1908, the National New Thought Alliance was organized with headquarters in Hollywood, California. Its purpose is "To teach the infinite of the Supreme One, the Divinity of Man and his Infinite Possibilities through the creative power of constructive thinking and obedience to the voice of the indwelling Presence which is our source of Inspiration, Power, Health, and Prosperity." Its principal teachings include, "The immanence of God, the divine nature of man, the spiritual character of the universe, and the fact that sin, human disorders, and human disease are basically matters of incorrect thinking. . . . Man can live in oneness with God in love, truth, peace, health, and plenty."[46]

Theosophy and New Thought present many of the key teachings of Hinduism and popularize them in writings and organizations. New Age views are an outgrowth of these writings and spokespersons and organizations.

By the late 1800s The Church of Jesus Christ of Latter-Day Saints, Christian Science, and the Unity School of Christianity had become a part of the religious and philosophical stream of thought. Joseph Smith had offered his Mormons the belief that as God had become man, so man may become God. Mary Baker Eddy had established her First Church of Christ Scientist emphasizing mind over matter, suffering and death as not real, and Jesus as a way-shower to truth. Clarence and Myrtle Fillmore founded the Unity School of Christianity emphasizing holistic health, teachings of one's own innate divinity and perfectability as one's mind is connected to the Divine Mind, and religions as spokes on the wheel with the hub being God. These religious movements serve as a background for New Age views on God within or the divinity of the soul, mind over matter, self realization, Jesus as one of the avatars or reincarnated ascended masters, and the truth of all religions.

Not only have nativistic movements, particularly of nineteenth century America, been influential upon New Age, but also religious and philosophical movements from abroad have impacted it. The first Parliament on World Religions was held in 1893 in Chicago. Swamis, gurus, and lecturers from the major world religions presented their religious and philosophical views of their Eastern traditions. Americans were offered a glimpse of Eastern mysticism which later became a major offering.

Swami Vivekananda, a major presenter at the parliament, remained in America to found the Vedanta Society. Swami Yogananda in 1920 began the Self Realization Fellowship. Meher Baba, the self-proclaimed avatar, established the Friends of Meher Baba group. Later, Zen Buddhist monks from Japan came to build their Zen Buddhist centers or Zendos.

By the 1960s many religious and philosophical ingredients were in place in American society from nativistic movements to those from abroad which influenced the New Age movement.

Major Voices and Visionaries of New Age

Some say that New Age has no singular voice and no one administration or organization; it is eclectic and diverse. There are overarching themes using similar ideas, phrases, and terminologies, and which display an integrated and coherent emerging world view and ethos. A loose network, or association of peoples with these similar themes, is evident as authors and speakers utilize the same roots in nativistic movements in America as well as the movements which have come from abroad.

Some select voices of New Age world view and ethos, such as Alice Bailey, David Spangler, and Marilyn Ferguson, have impacted American culture through their writings, lectures, and organizations. These thinkers and writers will be presented in more detail, and others more briefly.

Alice Bailey

Alice Bailey was schooled in the Theosophical Society of Madame Blavatsky. Married to an Episcopal rector, her marriage faltered and ended in divorce. Early in her life she had contact with a "master," and in her Christian pursuit had spent some time in India. She married Foster Bailey; and the two of them, informed of occultism and eastern mysticism, set out to speak and teach their views. The phrase, "New Age," is liberally scattered throughout her dozen books, and she is considered a foundational figure for New Age thinking of post World War II.

She was a prolific writer as well as organizer, establishing the Arcane School, the New Group of World Servers, Triangles, and World Goodwill. Lucis Publishing Company, originally known as Lucifer Publishing Company, was founded to distribute her works.

In her book, *The Reappearance of the Christ,* Bailey projects the seeds for a new world order, a new world religion, and a new age Christ. She writes of the avatar of synthesis who is a close associate of the Christ. "He works under the great natural law of Synthesis, producing at-one-ment, unification, and fusion." This avatar's function is to produce spiritual will within the spiritual hierarchy, within the assembly of the United Nations, and within humanity everywhere.[47]

There have been many avatars or sons of God or Christs according to Bailey. For example, Buddha was the messenger of light for the East, and Christ was the messenger of love for the West. The avatar of synthesis will be assisted by a New Group of World Servers who will bring in the New Age. This synthesis, or unity, will result in the universal recognition of one humanity, one world, the oneness of the sons of men.

Bailey writes, "The dream of brotherhood, of fellowship of world cooperation and of a peace, based on right human relations, is becoming clearer in our minds. We are also visioning a new and vital world religion, a universal faith which will have its roots in the past, but which will clear the new dawning beauty and the coming vital revelation."[48]

She indicates that in the return of the Christ, those who seek right human relationships will automatically gather around this avatar, whether they are in world religions or not. Those acceptable to the Christ are those who see no true or basic difference between religion and religion, man and man, or nation and nation. Those who do see differences because of their exclusivity and separateness will stand revealed.

The metaphysics of Bailey includes charts of gods and masters—Solar Trinity (Logos) of Father (Will), The Son (Love-Wisdom), and Holy Spirit (Active-Intelligence). Below this Trinity are Seven Rays and below the Rays (Energies) is S. Sanat Kumara which may be interpreted as God. Further down the charts are Kumaras, department heads, Bodhisattvas, and many masters in a hierarchy of masters.

There is also a chart composed of three terms, Shamballa, Hierarchy, and Humanity. Shamballa is the focal point of energies, the place or center where the will of God is known and there is peace, the center symbolically of plentary life. Shamballa focuses will, love, and intelligence in "one great and fundamental Intention" expressed in the life cycle of a planet. This "Intention" also is expressed in the medium of "The Plan." "From it the great political movements and the destiny of races and nations and their progress are determined, just as the religious movements, the cultural unfoldments and spiritual ideas are sent forth from the hierarchical centre of Love and Light. . . . There are, therefore, three great spiritual centres on the planet: Shamballa, the spiritual Hierarchy and humanity."[49]

Shamballa is described as synthesis, will, spirit, power, energy, and direction. Hierarchy is unity, purpose, soul, consciousness, transmission, and distribution. And Humanity is separation, plan, appearance, organization, action, focus of activity, and reception.

The themes which Bailey enunciates are fertile ground for the New Age of the 1960s onward. The worldview of Hinduism, including monism and reincarnation, is evident. The enlightenment of Buddhism is influential upon her. Planetary worlds, gods and ascended masters and avatars are a part of her teachings. Evolutionary development of all organisms and organizations is taught. The interconnectedness of all things is primary in her metaphysics.

Alice Bailey died in 1949, but she left many of her writings. In *The Destiny of the Nations,* she wrote that a nation is an evolving spiritual entity. *Discipleship in the New Age* contains teachings on Meditation, Initiation, and Six Stages of Discipleship. They emphasize the New Age. *The Externalization of the Hierarchy* presents the interdependence of all states of consciousness and kingdoms in nature within the planet. The book discusses the interaction of humanity, the Hierarchy, and Shamballa and projects the essentials of Plan and Purpose.

She wrote *A Treatise on the Seven Rays* which includes volumes on *Esoteric Psychology, Esoteric Astrology, Esoteric Healing,* and *The Rays and the Initiations.* In her *A Treatise on White Magic,* she describes the fifteen rules for magic (for soul control). Man is essentially and inherently divine. "The soul is the means whereby mankind evolves a consciousness of divinity, redeems gross matter, and liberates the pure flame of spirit from the limitations of form."[50]

David Spangler

David Spangler is considered to be one of the major spokespersons of New Age thought. In 1970 he became a member and co-director of the Findhorn Foundation in the Scottish community of Findhorn. His writings, along with those of Alice Bailey, were the seminal teachings of Findhorn. Peter and Eileen Caddy were the leaders at Findhorn, and it was Eileen Caddy who claimed to receive guidance that Spangler had "Christ energies."

Spangler returned to the United States in 1973 to found the Lorian Association with headquarters in Madison, Wisconsin. He serves on the board of directors of Planetary Citizens and is a contributing editor of *New Age Magazine.* His writings include *Revelation: the Birth of a New Age, Reflections on the Christ, New Age Rhythms, Towards a Planetary Vision,* and *Emergence: The Rebirth of the Sacred.* The latter writing was published by Doubleday.

Groothuis states that Spangler's earlier works were published by Findhorn and were difficult for the uninitiated to understand. These works included the perplexing esotericism from Theosophy and Alice Bailey. Spangler wrote about occult doctrines and the "Luciferic initiation." His Doubleday publication is aimed at a general audience. "His ideas have not changed, but they are more popularly available and attractive."[51]

Included in the themes of Spangler are the unity of all in the Primal Oneness, evolution, the New Age Christ or Cosmic Christ, and the coming of the New Age. Spangler has claimed to receive messages from "John" and from "Limitless Love and Truth." He writes, "I am Limitless Love. I embrace all that lives. I assist the descent of One from beyond the planet who carries New Age energies. We seek to bring down the barriers between all men and all Kingdoms of life, for our name is Oneness, Communion."[52]

It is possible to reunite with the "Primal Oneness" which underlies the created world. "It involves indeed a blending of consciousness in heightened awareness with beings from higher planes. This is the new and true communion for our age, which carries us from the trance mediumship which characterized the earlier generations of spiritualism. . . the possibility of blending in full consciousness with the thoughts of beings in higher spiritual planes opens the possibility for an undreamt of extension of human knowledge. . . there is nothing which could not be done by man in co-operation with higher worlds."[53]

Spangler writes concerning evolution and New Age that the "evolution of the race is for man to learn not how to obey the law, but how to be the law . . . there is a vast, vast difference. If you are the law it means that you are at one with the whole. For divine law simply exists. . . . When a person understands this, when he begins to have that attunement, when he is the law, he is not going to act in any way that will disturb or distort the true balance of the true wholeness. . . . The New Age is an age when there is needed that group of people who through attunement can be self governing, act as the law, as the divine, as the right, as the love."[54]

In referring to religions and scriptures, he asserts, "We can take all the scriptures and all the teachings, and all the tablets, and all the laws and all the marshmallows, and have a jolly good bonfire and marshmallow roast, because that's all they are worth. Once you are the law, once you are the truth, you do not need it externally represented for you."[55]

Spangler writes that the New Age needs something better than the mainstream Christian traditions with regard to Christ. "It must be a cosmic Christ, a universal Christ, a New Age Christ." This Christ is a universal presence which lifts humankind to a higher evolutionary standing. This presence may be in all philosophies and all religions which assist humanity in unity with the spirit.[56]

With regard to the "Luciferic Initiation" associated with Spangler, he writes that "the true light of Lucifer cannot be seen through sorrow, through darkness, through rejection. The true light of this great being can only be recognized when one's own eyes can see with the light of Christ, the light of the inner sun. Lucifer works within each of us to wholeness, and as we move into a new age, which is the age of man's wholeness, each of us in some way is brought to that point which I term the Luciferic initiation, the particular doorway through which the individual must pass if he is to come fully into the presence of his light and his wholeness. Lucifer comes to give us the final gift of wholeness. If we accept it, then he is free and we are free. That is the Luciferic initiation. . . it is an initiation into the New Age."[57]

Spangler, thus, is an influential thinker of New Age, serving on boards and lecturing around the world, including a sermon in St. John the Divine in New York City. Concerning New Age activities, he has written, "The value of New Age centers is that they are developing around people and places relatively uncontaminated by the taught forces, energies, and patterns of the past. Not being a part of the old web of power lines and influence, these new centers are not faced with having to overcome the inertia and ambiguous energies from past patterns. Thus a new world is being born and shall be born."[58]

In the introduction to *The New Age Catalogue* of which Spangler is an editor, he writes, "The New Age is essentially a symbol representing the human heart and intellect in partnership with God building a better world that can celebrate values of community wholeness and sacredness. . . we can forget the New Age of channels, crystals, and charisma and get on with discovering and cocreating a harmonious world that will nourish and empower all of us." According to Lowell Streiker, Spangler is saying that New Age has little to do with paganism, Eastern philosophy, the occult, channeling, crystals, reincarnation, or psychic phenomena. Yet, his introduction precedes a catalogue whose contents are full of the same which he has discounted.

The New Age Catalogue's contents include a variety of topics. There is intuitive development which includes channeling, psychic functioning, crystals, astrology, numerology, tarot, palmistry, and oracles. Emphasis is on creating one's own reality with transformational journeys, astral projection, out-of-body experiences, and dreamwork. There is holistic health and healing with acupressure, yoga, and t'ai chi. A topic deals with death and dying and reincarnation. All the products and services mentioned in the 244-page catalogue may be ordered directly from Body, Mind and Spirit.[59]

Marilyn Ferguson

The Aquarian Conspiracy has been called the "Bible" of the New Age. Written by Marilyn Ferguson, it became a Book-of-the-Month Club selection. Ferguson is a popular and respected lecturer as she enunciates her philosophical vision and New Age social agenda.

She explains that Aquarius was the waterbearer in the ancient Zodiac who symbolized the flow and the quenching of an ancient thirst. The Age of Aquarius forebodes the true liberation of the mind and the entrance into a millennium of love and light. The word *conspire* means "to breathe together," an intimate joining. Ferguson writes that there is a benevolent conspiracy to usher in the Aquarian age.[60]

This benevolent conspiracy composed of a powerful network is active to bring about radical change in the United States and is "triggering the most rapid cultural realignment in history."[61] Ferguson writes of a paradigm shift of the Aquarian Conspiracy in which it promotes the antonomous individual in a decentralized society. Human nature is seen to be neither good nor bad and open to a continuous transformation and transcendence.[62]

Ferguson discusses systems for a deliberate change in consciousness; these systems are called psychotechnologies. They include biofeedback, autogenic training, music in combination with imagery and meditation, self-help networks, meditation of every description, Theosophy and other systems, science of mind, a course in miracles, countless Yogas, and contemporary psychotherapies. The entry point for transformation and psychotechnologies has been the use of psychedelics.

Ferguson writes that "it is impossible to overestimate the historic role of psychedelics as an entry point drawing people into other transformative technologies. For tens of thousands of "left-brained" engineers, chemists, psychologists, and medical students who never before understood their more spontaneous, imaginative rightbrained brethren, the drugs were a pass to Xanadu, especially in the 1960s. The changes in brain chemistry triggered by psychedelics cause the familiar world to metamorphose. It gives way to rapid imagery, unaccustomed depths of visual perception and hearing, a flood of "new" knowledge that seems at once very old, a poignant primal memory. . . . the annals of the Aquarian Conspiracy are full of accounts of passages: LSD to Zen, LSD to India, psilocybin to Psychosynthesis."[63]

The transformation or paradigm shift which Ferguson envisions for the New Age has to do with the perception of one's nature and that of others. "The separate self is an illusion. . . . The self is a field within larger fields. When the self joins the Self, there is power. Brotherhood overtakes the individual like an army . . . not the obligatory ties of family, nation, church, but a living, throbbing connection, the unifying I-Thou of Matin Buber, a spiritual fusion. This discovery transforms strangers into kindred, and we know a new, friendly universe. . . . Even beyond the collective Self, the awareness of one's linkage with others, there is a transcendent, universal Self."[64]

In discussing the concept and experience of God in New Age, Ferguson draws upon the thought of Alan Watts, J. D. Salinger, Meister Eckhart, John Robinson, Buckminster Fuller, and Nikos Kazantzakis within the same several paragraphs. Ferguson writes, "God is experienced as flow, wholeness, the infinite kaleidoscope of life and death, Ultimate Cause, the ground of being. . . . . God is the organizing matrix." She quotes Salinger's short story about Teddy, a precocious youth who remembers his experience of immanent God while he watches his little sister drink her milk, "All of a sudden I saw that she was God and the milk was God. I mean, all she was doing was pouring God into God."[65]

Ferguson observes that her writing has been more a phenomenon than a book, like a spider spinning a web from a community of ideas and people. She considers herself more a midwife than an author. The paradigm shift which she describes and anticipates involves all fields including spirituality, health, economics, politics, education, art, and music.

In concluding *The Aquarian Conspiracy,* she notes fourteen areas of reflection. They include learning that bad news may be good news, the rise of the Pacific Culture, the advent of citizen diplomats, the rediscovery of bodymind, a new respect for whole-brain thinking, and a search for methods to achieve positive mental states. Other areas are the arts and entertainment as parts of broad cultural change, the rediscovery of myth and metaphor as reshaping social purpose, and the cultivation of intelligence.[66]

There is an invaluable listing of books, periodicals, directories, and networks in Ferguson's Appendix B "Resources for Change" in *The Aquarian Conspiracy.*[67] She has found these networks and networking important for "personal and social transformation in our time." There are tens of thousands of entry points in the "conspiracy" in networking such as "conferences, phone calls, air travel, books, phantom organizations, papers, pamphleteering, photocopying, lectures, workshops, parties, grapevines, mutual friends, summit meetings, coalitions, tapes, and newsletters." All of these help in spreading the transformative vision.[68]

Persons and Networks: Shapers of New Age

The last quarter of the twentieth century has witnessed a plethora of New Age philosophy, religion, publications, movements, and expressions. Included in this myriad of development are visionaries and organizations, writers and lecturers and publishers, channeling and crystals and astrology, gurus and churches and spirituality, and a host of clusters of concern in areas of health, education, politics, and the environment. Below are varied expressions of persons, organizations, and networks which make their contributions large and small to personal and social transformation in what is called New Age.

Findhorn

The Findhorn community of Northern Scotland was the seedbed for creating a new culture based on spiritual values during the 1960s and 1970s. Peter and Eileen Caddy were among its founders who were influenced earlier by Theosophy. David Spangler joined the community and became a codirector.

Residents of Findhorn claimed to communicate with plants and spirits of nature as well as other spirit beings. They focused on an evolutionary expansion of consciousness which would influence all civilization. Groothuis observes, "During the sixties and seventies, Findhorn served as Mecca and model for the New Age community. Mixing occultism, animism, Eastern religions and other ingredients, Findhorn made the animistic-pantheistic world view palatable and intriguing."[69]

Esalen

The Esalen Institute was opened in 1961 in Big Sur, California, under the leadership of Michal Murphy and Richard Price. Marilyn Ferguson writes that this residential center helped midwife what later was called the human-potential movement. Early seminar leaders included Alan Watts, Arnold Tonybee, Linus Pauling, Carl Rogers, Paul Tillich, Rollo May, and Carlos Castaneda.

Other participants and residents have been Abraham Maslow, Fritjof Capra, Buckminster Fuller, former California governor Jerry Brown, and Swami Muktananda and other gurus and yogis. Chandler asserts that in the counterculture of the 1960s, Esalen was known as the "wild frontier" of the touchy-feely and the primal hot tub. "Some of Esalen's outlandish excesses have been curbed, and less extravagant claims are being made these days. But the meat and potatoes seminars are still meditation, psychotherapy, Eastern religion, and massage and body work—the core of New Age consciousness."[70]

Esalen is known to have sprouted most of the avant-gard psychological methods of the 1960s. "A recent Esalen catalogue of events promises an experience where 'your discoveries are your truth without needing outside validation.'"[71]

The Forum (Formerly EST)

Werner Erhard established the Erhard Seminar Training (EST) in the 1970s to appeal to businesses in training their personnel in overcoming stress and in instigating assertiveness and efficiency in the work force. The name of EST was recently changed to The Forum. The Forum publicity describes itself as a powerful, practical inquiry into issues that determine one's personal effectiveness. The Forum promises to produce an extraordinary advantage in one's effectiveness and to give one a decisive edge in the ability to achieve.

A Forum seminar covers two consecutive weekends and one evening for $545. One is said to get in touch with one's being in order to have the power to change things. Being is not explained, but assurance is given that one will experience it. The Forum claims not to be a philosophy or a religion, although Erhard has claimed that Zen Buddhism and Scientology were the most influential forces in EST.

Chandler says The Forum's seminars tear down old beliefs and reconstruct values through a mixture of Freudian theory, behavior modification techniques, Eastern philosophy, and transpersonal psychology. He quotes Francis Adeney who wrote about human potential movements in general and of EST in particular.

> It is geared toward stripping a person of values, mores, and religious beliefs so that one may begin "freely" choosing values and creating one's own reality. The humanistic assumptions of the perfection of the individual and the potential for transcendence are crucial for EST. . . . The world is illusion; you see whatever you choose to see. You may create anything you like around you, and in fact, all you see is your own creation. Everything in essence is one; you are perfect; you are God.[72]

Lucis Trust

The Lucis Trust was founded by Alice and Foster Bailey in 1922 as a world service organization. The trust serves as an umbrella for the activities of the Lucis Publishing Company, the Arcane School, the World Goodwill, Triangles, and Lending Libraries.

The Arcane School is a correspondence school in meditation techniques and the development of spiritual potentiality.

World Goodwill purposes to establish right human relations through the practical application of the principle of goodwill. It cooperates with the United Nations and its specialized agencies. Triangles is an activity of the mind, using the power of thought and prayer to invoke light and goodwill for all humanity. This activity is done by units of three people linked in a worldwide network. The lending libraries are by mail and deal with esoteric and occult books. The Lucis Publishing Company publishes the books of Alice Bailey. It also publishes a bimonthly magazine, *The Beacon,* composed of esoteric philosophy and ageless wisdom.[73]

From Arica to Planetary Citizens

As Marilyn Ferguson indicated, there are thousands of clusters and entry points in the personal and social transformation into the New Age.

Arica is another psychotechnology in search of the Self. Its goal is to achieve the divine life through such means as chanting mantras, African dances, Egyptian gymnastics, and concentrating on colorful wall symbols called *yantras.* It holds workshops across the nation.

Planetary Citizens was founded in 1972 by Donald Keys, consultant to delegations and committees of the United Nations. Keys asserts that humanity is progressing toward the Omega point, the higher consciousness level, and claims that leading the way to planetization are groups such as Findhorn, Esalen, and the Association for Humanistic Psychology. The United Nations is seen as a central hub and catalyst in this effort of planetization.

A Planetary congress has been held in which representatives from twenty countries addressed the subjects of ecology, economics, and politics. The congress issued statements indicating the need to achieve individual human potential and the spiritual identity of each person to help achieve unity with all life. It also voiced the need for a new economic order, a strong United Nations, and a centralized global government.[74]

Board members and advisors of Planetary Citizens have included David Spangler and Peter Caddy, formerly of Findhorn; Michal Murphy of Esalen Institute; Edgar Mitchell, ex-astronaut; Isaac Asimov; Rene Dubos; Norman Cousins; and the president of Notre Dame, Theodore Hesburg.

Other visionaries and/or organizations whose views and practices are associated with New Age thought would include Silva Mind Control, Ron Hubbard's Scientology, Eckankar, Edgar Cayce's Association for Research and Enlightenment, and Lifespring.

Gurus, Spirituality, Churches

Baba Ram Dass

Richard Alpert was a Harvard psychologist in the 1960s who was expelled from the university for using LSD. In India, he studied with a guru and changed his name to Guru Ram Dass, meaning "Servant of God." He returned to the United States as the "Age of Aquarius" was dawning, and with his writings and lectures contributed to the New Age. His book, *Be Here Now,* published in 1971, was considered to be one of the catalysts for the New Age movement.

Baba Ram Dass "preached a new, hybrid message of spiritual ecstasy and 'nowness,' which he committed to print as a crazy pastiche of bold-face words strewn all over the pages in scissor-and-paste fashion."[75] Over time he changed his clothing and hairstyle to address the middle class, not the hippie culture. "I can go to Omaha, Idaho City, Seattle, Buffalo, or Tuscaloosa, and everywhere thousands of people are ready to hear. They are growing spiritually in their daily lives, without putting on farout clothes and wearing beads around their necks. Their spiritual awakening grows from within."[76] Ram Dass moved to the Hindu practice of Karma Yoga, "using service to others as a path to transformation." "I have never thought of my humanity as a practice. I was too busy trying to become divine."[77]

Transcendental Meditation (TM)

Maharishi Mahesh Yogi was the founder of Transcendental Meditation, known as TM. In India he studied under the noted Guru Dev. Maharishi brought his teachings and meditation practices to the United States and introduced them through workshops across the nation. He founded Science of Creative Intelligence (SCI), which is a curriculum in his Maharishi International University, emphasizing astronomy, cosmology, and vedic philosophy. After buying the former Presbyterian school, Parsons College, in Fairfield, Iowa, he renamed it Maharishi International University.

He has formulated a World Plan known as the "World Government of the Age of Enlightenment." He believes that the proper study and meditation techniques among meditators who learn and are trained in TM and in his university can have a global impact to effect change to solve problems in the political, economic, social, and religious systems of the world regardless of ideology. Some of his noted practitioners have been the Beatles, the Rolling Stones, and Shirley MacLaine.

Transcendental Meditation has its foundations in the Hindu Vedic scriptures, including the Upanishads and the Bhagavad Gita. Its emphases include Hindu worship *(puja)*, karma, reincarnation, and the transmigration of souls.

Tara Center and Benjamen Creme

The Tara Center in North Hollywood, California has promoted the teachings of Benjamen Creme, an English occultist. Creme's works rely heavily on Alice Bailey's writings, especially *The Reappearance of Christ*.

He is an author, lecturer, and artist, and has traveled and lectured extensively in America and Europe. His basic message has been that a few great teachers prepare the way throughout history for religious and spiritual movements. As a high initiate who receives messages from Lord Maitreya the Christ, Creme proclaimed the coming of the Christ. He stated that the New World Teacher (Christ) in 1977 entered a well-known country. He would become more visible during 1981, but would withhold his true identity until 1982.

In 1982 the Tara Center placed a full-page ad in major newspapers of the world announcing, "The Christ Is Here Now." This great revelation and the return of Lord Maitreya (Eastern term) or Christ (Western term) would lead to the end of world hunger, war, and strife. Sickness and evil would disappear. The Tara Center placed the "Great Invocation" from the works of Alice Bailey in newspapers so people could invoke the Christ's coming.[78]

Creme said that he had been chosen by Lord Maitreya the Christ to tell the world of his coming. In Creme's message of hope on the lecture circuit, he spoke of ending world hunger, sharing world resources, resolving today's violence, talking of World War III, breakdown of old institutions, the New Age, the women's movement, a new economic order, and a new world religion.

Lord Maitreya did not appear. Followers of Creme gathered regularly in "transmission groups" to recite the "Great Invocation" in order to create an atmosphere for the Maitreya's coming. Creme continued to lecture.

Church Universal and Triumphant: Elizabeth Clare Prophet

The Church Universal and Triumphant was founded in 1958 by Mark Prophet as the Summit Lighthouse. When he died in 1978, his wife, Elizabeth Clare Prophet, assumed leadership and became known to her followers as Guru Ma. She claimed that the ascended masters of the Great White Brotherhood had summoned her late husband and herself to be messengers of God releasing the sacred scriptures of the Aquarian Age to the world. The Great White Brotherhood is composed of spirit guides who use Guru Ma as a mouthpiece.

Through her writings, including *The Lost Years of Jesus* and *The Science of the Spoken Word,* and through her Summit University in Los Angeles, and through clusters of her church members in some one hundred American cities, she disseminates her teachings from the ascended masters. The earth is in a revolution of higher consciousness in which heightened awareness will make initiated students recognize the fact that life, God, and persons are energy. Her teaching is the way to enlightenment through contact with the inner Christ Self, the individual reality that knows itself as God.[79]

Official literature of Summit University describes it as sponsored by Gautama Buddha with the assistance of world teachers like Jesus and Kuthumi. Those who teach at Summit are the "I Am Presence" and the "Christ Self" and the ascended masters. Prophet herself is the "Vicar of Christ" and claims to receive direct dictations as God's chosen messenger from the ascended masters such as Buddha, Jesus, Pope John XXIII, Christopher Columbus, and K-17, the "head of the Cosmic Secret Service."

Course offerings at Summit include "Consciousness of the Cosmic Christ and Planetary Buddha," "Mother Mary's Scriptural Rosary for the New Age," and "Meditations for the Conception of New-Age Children."

Prophet moved her church from Southern California to a large ranch near Yellowstone National Park. She has had difficulties with some of the rural Montana townsfolk over several issues, including the arming of her community. The church is founded on eclectic teachings of world religions and the occult. Prophet teaches a sharp distinction between Jesus and the Christ. The universal Christ consciousness which Jesus possessed may be achieved by any willing individual.

From Hare Krishna to Church of Scientology

A variety of gurus and teachers and writers saturated the American scene during the 1960s and 1970s. Many contributed seminal ideas to New Age as well as their culture of values and life-styles.

A. C. Bhaktivedanta, affectionately called Prahupada by his devotees, came from India in the 1960s to establish his International Society for Krishna Consciousness. Known as the Hare Krishna, he popularized the Bhagavad Gita with his translation. The chanting of the Hare Krishna mantra became a form of meditation. The building of temples ensued across the nation, and a strictly disciplined life-style on a commune with uniform clothing became standardized. God consciousness became the focus for attainment.

Swami Muktananda offered his SYDA Foundation with headquarters in New York. Considered one of the largest yoga movements in the world, he was looked upon by his followers as divine essence. He taught that God was within the individual, and the individual ought to worship oneself. He died in 1982, having influenced hundreds of thousands around the world, including Werner Erhard of EST.

Guru Maharaj Ji established the Divine Light Mission in America in the 1970s. His devotees, called premies, absorbed his teaching of the future light of inner peace. Also, Bhagwan Shree Rajneesh built his commune in Oregon, having attracted thousands of followers to Puma, India, for years before bringing his teachings to America.

The Church of Scientology evolved from the thought of L. Ron Hubbard, who through his science fiction writings impacted the public with his bestseller *Dianetics*. His system of Dianetics or Scientology states that humans are Thetans who are uncreated gods. Thetans continue to be reincarnated through their ignorance until they are able to gain their true identities in the counseling programs of the Church of Scientology. Scientology is a blend of eastern mysticism with the occult and human potential.

A Course in Miracles

A Course in Miracles is a twelve hundred-page, three-volume work, written by Helena Schucman, a Jewish psychologist of Columbia University in New York. Being an atheist, she claimed that in 1965 she heard an inaudible voice whose words she dictated for seven years. The result is "The Course."

Over a million copies have been sold, and hundreds of study groups on its teachings have surfaced. Robert and Judityh Skutch, through their Foundation for Inner Peace, publish *A Course in Miracles,* translated into over a dozen languages with teacher and study guides. Schucman died in 1981. Mary Ann Williamson lectures on "The Course" to Hollywood stars and holds lectures nationally. She has authored her own experience and interpretations from "The Course," entitled *A Return to Love.*

Russell Chandler observes, "While the Course's teachings are complex, arcane, and couched in Christian terminology with a psychological application, the nub of Schucman's channeled revelation is that each person is God. The universe is one. And evil is illusion—a spirituality that squares nicely with the ancient nondualistic Vedanta of Hinduism as well as with modern New Age fundamentals."[80]

The main tenets of "The Course" about God, Jesus, and the condition of humanity are that God did not create the world; that Jesus was not the only Son of God; all are equally Christ; and that Jesus did not suffer and die for sins for they are illusion.

Trance-Channeling and Crystals and Stars

Trance-channeling of the New Age has precedents in ancient history. In the Old Testament, King Saul approached a woman with a "familiar spirit" at Endor to seek communication with the dead prophet Samuel. She served as a "medium" to facilitate conversation with a deceased spirit. History is replete with mediums. Spiritualism was known for its seances with deceased spirits or with beings in other worlds.

Modern trance-channeling involves altered states of consciousness. It is a form of the occult dealing with esoteric knowledge. Trance-channelers say that this knowledge is only available to a few. The trance channeler differs from the traditional medium in that another being inhabits the channeler's body and/or mind. This being is described differently by channelers, including a higher being, a guide, a spirit, and a specified name such as Ramtha.

Trance-channelers claim that a particular entity comes to them, taking the initiative to deliver its own message to a person or group, and communicating with those individuals. Channelers say that they go into a meditative trance and are unaware of the entity speaking through them. Channelers have different styles and techniques which may include crystals, astral projection, recitation of mantras, and light and sound therapy along with visualization.

There are channelers little known outside their close associates who channel in private. Some channelers have become widely known through their clientel and the mass media. The *Urantia Book* was given through automatic writing by unnamed individuals in the 1930s. *A Course in Miracles* was dictated to Schucman. J. Z. Knight has channeled an ancient entity named Ramtha. Jack Pursel channels an entity known as Lazaris. Other notable channelers are Penny Tower of Mafa and Kevin Ryerson of various entities.

Shirley MacLaine

Mass media have called Shirley MacLaine "the New Age's reigning whirling dervish," and "the celebrity evangelist of New Age metaphysics." As a Hollywood actress, she has won an Oscar. As an author, she has best-sellers. As a traveling lecturer, she has gathered thousands of people into lecture halls. Her topic, "Connecting with the Higher Self," and all its ramifications have been heard or read by millions.

MacLaine grew up attending a Baptist church in Northern Virginia. Having been at one time an atheist, she unfolds her changing spiritual experiences through her writings, lectures, and television appearances on talk shows and a mini-series. *Out on a Limb,* published in 1983, chronicles her conversion to metaphysics and spirituality. The book describes her seances or trance channeling, communication with other world entities, reincarnation, and out-of-body travels. She says, "Perhaps as philosophies and even some scientists have claimed, reality is only what one perceived it to be."[81]

Her second book, *Dancing in the Light,* published in 1985, describes her journey further into reincarnation, yoga, meditation, the power of crystals, and various communications with her spirit guides. In her first book she was told by her spirit guides that individuals are cocreators with God. In this second book she writes, "If everyone was taught one basic spiritual law, your world would be a happier, healthier place. And that law is this: Everyone is God. Everyone. . . . You are unlimited. You just don't realize it."[82]

MacLaine had prime time exposure with her five-hour ABC-TV movie, *Out on a Limb,* in 1987. Russell Chandler describes her as she played the lead role, "Primed by voluminous reading and much conversation with mystics, MacLaine's 'moment of naked truth' comes in a hot sulfur pool in the Andes where she feels her conscious self drift from her body and soar high into the Peruvian sky. In her luminous description, her 'spirit, or mind, or soul, whatever it was, flowed out of her body—though the two were connected by a 'thin silver cord.' She rose so high, she said, she could see the Earth's curvature."[83]

In a later book, *It's All in the Playing,* she describes what went on in making the mini-series, including help from the deceased Alfred Hitchcock. MacLaine has sought the help of various popular channelers including Kevin Ryerson and J. Z. Knight.

Thus, MacLaine draws on Hindu metaphysics, mysticism, and occult esotericism to state her teachings and experiences to a wide public. To understand developments of New Age is to take into account the MacLaine phenomenon.

J. Z. Knight (Ramtha)

J. Z. Knight trance-channels Ramtha. She is one of a host of channelers who has found acclaim through the mass media by channeling for Hollywood notables and through her presentations to paying groups.

Knight lives in the farming community of Yala, Washington. She grew up in New Mexico with an alcoholic father who left the family and with a fundamentalist Christian mother. She claims that Ramtha first spoke to her in 1977 while she was experimenting with crystal pyramids in her kitchen.

Ramtha is a thirty-five thousand-year-old ascended master from the lost continent of Atlantis. His primary message is that God resides within oneself. Reality is what one makes of it, and the individual is the measure of right and wrong. There is no message of judgment, sin, or guilt from Ramtha. He does speak of possible earthquakes and other devastation which might come to America and says the safest possible refuge is the Pacific Northwest.

Knight has attracted clientel like Shirley MacLaine, Linda Evans, and Burt Reynolds. Many individuals and families have moved to the Northwest to be closer to their channeler and to escape possible devastation which Ramtha has predicted. Knight lives in a mansion, raises Arabian horses whose stables are furnished with chandeliers and carpets, appears on TV talk shows channeling Ramtha, and holds seminars which attract thousands and cost hundreds of dollars.[84]

Crystals

A belief and practice associated with New Age is the use of crystals and gemstones such as citrine, tourmaline, and amethyst. It has been called "crystal consciousness." Many books have been written about crystals, including Uma Silbey's *The Complete Crystal Guidebook*.

The use of crystals is believed to have paranormal healing effects and restorative powers. Combined with Eastern metaphysics, mysticism, and meditation together with occultic esotericism, reliance on the presence and power of crystals has also become associated with New Age. Therapists use them to treat their patients or counselees.

One who practices metaphysical counseling and healing may place crystals over the body of a person in a hypnotic trance. Suspended quartz crystals from room ceilings may filter out all the negative energy. A business executive may have a $10,000 amethyst cluster on his desk to help keep him and others calm during the business hours.

Crystals in the New Age have become a fad, a fashion, and a phenomenon. Science has done little to investigate crystal use. Users of crystals are certain that there are spiritual energies in crystals that science cannot measure.[85]

Astrology and Outer Space

The study of the stars and heavens is not new. In the modern age, however, people have latched onto the stars and other space phenomena like UFOs and ETIs not only for curiosity and knowledge, but for an understanding of and dependence on these phenomena for everyday living and for their destinies.

Daily horoscopes are applied to individuals and to businesses. Some members of the White House during President Ronald Reagan's administrations relied on communication with an astrologist before making certain decisions. Brad Steiger has written 107 books concerning psychic phenomena with sales of over $15 million. Hollywood films of Stephen Spielburg like *E. T.* and *Close Encounters of the Third Kind* portray UFO phenomena. Extra terrestrials are portrayed in Whitley Strieber's *Communion,* a best-selling novel, which he claimed was his true experience.

Major messages of the New Age that come from phenomena and entities of other spaces are that other intelligences inhabit other planets, that they assist us to the higher consciousness, that there is a changing and impacting of energy fields and forces, and that all entities are interrelated. Margaret Mead, an influential anthropologist, said that there is no reason to deny the reality of psychic phenomena we cannot as yet explain.

Other Thinkers, Publishers, Fields of New Age

Physics, Politics, Psychology

There are writers whose seminal thoughts contribute to New Age emphases upon personal and social transformation and whose writings are quoted by the vast network or clusters of the "Aquarian conspiracy."

Fritz Capra is an Austrian physicist in the lineage of the thought of Pierre Teilhard de Chardin. Capra wrote *The Tao of Physics* and *The Turning Point*. Capra, called a mystic physicist, holds to the unity of all things including opposites, and the nonexistence of an independent external world. He relates an early vision he had: "I suddenly became aware of my whole environment as being engaged in a gigantic cosmic dance. . . . I 'saw' cascades of energy coming down from outer space, in which particles were created and destroyed in rhythmic pulses. I 'saw' the atoms of the elements and those of my body participating in this cosmic dance of energy. I felt its rhythm and 'heard' its sound, and at that moment I knew that this was the Dance of Shiva, the Lord of Dancers worshipped by the Hindus."[86]

Mark Satin is the editor of the political newsletter "New Options" and author of *New Age Politics*. He covers post-liberal, post-conservative, post-socialist options in labor, business, economics, feminism, the peace movement, global development, religions and minority group activism. As with Satin, so there is the politics of transformation supported by Planetary Citizens whose founder is Donald Keys. This politic is concerned with a paradigm shift in which patriotism and nationalism give way to unity and interdependence on a global scale. The political order should be consonant with the cosmic order.

Robert Muller, the author of *New Genesis,* has served as secretary of the United Nation's Economic and Social Council, and as an assistant secretary general. His book's subtitle is "Shaping a Global Spirituality." He writes, "The supreme unity of the human family, universal and interdependent, as seen by all great religions must now become a political reality; the hour has struck for the implementation of a spiritual union of world affairs; the next great task of humanity will be to determine the divine or cosmic laws which must rule our behavior on this planet." He sees humankind reuniting with the divine, and the United Nations as a catalyst for planetary transformation.[87]

Ken Wilbur, author of *Up from Eden* and *A Sociable God,* delineates his transpersonal psychology and reliance on Eastern mysticism. He points to further levels of psychological growth for humanity and refers to the seven yogic chakras of Hinduism. At the highest level, self realization, one comes to the higher consciousness or enlightenment.

Health and Healing; Education and Music

Holistic health is a major focus in New Age writings and practices. Marilyn Ferguson, publisher of "Brain/Mind Bulletin," says that the mind has the ability to alter every physiological system and every cell in the body. The mind, body, and spirit are integrally interconnected so that the proper interaction and alignment of all three are necessary for holistic health and healing. Ferguson indicates that the mind is primary or co-equal in all illness.

The Aquarian conspiracy in medicine and health includes new therapies of meditation, visualization, biofeedback, acupuncture, hypnosis, psychic healing, and folk healing.[88] Also, there are homeopathic remedies, New Age health spas, and healing through trance-channeling.

Groothuis observes that ten themes summarize New Age health care:

1. Whole is greater than the parts.

2. Health is more than the absence of disease.

3. Humanity is responsible for its own health.

4. Natural forces of healing are preferable to drugs and surgery, e.g., diet, life-style, attitude.

5. Holistic methods like acupuncture, biofeedback, Eastern meditation, psychic healing, are promoted.

6. Health implies evolution.

7. Understanding of energy, not matter, is the key.

8. Death is final stage of growth.

9. Thinking and practice of ancient civilizations are a rich source.

10. Holistic health must be incorporated into fabric of society through public policy.[89]

Educational philosophy and methods which are nurtured in New Age include visualization, guided imagery, and value clarification. Children are taught that they are one with the sun's rays or a part of God. They are led to visualize it, sense it, and feel it. Children are to discover their own Self, their own values, and not have those values imposed on them from without. They are to become autonomous.

John Dunlop, in his award-winning essay "A Religion for a New Age," wrote, "I am convinced that the battle for humankind's future must be waged and won in the public school classroom by teachers who correctly perceive their role as the proselytizers of a new faith: a religion of humanity that recognizes and respects the spark of what theologians call divinity in every human being." Marilyn Ferguson portrays the new paradigm over the old one in education as urgent and needed.[90]

New Age sounds and music have impacted modern culture. The music is mostly instrumental. "It includes the sounds of plant vibrations, animal and nature noises, Celtic harps, gourd-shaped sitars, turnable table drums, drone generating tambouras, and digital synthesizers." Windham Hill recordings turned a $300 investment into a multimillion dollar enterprise. George Winston's "December" recording went platinum and helped create a New Age division of music in recording companies and music stores.[91]

Communications of New Age

There are several publishing companies associated primarily with New Age. An example is Jeremy P. Tarcher, Inc., which has published books such as Marilyn Ferguson's *The Aquarian Conspiracy, Channeling* by Jon Kilmo, and *The Meditative Mind* by Daniel Goleman.

Streiker summarizes the assumptions of Tarcher as follows:

1. The world, including the human race, constitutes an expression of a higher, more comprehensive divine nature.

2. Hidden within each human being is a higher divine Self, which is a manifestation of the higher, more comprehensive divine nature.

3. This higher nature can be awakened and can become the center of the individual's everyday life.

4. This awakening is the reason for the existence of each individual life.[92]

Marilyn Ferguson presents a list of periodicals and resource directories which she labels "Resources for Change." They include *Advances* (Institute for the Advancement of Health); *The Essential Whole Earth Catalogue; The Networking Book: People Connecting With People; New Age Journal; New Options; Revision: A Journal of Consciousness and Change; Whole Earth Review;* and *Windstar Journal.* She also gives an invaluable list of "Networks and Organizations" with addresses.[93]

New Age and Christian World Views

New Age may not be a monolithic movement with a hierarchical leadership and organization. It may not have one central voice or one official book. Individual New Age thinkers, authors, and organizers may not interpret and implement a world view or practice in the same fashion. Yet, there are central themes. Christianity, too, has much diversity among its constituencies. The Bible, however, is the primary and central focus upon which Christian thinkers, authors, and organizers have expressed their world view and ethos.

Perhaps a general typology of comparisons between New Age and Christian world views and values may offer clarifications. The themes of God, creation, humanity, humanity's dilemma and solution, Jesus Christ, history and eschatology are considered.

The concept of *God* in New Age thinking revolves around the words Higher Self, Higher Consciousness, Ultimate Reality or Spirit, Energy, The Force, and Oneness or Unity with All. There is the idea that God is in all things and all things are in God. In traditional Christian thought, the concept of God focuses God as a personal Spirit or Being, transcendent to His creation, with personal attributes including holiness, righteousness, and love. God reveals Himself as Father, Son, and Holy Spirit with personal attributes, but without division of His being or nature.

Creation in New Age thought centers on unity and oneness. There is little if any distinction between God and creation or cosmos. All is Spirit or Consciousness or Self. God is not One who transcends creation or is over against it as a separate being. Creation is of one piece with God and all its parts interrelated. In traditional Christian thinking, creation is the result of the God who creates. The God who creates is the God who preserves, saves, judges, and rules. Creation is good but is fallen and distorted and needs restoring and renewal. God is related to His creation but transcends it.

New Age addresses *humanity* as divine. Humanity is not distinct from God, but is God. Humanity is, in reality and truth, pure consciousness, or self, or divinity when it comes to self-realization. Humanity is the ultimate reality. God is in creation and humanity. Every individual has the potential of the "Christ spirit" and is good. Traditional Christian thought sees humanity as created by God as good, as rebellious against God's laws and therefore sinful, and as bearing the image of God with the hope to be saved by God. Humanity is a part of God's creation which bears the image of God to become the sons and daughters of God.

The *human dilemma* for the New Age is that humanity lives in a state of ignorance and illusion. Humanity does not know its true nature. Humanity does not realize that it is unlimited or infinite. It does not realize that it does not have to live with death and rebirth. Humanity does not grasp the knowledge that it is divine and only has to realize it. The dilemma is the lack of knowledge, perception, and will to be what humanity really is.

Traditional Christian thought concerning the human dilemma is that humanity has a broken relationship with its Creator God. The problem is spiritual alienation and lack of fellowship with God. The problem is that humanity chose to rebel against God's authority and desire for humanity. Humanity is unable on its own to restore the relationship; it needs help beyond itself and other selves; it needs God.

The solution to the human problem, according to New Age, is to turn inward to the self for enlightenment and self-realization. Humanity can overcome its ignorance and its resting on illusions by exploring its own human potentiality, which is in reality its divinity. Most often humanity needs to turn for help to self-helps of types like the return of ascended masters, prominent gurus, enlightened teachers, guides; as well as techniques and methods like meditation, channeling, and altered states of consciousness. One can attain the "Christ consciousness" within oneself.

On the other hand, traditional Christian thought says that the solution to the human problem is to turn away from self to God. To overcome rebellion against God and to be forgiven of sin, humanity's need is to turn to God through Jesus Christ who, by His sinless and reconciling love, died a sacrificial death and was raised in a victorious resurrection. Humanity needs salvation in Jesus Christ through personal faith in God's revelation and action in Him. The dilemma is overcome through God's initiative of love and humanity's response in faith and obedience.

Jesus Christ, in New Age thought, is like one of the many avatars or ascended masters who comes to show the way to God-consciousness, to self-realization, and to Christ-consciousness. Jesus is the historical figure, and Christ is the universal consciousness or truth or being. Jesus is similar to a type like the Buddha and other manifestations of various ages who demonstrate for their age a type of pure consciousness or unity with being. Individuals can learn from

Jesus, can be enlightened according to their own divinity or Christ consciousness to attain as Jesus had.

Jesus Christ, according to traditional Christian thought, is fully God and fully man. He is the unique, divine Son of God who was born, lived, died, and was resurrected for the salvation of all humanity. Jesus Christ is not one of the avatars or ascended masters. Jesus Christ is not just one whose example is to be followed or emulated. He is not one who awakens in one a slumbering god. He is called the Redeemer, the Savior, the Lord.

New Age thought views *history* as cyclical with individuals having many cycles of births and reincarnations in various ages. One's karma for good or bad determines one's various states of existence. Traditional Christian reflection views history as linear with a beginning and an end. Ethics, morality, and the grace of God influence the individual's life. New Age envisions an ultimate reality of union of all entities, having realized all human and cosmic potentialities. Traditional Christian thought envisions last things, which include a judgment, a heaven and a hell, and the final sovereignty and grace and love of God.

NOTES

■　　　　　　　　　　　　　　　　　　　　　　　　　　■

Chapter 1

1. For a full listing of the prophet/presidents of the church together with their counselors, see Leonard J. Arrington and Davis Britton, *The Mormon Experience* (New York: Alfred A. Knopf, 1979), 339-340.

2. Joseph Smith, *The Pearl of Great Price* (Salt Lake City: The Church of Jesus Christ of Latter-Day Saints, 1982), 47.

3. Ibid., 49-50.

4. See Arrington and Britton, The Mormon Experience, 127-144 for further data on immigration and growth.

5. See Joseph Smith, *Doctrine and Covenants* (Salt Lake City: The Church of Jesus Christ of Latter-Day Saints, 1982), 265. May be referred to as D. & C.

6. *D. & C.,*132.

7. *D. & C.,*128.

8. *D. & C.,*132.

9. *D. & C.,* Official Declaration 1, 291-293.

10. Smith, *Pearl of Great Price*, 60. (See article 8 in Articles of Faith which contains 13 articles.)

11. Joseph Fielding Smith, *Teachings of the Prophet Joseph Smith* (Salt Lake City: Deseret Book Co., 1958), 194.

12. Mormons believe that the Bible cannot stand alone; it needs the Book of Mormon as the second witness. The Book of Mormon attributes "many plain and precious things" to the Bible, but it later describes as fools those who believe the full inspiration of the Bible. See in the Book of Mormon, 1981 edition, the following books, chapters, verses: Mormon 7:9; I Nephi 13:29; II Nephi 29:3, 4, 6, 10.

13. Thomas F. O'Dea, *The Mormons* (Chicago: The University of Chicago Press, 1957), 24.

14. Ibid., 40.

15. Anthony A. Hoekema, *Mormonism* (Grand Rapids: Eerdmans Publishing Company, 1963), 19.

16. See introduction in *D. & C.*

17. Ibid.

18. See Jerald and Sandra Tanner, *Mormonism: Shadow or Reality?* (Salt Lake City: Utah Lighthouse Ministry, 1982), 294-369. The Tanners are former Mormons who present their research in this publication.

19. *D. & C.* 20:46.

20. See O'Dea, 174-182 for descriptions of the offices in the Mormon church.

21. *Church News,* March 5, 1980, 3.

22. Arrington and Britton, 297.

23. Joseph Fielding Smith, *Teachings,* 370, 372.

24. Ibid., 345-346.

25. John A. Widtsoe, *Discourses of Brigham Young* (Salt Lake City: Deseret Book Co., 1954), 22-23.

26. Milton R. Hunter, *The Gospel Through the Ages* (Salt Lake City: Deseret Book Co., 1958), 105-106.

27. Joseph Fielding Smith, *Teachings,* 346-347.

28. Joseph Fielding Smith, *Doctrines of Salvation,* 3 vols. (Salt Lake City: Bookcraft, 1960), I, 96.

29. Bruce McConkie, *Mormon Doctrine* (Salt Lake City: Bookcraft, 1958), 467.

30. O'Dea, *The Mormons,* 125.

31. James E. Talmage, *Articles of Faith* (Salt Lake City: The Church of Jesus Christ of Latter-Day Saints, 1981), 471-473.

32. Smith, *Doctrines of Salvation,* I, 102.

33. Ibid., I, 19.

34. Ibid., I, 18.

35. Talmage, *Articles,* 472.

36. As quoted in Harry L. Ropp, *The Mormon Papers* (Downers Grove, Ill.: InterVarsity Press, 1977), 18.

37. Joseph Fielding Smith, *Doctrines of Salvation,* II, 82. Jesus is also placed in the context of polygamy in *The Seer,* 1:160.

38. A pamphlet "Your Pre-Earth Life" published by The Church of Jesus Christ of Latter-Day Saints, Salt Lake City, Utah, 7/78.

39. *Journal of Discoveries,* Vol. 6, 163.

40. See Mormon pamphlet "Temples of the Church of Jesus Christ of Latter-Day Saints" published by the Corporation of the President of The Church of Jesus Christ of Latter-Day Saints, Salt Lake City, Utah, 1981, for a pictorial and commentary on baptism for the dead, 59-69.

41. Ibid., 19.

42. O'Dea, 59.

43. Ibid., 57. See Jerald and Sandra Turner, *Mormonism,* 484 ff. for discussion on Joseph Smith's relationship to Masonism.

44. Ibid., 44-48, for an article by Spencer W. Kimball on "Temples and Eternal Marriages" with pictorial descriptions of the sealing rooms.

45. Joseph Fielding Smith, *Doctrines of Salvation,* II, 44.

46. McConkie, *Mormon Doctrine,* 238.

47. O'Dea, 59.

48. Arrington and Britton, 189.

49. See pamphlet "Temples of the Church of Jesus Christ of Latter-Day Saints" as cited above, 48.

50. *Doctrine and Covenants,* Official Declaration I, 291-292.

51. Ibid., Official Declaration II, 293-294. See *Time,* August 7, 1978, for reporting of this decision.

52. See article on Mormon leadership in *Newsweek,* October 9, 1981, 109.

53. Address given at Brigham Young University, March 25, 1984.

54. Joseph Fielding Smith, *Salvation Universal* (Salt Lake City: Deseret Book Co., 1957), 73.

55. McConkie, *Mormon Doctrine,* 670.

56. See the critical review by Alexander Campbell (1788-1866), early leader of the Disciples of Christ, of the Book of Mormon first published in 1831 and now in print in *Restoration: News and Views of the Latter-Day Saint Movement,* Vol. 1, No. 3 (July 1982).

Chapter 2

1. Unauthored title. *The Watchtower,* January 1, 1992, published by Watchtower Bible and Tract Society of Pennsylvania. (Unless otherwise noted, Witness literature is unauthored and is published by their Tract Society.)

2. *The Watchtower,* September 15, 1910, 298, as quoted in Walter R. Martin, Jehovah of the Watchtower (Chicago: Moody Press, 1974), 25.

3. Heather and Gary Botting, *The Orwellian World of Jehovah's Witnesses* (Toronto: The University of Toronto Press), 41.

4. Ibid.

5. *The Watchtower,* October 15, 1966, 631.

6. Yearbook 1979, 30-31.

7. Richard N. Ostling, "Ostracized: A Sect Leader Falls." *Time,* February 22, 1982, 41.

8. See *Make Sure of All Things* (1953), 193.

9. Ibid., 200-203.

10. *The Watchtower,* February 15, 1981, 19.

11. *The Watchtower,* October 1, 1967, 587.

12. *The Watchtower,* September 15, 1954, 528.

13. See chapters 4 and 5 in *Organization for Kingdom-Preaching and Disciple-Making* (1972).

14. See the program of Weekly Meetings from which the following quotes are taken in *The Watchtower,* January 15, 1966, 45-46.

15. *You Can Live Forever in Paradise on Earth* (1982), 55-56.

16. Unauthored Title. *Babylon the Great Has Fallen* (1963), 83. Also see *You Can Live Forever in Paradise on Earth* (1982), 39-40, for discussion of the view of the Trinity.

17. *Make Sure of All Things* (1953), 188. Also see discussion of the idea of God in You Can Live Forever in Paradise on Earth (1982) 41-46.

18. *You Can Live Forever in Paradise on Earth* (1982), 66.

19. Ibid., 57.

20. *Holy Spirit* (1976), 88. Also see *Aid to Bible Understanding* (1971), 920.

21. *New Heavens and a New Earth,* 151.

22. *Holy Spirit* (1976), 94.

23. *You Can Live Forever in Paradise on Earth* (1982),60. See also *New Heavens and a New Earth* (1953), 151.

24. *You May Survive Armageddon,* 39.

25. *You Can Live Forever in Paradise on Earth* (1982), 194. See also *The Truth Shall Make You Free,* 264.

26. *Let God Be True* (1946), 40.

27. Bruce M. Metzger, *The Jehovah's Witnesses and Jesus Christ* (Princeton, N.J.: The Theological Book Agency, 1953), 70.

28. Anthony Hoekema, *Jehovah's Witnesses* (Grand Rapids, Mich.: Eerdman's Publishing Company, 1972), 67. See also 65-67.

29. *Let God Be True* (1946), 145.

30. *You Can Live Forever in Paradise on Earth* (1982), 78.

31. Ibid., 80.

32. Ibid., 140.

33. Ibid., 141.

34. Ibid., 136.

35. *The Watchtower,* February 1, 1975. 84.

36. *You Can Live Forever in Paradise on Earth* (1982), 126.

37. *Things in Which It Is Impossible for God to Lie* (1965), 364-365.

38. *Let God Be True* (1946), 80.

39. Heather and Gary Botting, *Orwellian World. . . .,* 107.

40. *The Watchtower,* January 15, 1966. 44.

41. See Anthony Hoekema, *Jehovah's Witnesses,* especially 122-141 for a discussion of Jehovah's Witnesses' view on Jesus Christ.

42. See Heather and Gary Botting, 99, for the outline of Ephesians 6:4.

43. See *Organized to Accomplish Our Ministry* (1983), 81-110, "Ministers of the Good News" and 110-118 "Ways to Expand Your Ministry."

44. Ibid., 98-99.

45. *The Watchtower,* January 1, 1992.

46. *You Can Live Forever in Paradise on Earth* (1982), see 208-216 "For Satan's World, or for God's New System."

47. Ibid., 215.

48. Ibid., 216.

49. See Heather and Gary Botting. *Orwellian World . . .,* "Crisis at the 'Top,'" 150-165.

50. See ex-Witnesses' statements in Edmund C. Gruss, *We Left Jehovah's Witnesses* (Grand Rapids: Baker Book House, 1982); and the recent book by Raymond V. Franz, Crisis of Conscience: *The Struggle between Loyalty to God and Loyalty to One's Religion* (Atlanta: Commentary Press, 1983).

51. See William J. Schnell, 30 *Years a Watchtower Slave* (Grand Rapids: Baker Book House, 1978), especially, 190-192.

Chapter 3

1. Young Oon Kim, *Unification Theology* (New York: The Holy Spirit Association for the Unification of World Christianity, 1980), 19. See 19-23 for a brief sketch of Moon's life.

2. Ibid., 20.

3. Ibid., 21-22.

4. Neil Salonen. "History of the Unification Church in America." in Richard Quebedeaux. (ed.), *Lifestyle Conversations with Members of the Unification Church* (New York: Rose of Sharon Press, 1982), 164-65.

5. Ibid., 182.

6. Pamphlet, unauthored and undated. "Word and Deed, The Unification Movement: Toward an Ideal World."

7. Salonen, 167-68.

8. Ibid., 177.

9. Ibid., 177-178.

10. *The News and Observer,* Raleigh, N.C., July 22, 1984, 4A.

11. *The News and Observer,* Raleigh, N.C., May 12, 1985, 37A.

12. Kim, 43-44.

13. Ibid., 44.

14. Ibid., 45.

15. Frederick Sontag, *Sun Myung Moon and the Unification Church* (Nashville: Abingdon, 1977), 134.

16. *God's Warning to the World.* Reverend Moon's Message from Prison (New York: Rose of Sharon Press, 1985), 126.

17. Ibid., 128-129.

18. Ibid., 152.

19. Ibid., 153.

20. Sontag, 98.

21. *Outline of The Principle Level 4* (New York: Holy Spirit Association for the Unification of World Christianity, 1980), 2.

22. *Divine Principle* (New York: Holy Spirit Association for the Unification of World Christianity, fifth edition, 1977), 9.

23. Ibid., 131.

24. See discussion on Divine Principle in *Evangelical-Unification Dialogue,* Richard Quebedeaux and Rodney Sawatsky, eds. (New York: Rose of Sharon Press, 1979) 174-248; and Herbert Richardson, ed. *Ten Theologians Respond to the Unification Church* (New York: Rose of Sharon Press, 1981), 109-139.

25. *Divine Principle.* 43.

26. Kim, 72. See *Divine Principle.,* 32.

27. Kim, 64. See *Divine Principle.,* 19-64; for data on creation.

28. Ibid., 63. See *Divine Principle.,* 20; 25; 29; 53; 217-218; for data on nature of God.

29. Ibid., 118.

30. *Divine Principle,* 75.

31. Ibid., 77.

32. Ibid., 76.

33. Ibid., 210-211.

34. *Outline of the Principle Level 4.,* 97.

35. *Divine Principle.,* 209.

36. Kim. 197.

37. *Divine Principle.,* 147.

38. Kim. 148.

39. *Divine Principle.,* 143.

40. Ibid., 145.

41. Ibid., 147-148. See *Divine Principle.,* 142. *Divine Principle* presents a consistently negative attitude toward Israel and Jews, 113; 118; 143; 144; 147; 152; 153; 154; 156; 157; 196; 232; 343; 357; 359; 369-370; 418; 479-480; 516-519; 480.

42. *Outline of the Principle Level 4.,* 169, 171.

43. Kim., 190. See *Divine Principle* 348; 371; 221-225; for data on indemnity and on Jesus' suffering the tribulations which John the Baptist was to suffer.

44. *Divine Principle.,* 497.

45. Ibid., 519.

46. Ibid., 520.

47. Ibid., 521-532.

48. *God's Warning to the World.* See Moon's departing remarks in "The Path I Am Walking," 155-163.

49. *Divine Principle.,* 222-227.

50. Kim., 232.

51. Ibid., 231.

52. See articles on the Unification Seminary by Joseph M. Hopkins. "Meeting the Moonies on Their Territory" in *Christianity Today.* August 18, 1978. 40-42; and by Rodney Sawatsky. "Dialogue with the Moonies" in *Theology Today.* April 1, 1978. 88-91.

53. Quebedeaux, 5.

54. Ibid.

55. *Word and Deed.* 1.

56. Ibid., 31.

Chapter 4

1. Stephen Gottschalk, *The Emergence of Christian Science in American Religious Life* (Berkeley: University of California Press, 1973), 23.

2. See Robert Peel, *Mary Baker Eddy, the Years of Discovery 1821-1875* (New York: Holt, Rinehart and Winston, 1966), for an excellent study of Mrs. Eddy's formative years.

3. Thomas Linton Leishman, *Why I Am a Christian Scientist* (Boston: Beacon Press, 1958), 189, gives quote of Mrs. Eddy.

4. Mary Baker Eddy, *Science and Health with Key to the Scriptures* (Boston: The First Church of Christ, Scientist, 1971), 109.

5. Ibid., 107.

6. Ibid., 110.

7. Ibid., 126.

8. Ibid., 110.

9. *Questions and Answers on Christian Science* (Boston: The Christian Science Publishing Society, 1974), 28-29.

10. Ibid., 29.

11. Leishman, 171.

12. Science and Health, 497.

13. Ibid., 587.

14. Ibid., 589.

15. Ibid., 583.

16. Ibid., 588.

17. Ibid., 331-332.

18. Leishman, 61.

19. Ibid., 62.

20. *Facts About Christian Science* (Boston: The Christian Science Publishing Society, 1959), 4.

21. *Science and Health, 476-477.*

22. Ibid., 472.

23. Ibid.

24. Ibid., 593.

25. *Facts About Christian Science, 6.*

26. Leishman, 103.

27. *Science and Health,* 593.

28. See *Science and Health,* 362-442 for Christian Science Practice.

29. See Journal of Pastoral Counseling. Spring 1969, Vol. IV. No. 1, 39-42 for Robert Peel, "The Christian Science Practitioner."

30. Science and Health, 167.

31. Ibid., 193.

32. See Leishman, 65-83 for an excellent description of services in the church.

33. *Science and Health,* 16-17.

34. Ibid., 468.

35. King James Version, Bible, 1 John 3:1-3.

36. *Facts About Christian Science,* 21.

37. Eric Butterworth, *Unity: A Quest for Truth* (New York: Robert Speller and Sons, Publishers, Inc., 1965), 9. Also see James D. Freeman, *The Story of Unity* (Lee's Summit, MO.: Unity School of Christianity, 1954), for an overview of the Unity School.

38. Freeman, 55.

39. See A. Jase Jones. "The Unity School of Christianity" Home Missions magazine. (March 1975), 28-32 for an excellent statement on the Unity School and also Mission magazine 1984 on "Unity." 85-86.

40. Butterworth, 50-51.

41. Unity, January, 1985. 63.

42. Charles R. Fillmore, "The Adventure Called Unity," a pamphlet, n.d., 11.

43. Ibid.

44. Ibid., 12.

45. Butterworth, 28.

46. What is Unity. n.d. a handout from Unity Center.

47. Charles R. Fillmore. *The Revealing Word* (Lee's Summit, MO.: Unity School of Christianity, 1963), 212.

48. H. Emilie Cady. *Lessons in Truth* (Kansas City: Unity School of Christianity, 1940), 83.

49. Butterworth. 38.

50. Ibid., 32.

51. Ibid., 37.

52. Charles R. Fillmore, *Jesus Christ's Atonement* (Lee's Summit, MO.: Unity School of Christianity, 1960), 13-21.

53. Butterworth, 51.

54. See Butterworth, 78-89 for his chapter in "Techniques for Abundant Living."

55. L. Ron Hubbard. *Mission Into Time* (Los Angeles: The American Saint Hill Organization, 1973), 6.

56. L. Ron Hubbard. a pamphlet. Clearwater: Church of Scientology, 1981.

57. Ibid.

58. Ibid.

59. Hubbard. *Mission Into Time,* 16.

60. Ibid., 21.

61. Ibid., 97.

62. Ibid., 102.

63. *Scientology A Religion Helping Others,* published by the Church of Scientology Information Service, 1978. 15-17.

64. *Time.,* April 5, 1976. 57.

65. *Scientology A Religion Helping Others.,* 15.

66. See *Time.* January 31, 1983. 64-67.

67. *Christianity Today.* February 18, 1983, 30.

68. See *Time.,* January 31, 1983. 64-67.

69. *The News and Observer.* Raleigh, N.C. May 21, 1985.

70. *Time,* May 6, 1991., 51.

71. *Time,* April 5, 1976., 5.

72. Ibid., 57.

Chapter 5

1. See the articles on the occult in *U.S. News and World Report.* November 7, 1983. 83 for general characteristics of its presence in the U.S. Also, see John Charles Cooper, *Religion in the Age of Aquarius* (Philadelphia: The Westminster Press, 1971) for an overview of the occult.

2. See an excellent description of astrology in John Stevens Kerr, *The Mystery and Magic of the Occult* (Philadelphia: Fortress, 1971) 12-43. "What's Written in the Stars."

3. Ibid., 25-31 for a detailed outline of the zodiac.

4. See Kerr, 88-118; and David Farren, *The Return of Magic* (New York: Harper and Row, 1972), 56-69; and H. Richard Neff. *Psychic Phenomena and Religion* (Philadelphia: The Westminster Press, 1971) 21-63; 114-153; for descriptions of Spiritualism and psychic phenomena.

5. Frank S. Mead, *Handbook of Denominations in the United States* (Nashville: Abingdon Press, 1956), 198.

6. See James A. Pike, *The Other Side* (New York: Dell Publishing Co., 1968).

7. Morey Bernstein. *The Search for Bridey Murphy* (New York: Doubleday and Company, Inc., 1956).

8. See Hans Holzer, *The Truth About Witchcraft* (New York: Doubleday and Company, Inc., 1969), especially pages 78-173 on witchcraft in America and Great Britain.

9. See Margaret A. Murray, *The God of the Witches* (New York: Oxford University Press, 1970), for an overview of witchcraft; and Arthur Lyons, *The Second Coming* (New York: Dodd, Mead and Company, 1970), 45-62 for a description of esbat and sabbat.

10. For descriptions of black magic and Black Mass, see Kerr, 68-87; Lyons, 63-85; Holzer, 229-248.

11. For general background reading on demonology, see Henry Ansgar Kelly, *The Devil, Demonology, and Witchcraft* (New York: Doubleday and Company, Inc., 1968); and Lyons, 87-169.

12. See Lyons, 171-193, for a description of LaVey's The Church of Satan, San Francisco.

13. Angon Szander LaVey, The Satanic Bible (New York: Avon Books, 1969), 14.

14. Ibid., 16.

15. Ibid., 17.

16. Ibid., 25.

17. Ibid., 46.

Chapter 6

1. George W. Braswell, Jr. *Understanding World Religions* (Nashville: Broadman Press, 1983), 27.

2. Ibid. See the following pages for an overview of the concepts and practices of Hinduism: 12-13; 27-30; 45-52; 75-82; 117-120; 141-147; 192-195.

3. Satsvarupa Dasa Goswam: Prabhupada (Los Angeles: Bhaktivedanta Book Trust, 1983), ix.

4. Ibid., xxi.

5. Ibid., xl.

6. *Back To Godhead*. Vol. 19. No. 7. July 1984, inside front cover.

7. A. C. Bhaktivedanta. Bhagavad-Gita As It Is (Los Angeles: The Bhaktivedanta Book Trust, 1975), xxi.

8. A. C. Bhaktivedanta Swami Prabhupada. Krsna Consciousness (New York: The MacMillan Company, 1970), 11.

9. Bhagavad Gita As It Is, xxiii.

10. Krsna Consciousness, 51.

11. Bhagavad Gita as It Is, xxxiii.

12. Krsna Consciousness, 19.

13. Bhagavad Gita as It Is, xxxix.

14. Ibid., xl.

15. Ibid., xli.

16. Ibid., See the list of the disciplic succession.

17. Krsna Consciousness, 73.

18. Ibid., 14.

19. Ibid., 31.

20. Ibid., 31-32.

21. Ibid., 52.

22. Ibid., 12.

23. *Back to Godhead.*, 7.

24. Steven J. Gelberg, editor, *Hare Krishna, Hare Krishna* (New York: Grove Press, Inc., 1983), 85. See the article on chanting "The Nectar of the Holy Name." *Back to Godhead,* 15(3-4); 21-28, 1981.

25. See *Back to Godhead,* Vol. 17. No. 11. November, 1982., 9 for a description of the Jagannatha festival in D.C. Also see *U.S. News and World Report.* July 15, 1982., 39 for article on the Palace of Gold; and the magazine *Plain Living High Thinking.*, Bhaktipada Books, 1984 for a description of the New Vrndavana or Palace of Gold in West Virginia.

26. Iskon Review. Vol. 1, Number 1. Spring 1985, 7. The first issue of a journal by the Bhaktivedanta Institute of Religion and Culture. All correspondence should be addressed to Subhananda Das, c/o Iskon, 41 West Allens Lane, Philadelphia, Pa. 19119.

27. Ibid., 9.

28. Ibid., 10.

29. Ibid., 11.

30. Ibid.

31. Ibid., 12.

32. Ibid.

33. Prabhupada, 11.

34. Krsna Consciousness, 49.

35. Ibid., 33.

36. Found in the Certificate of Incorporation of the Spiritual Regeneration Movement in the office of secretary of state in California. July 7, 1959. Article 2. Paragraph 1.

37. From standard TM publicity.

38. *Time* magazine. (various issues, no page numbers)

39. *U.S. News and World Report.*, June 24, 1984, 60-61. See also *Richmond Times-Dispatch* newspaper, June 4, 1985, page B-4 for an article on TM.

40. *Time* magazine.

41. Update. Vol. 6. No. 4, Dec. 82, 53.

42. Maharishi Mahesh Yogi, *The Science of Being and the Art of Living* (New York: Signet Books, 1963), 64.

43. Ibid., 33.

44. Maharishi Mahesh Yogi, *Meditation of Maharishi Yogi* (New York: Bantam Books, 1973), 17-18.

45. Update. Vol. 7. No. 2. June 1983, 5-6.

46. See "The Guru Down the Road." *Christianity Today.* April 23, 1982, 38-40.

47. Gary Leazer. "Bhagwan." Beliefs of Other Kinds. A Home Mission Board of the Southern Baptist Convention publication. October, 1984, 134.

48. See R. C. Prasal. *Rajneesh: The Mystic of Feeling* (Delhi, 1978), and Bhaganan Shree Rajneesh. *Book of the Secrets* Vol. 2. (Poona, India: 1975).

49. Update, Vol. 6, No. 4. December 1982, 12.

50. See the description of the Celebration in Update. Vol. 6. No. 4. December 1982, 47-52.

51. Ibid., 49.

52. *The News and Observer,* a newspaper of Raleigh, N.C. October 28, 1984, 13A.

53. *The News and Observer,* September 18, 1985, 5A.

54. Church bulletin cover of Self-Revelation Church of Absolute Monism. May 15, 1983.

55. "The Gandhi Message." Vol. XIX. No. 3. 1985, 6. published quarterly by The Mahatma Gandhi Memorial Foundation, Inc., 4748 Western Avenue, O. Box 9515, Washington, D.C. 20016.

56. "The Mystic Cross," New Year 1985, 13, a pamphlet printed by Golden Lotus Press.

57. *News India.* May 16, 1980, "Srimati Kamala: The United States' First Lady of Vedanta." See "An American Ghandian" in *The Times of India,* February 3, 1980.

58. Church bulletin cover of Self-Revelation Church of Monism. May 12, 1985.

59. Ibid.

60. "Kriya Meditation Series" bulletin by the Self-Revelation Church of Monism. Seven weeks beginning April 25th, 1984.

Chapter 7

1. George W. Braswell, Jr. *Understanding World Religions* (Nashville: Broadman Press, 1983), 30.

2. Ibid., 83.

3. Ibid., 87.

4. See Charles S. Prebish. *American Buddhism* (North Scituate, Mass.: Duxbury Press, 1979), 1-55, for an overview of Buddhist groups in America.

5. See Henrich Dumolin, ed., *Buddhism in the Modern World* (New York: MacMillan Publishers, 1976), 320.

6. *The Teaching of Buddha* (Tokyo, Japan: Kosaido Printing Co., 1966).

7. See Prebish, American Buddhism, 83-96 for information on the San Francisco Zen Center.

8. See Christmas Humphreys, *Buddhism* (London: Cox and Wyman, Ltd., 1951), 179-187 for a general overview of Zen Buddhism.

9. From a handout sheet, Zen Buddhist Center, Washington, D.C.

10. See Nancy Ross Wilson. *The World of Zen* (New York: Vintage Books, 1960), for an East-West Anthology.

11. From a pamphlet "Introduction to NSA" provided by the Nichiren Shoshu of America Center in Washington, D.C.

12. Noah Brannen, *Soka Gakkai* (Richmond, Va.: John Knox Press, 1968), 77.

13. Ibid., See 91-130 for data on the Soka Gakkai movement in modern Japan.

14. "Introduction to NSA."

15. Ibid.

16. See Prebish, *American Buddhism,* 70-82 for an overview of NSA, and Brannen, *Soka Ga Kkai,* 152-154 for a brief description of worshi

17. *World Tribune.* Monday, January 31, 1983. 9. published weekly by NSA at their world headquarters in Santa Monica, California.

18. Ibid., 2.

19. Prebish, *American Buddhism,* 76-77 for information on profile of members of NSA.

20. Pamphlet from Buddhist Vihara Society, Washington, D.C.

21. Ibid.

22. Ibid.

23. From the minutes of "The Sixteenth Annual Report of the Buddhist Vihara Society, Inc." dated December 12, 1982, 3.

24. Pamphlet "Washington Buddhist Vihara a New Center" from the Buddhist Vihara Society of Washington, D.C.

25. See Braswell, *World Religions,* 195-198, for a Christian perspective upon Buddhist peoples.

26. Ibid., 198.

Chapter 8

1. See the following articles by George W. Braswell, Jr., on Islam and Iran: "Civil Religion in Contemporary Iran," *Journal of Church and State,* Spring, 1979; "Iran and Islam," *Theology Today,* January, 1980; and "Iran: Dreams and Nightmares," *The Christian Century,* July 16-23, 1980.

2. See the following pages for an overview of the doctrines and practices of Islam: George W. Braswell, Jr., *Understanding World Religions* (Nashville: Broadman Press, 1983), 19-20; 34-40; 66-70; 103-110; 133-136; 156-159; 198-201.

3. The word *imam* generally refers to the prayer leader of the mosque, and it may also be used to mean the spiritual leader of the mosque. The word also is used by the Shi'ite branch to indicate the leaders of the prophet's family, namely the twelve imams, who headed the Imamate.

4. For an overview of Shi'ite Islam, see the author's book on Islam in Iran, George W. Braswell, Jr., *To Ride a Magic Carpet* (Nashville: Broadman Press, 1977).

5. See information on Muslims in America in Don M. McCurry, editor, *The Gospel and Islam* (Monrovia: MARC, 1979), 228-229 and R. Marston Speight, *Christian-Muslim Relations* (Hartford: National Council of the Churches of Christ in the U.S.A., 1983), 32.

6. *The News and Observer.* A newspaper of Raleigh, N.C., Sunday, June 3, 1984, 1A, 12A-14A.

7. A pamphlet by Imam A. M. Khattab. "A Brief Introduction to Islam," printed by Islamic Center of Greater Toledo, 25877 Scheider Road, Perrysburg, Ohio. Quoted from inside cover.

8. An excellent recent study of the American Muslim Mission has been made by a master of theology thesis: Steven T. Smith, "An Historical Account of the American Muslim Mission with Specific Reference to North Carolina." An unpublished thesis presented to the faculty of Southeastern Baptist Theological Seminary, November 1, 1984.

9. C. E. Lincoln, The Black Muslims in America, Rev. ed., (Boston: Beacon Press, 1973), 17.

10. See McCurry, *The Gospel of Islam,* 230.

11. See Speight, *Christian-Muslim Relations,* 33-34.

12. See Smith, *American-Muslim Mission . . .* North Carolina, 102 ff.

13. From pamphlet of Washington, D.C. Masjid.

14. See J. E. Esslemont. *Baha'ullah and the New Era* (National Spiritual Assembly of the Baha'is of the United States, 1980), for an overview of the history of the Baha'i religion.

15. Allan L. Ward, *230 Days Abdul Baha's Journey in America* (Wilmette, Illinois. Baha'i Publishing Trust, 1979). This is an excellent report of Abdul Baha's travels across the states and his reception by a variety of audiences.

16. Abdul Baha, "Promulgation," 1, pamphlet. n.d.

17. For information on the Baha'i condition in Iran, see: "The Baha'is in Iran, A Report on the Persecution of a Religious Minority," published by the Baha'i International Community, June, 1981; *Time* magazine, February 20, 1984, 76. An article on "Slow Death for Iran's Baha'is." *The News and Observer.* A Raleigh, N.C. newspaper. Sunday, July 31, 1983. "Baha'is in Iran forced to choose between life, faith."

18. A pamphlet "The Baha'i Faith and its World Community" issued by the Baha'i Information Office in March, 1979.

19. See "The Baha'i Faith," by Firuz Kazemzadeh. A pamphlet printed by Baha'i Publishing Trust, Wilmette, Ill., 1976, 3-13.

20. "The Baha'i Faith and Its World Community."

21. Ibid.

22. "God's New Age," A pamphlet by Baha'i Publishing Trust. Wilmette, Ill. n.d. 6-7.

23. The News and Observer, (Raleigh, N.C.) June 25, 1984.

24. George W. Braswell, *Understanding World Religions,* 198-201. See for a discussion of Christian relations with Muslims.

Chapter 9

1. Ecclesiastes 1:9-10, The Holy Bible *New International Version,* Nashville: Holman Bible Publishers, 1986.

2. Marilyn Ferguson, *The Aquarian Conspiracy* (Los Angeles: J. Tarcher, Inc., 1980), 23.

3. Ibid.

4. Ibid., 29.

5. Russell Chandler, *Understanding the New Age* (Dallas: Word Publishing, 1991), 5.

6. Ibid., 7.

7. Douglas R. Groothuis, *Unmasking The New Age* (Downers Grove: Intervarsity Press, 1990), 9.

8. Lowell D. Streiker, *New Age Comes To Main Street* (Nashville: Abingdon, 1990), 10.

9. Constance Cumbey, *The Hidden Dangers of the Rainbow* (Lafayette: Huntington House, Inc., 1983), 17.

10. Ibid., 54.

11. Chandler, 15.

12. Ibid., 16-17.

13. Ibid., 16.

14. Ibid., 17.

15. Ibid., 18.

16. Ibid., 19.

17. Ibid., 20.

18. Groothuis,18.

19. Ibid., 19.

20. Ibid., 20.

21. Ibid., 22.

22. Ibid., 21-22.

23. Ibid., 25.

24. Ibid., 26.

25. Ibid., 27-28.

26. Ibid., 29.

27. Streiker, 10.

28. Ibid., 53.

29. Ibid., 53.

30. Ibid., 54.

31. Ibid.

32. David K. Clark and Norman L. Geisler, *Apologetics in the New Age* (Grand Rapids: Baker Book House, 1990), 118-120.

33. Ibid., 125-127.

34. Cumbey, Ibid., 40.

35. Ibid., 253-54.

36. Otto Friedrich, "New Age Harmonies," *Time* (December 7, 1987), 64.

37. George W. Braswell, Jr. *Understanding World Religions* (Nashville: Broadman Press, 1983), 27-30; 75-82.

38. Ibid., 30-31.

39. Ibid., 82-88.

40. Ibid., 32; 91-92.

41. Groothuis, 137.

42. J. Gordon Melton. *Encyclopedic Handbook of Cults in America,* 108.

43. Madame Helena Blavatsky. *The Secret Doctrine* (New York, 1985), 27, 42-45.

44. Chandler, 35.

45. Ibid.

46. Streiker, 39.

47. Alice Bailey, *The Reappearance of the Christ* (New York: Lucis Publishing Company, 1948), 77.

48. Ibid., 149.

49. Bulletin. "Shamballa," n.d., published by Arcane School, 2-3.

50. Bulletin, Lucis Publishing Company, n.d., 23.

51. Groothuis, 160.

52. David Spangler, *Revelation: The Birth of a New Age* (San Francisco: The Rainbow Bridge, 1977), 69.

53. Ibid., 16.

54. David Spangler, *Relationship and Identity* (Scotland: Findhorn Publications, 1986), 34.

55. David Spangler, *Emergence: Rebirth of the Sacred* (Scotland: Findhorn Publications), 144.

56. David Spangler, *Reflections on the Christ* (Glasgow: Findhorn Publications, 1978), 107.

57. Cumbey, 139.

58. Ibid., 60.

59. Streiker, Ibid., 33.

60. Ferguson, Ibid., 19.

61. Ibid., 23.

62. Ibid., 29.

63. Ibid., 89-90.

64. Ibid., 100-101.

65. Ibid., 382-383.

66. Ibid., 420-429.

67. Ibid., 435-449.
68. Ibid., 62-63.
69. Groothuis, 137.
70. Chandler,154.
71. Groothuis, 79.
72. Chandler, 160.
73. Pamphlet, Lucis Trust, n.d.
74. Groothuis, 119.
75. Chandler, 36.
76. Ferguson, 365.
77. Chandler, 50.
78. Cumbey, 217-219; 52-53.
79. Mark and Elizabeth Clare Prophet, *The Science of the Spoken Word* (Colorado Springs: Summit University Press, 1974), 73.
80. Chandler, 191-192.
81. Shirley MacLaine, *Out on a Limb* (New York: Bantam Books, 1983), 214.
82. Shirley MacLaine, *Dancing in the Dark* (New York: Bantam Books, 1985), 133.
83. Chandler, 39.
84. See *Time,* December 15, 1986, 36.
85. See *Time,* January 19, 1987, 66.
86. Fritz Capra, *Tao of Physics* (Berkley: Shambhala, 1975), 25.
87. Robert Muller, *New Genesis: Shaping A Global Spirituality* (Garden City, N.J.: Doubleday, 1982), 184.
88. Ferguson, 246-248.
89. Groothuis, 57-64.
90. Ferguson, 289-291.
91. Chandler, 139-140.
92. Streiker, 26-27.
93. Ferguson, 436-440.